CW00828290

The Mandarin's Tale

For Moya, James and Julia

THE MANDARIN'S TALE

ROY DENMAN

First published in Great Britain 2002
by Politico's Publishing
8 Artillery Row
Westminster
London SW1P 1RZ

www.politicos.co.uk/publishing

A catalogue record for this book is available from the British Library.

ISBN 1 84275 028 3

Printed and bound by Creative Print and Design, Wales

CONTENTS

ACKNOWLEDGEMENTS

I should like to make two acknowledgements.

One is to my editor, Sean Magee. When he was at Cassell he helped me with my previous book, *Missed Chances*. He has again displayed the humour, imagination and feeling for words which make him a prince of editors.

The other is to Moya. Her ability to convert rambling into readable prose is equalled only her patience at the absences of her husband as a time traveller in a past and future Europe.

INTRODUCTION

At the start of the twenty-first century Britain's public services are in a mess. Health care, education and the railways are failing to deliver standards comparable with those of our European neighbours.

Nor are Britain's troubles entirely domestic. In foreign policy it has lost its way. The biggest external problem before the country for the last fifty years has been its relationship with a uniting Europe. Yet Britain – at least until Tony Blair's speech in Birmingham in November 2001 when he spoke of 'missed opportunities' – has consistently failed to recognise the drive in Continental Europe towards unity and is still, after four years of New Labour, unable to decide whether or not to join the European single currency. Britain's leaders seem obsessed with dreams of an Anglo-American special relationship, which anyone who has lived for years in the United States can tell you is, in terms of present-day power politics, largely a mirage.

So the ship is adrift. The navigator cannot read the charts. The captain is constantly on the ship's loudspeaker promising exotic new cruises to unnamed destinations but complaining that the crew and the engine room are not delivering. The passengers become increasingly restive. The wind is rising and a storm is on the way.

How did this sorry state develop? In 1945 Britain at the Potsdam Conference was one of the three great world powers. Britain was widely admired as the country which had stood against Hitler, during six long years, for a time alone, and it had at the end liberated a good part of Europe. Its industry was intact, its pride was high; on the Continent whole cities were wrecked, factories reduced to rubble and political life had slowly to recover from the turmoil left by defeat and occupation. And the British Empire had brought good administration to vast expanses of the world's surface.

Many causes have been cited for the decline. For too long after 1945 Great Britain basked in the memory of the days of glory. Industrial management and unions alike were protected too long by high tariffs. British thinking remained profoundly insular. We never thought we could learn anything from our European neighbours.

Increasingly British public life is characterised by bitter partisanship and daily point scoring. Slogans abound. And projects such as 'rolling back the frontiers of the state' and 'marketising' public services are regarded as unfailing panaceas just as was the concept of nationalisation after 1945. Politics is a battleground where the main priority is to defeat one's rivals, not to forge a consensus on incremental change for the long-term benefit of the country.

One question remains. For 130 years since the Northcote Trevelyan reforms established a Civil Service recruited on merit, Britain has had one of the best administered governments in the world. An American journalist wrote of Britain in the 1930s that his office boy could fill the role of a Minister, but this would hardly matter as Britain was essentially ruled by the permanent heads of the great Departments. The Civil Service should not escape its share of the blame. If it has long been, as it has proudly boasted, a Rolls Royce machine, then why has it allowed Britain to sink so low both at home and abroad?

I offer later some not uncritical reflections on this theme, based on my own experience. But for reflections to be understood the reader needs to have some concept of the world to which they apply. Anyone seeking to explain the finer points of marine engineering to a hill tribe which had never seen the sea would find it heavy going. In most walks of life this difficulty hardly applies. It is not impossible to form some idea of the daily life of a school teacher, a seaman, a farmer or a salesman. But Whitehall remains a world of mystery and shadows. What do people do behind those tall windows in the stately ministries? Do they really spend all day penning minutes to each other and bowing gravely to their seniors?

Published sources do not greatly help. C. P. Snow's novels purport to offer leeringly knowing pictures of Whitehall life but are about as authentic as fake Chippendale. There are some good general surveys of the Whitehall machine and assessments of the major Departments but these cannot be expected to give the flavour and the texture of everyday. Nor do the few memoirs of the great of Whitehall. These are curiously stilted and humourless. ('After a number of years as Deputy Director of Widgets I became, I am glad to say to general satisfaction, Director. My colleagues were unfailingly helpful in the many widget problems we faced and when I left they gave me a handsome clock which I often gaze at in my retirement home in Purley.')

So as a prelude to some reflections on the role of our mandarins I give an account of what life among them was like in the second half of the last century. I cannot claim that my passage among them was a model. It had more than its fair share of cock-ups and miscalculations. And having been born in Liverpool and being thus of a questioning and quarrelsome disposition, I probably found the road bumpier than is customary. But I hope it gives a picture of the Whitehall world deeper in colour and depth than picture postcards or cartoons. It is against this that the limitations and the values of the mandarins should be judged.

ONE

Joining the Guild

On a cold, grey morning in February 1948 I made my way to central London. I was walking along Millbank, towards the imposing office block built before the war by Imperial Chemical Industries, when a figure hove into view. By coincidence it was a lecturer from the Cambridge world I had just left. He recognised me and expressed surprise.

'What are you doing in this part of the world?'

'I'm going to work here.'

'Here. Where is here?'

I pointed wordlessly to a plaque by the entrance to the office block. It read 'Board of Trade'.

He looked at it with widening, incredulous eyes. 'Good God', he said, 'You know, you had the makings of a good Germanist.' Then he strode off, back to his world of dreaming spires and the dreams of Nietzsche.

I felt more than a pang of doubt. In those days the thought of leaving a job if one did not like it and moving to another was hardly imaginable. A job was for life. But would I be happy with a lifetime as a bureaucrat? There was something mysteriously grand about the towering, grey buildings of Whitehall. I would be able to see what lay beyond their tall windows. But would I find myself condemned to nearly forty years of insular drudgery, barely able to afford even an occasional visit to the Europe I had read so much about? What had brought me here?

5

Seven years earlier I had won a scholarship in Modern Languages to Cambridge. My parents were not well off and the school I went to was a County Grammar School. The teaching was mediocre – until a new German teacher joined the school. He was a brilliant linguist and his teaching was inspired. He should have stayed at Cambridge and become a lecturer, but he spent too much time in his last year drinking coffee and did not get a First. For me his coming was a blessing. He changed my life. He introduced to me Hegel lecturing in a drowsy summer in a small German town and changing the world; Wagner immortalising the great clashes in the sky of the Nordic gods; Stefan George whose verses rang out like a trumpet of the angels. For the next four years I happily read more German than English.

In 1941 Roland Birch encouraged me to try for a scholarship at Cambridge. The other masters were dismissive. Scholarships at Cambridge were prizes much sought after. Did I seriously think that someone from a tinpot school like ours could compete with the carefully coached elite of the great public schools? This argument seemed to me to have a certain gloomy ring of truth. It was reinforced when in December I travelled to Cambridge for the scholarship exam. I felt out of place. Spires and battlements from the Middle Ages loomed out of the dusk. Seven centuries lay as lightly on the colleges as a powdering of snow on a winter's morning. And the other young men seemed frighteningly clever and worldly. They spoke in loud, self confident tones about the numerous friends and relations they already had at Cambridge. The few I spoke to seemed mildly surprised that I was not in this category.

The exam, like the curate's egg, was good in parts. I did not think I had distinguished myself in French or in the general paper. But the German paper I tackled with the enthusiasm of the club bore invited to tell his stories to a new audience. A few days later I got a telegram. I had been awarded a scholarship in Modern Languages at St John's.

I felt like Siegfried who understood the language of the birds and would set out to conquer the world.

In 1942 the system allowed one to do a first year at a university before being called up. If one survived the war, one's studies could be resumed later. So I spent a happy year at Cambridge, mainly in the Modern Languages Library, and then joined up. After a year I was sent out to Burma as a Signals Lieutenant in a Ghurka brigade. I took with me two books, a long German novel and the poems of Stefan George. My most vivid memory was of one day, when I was in a jeep visiting one of our battalions, and came under shell fire. One burst some hundred yards in front. We scrambled out and took cover. A second burst a hundred yards to our rear. This was what was known as a bracket; the next shot, splitting the difference, would land directly on us. I had wrenched my ankle getting out of the jeep and was hardly able to hobble. So there was nothing to do but wait. With thirty seconds before I left this life, I took from my pack the slim volume of Stefan George and read again my favourite:

Komm in den totgesagten park und schau
Der schimmer ferner lächelnder gestade
Der reinen wolken unverhofftes blau,
Erhellt die weiher und die bunten pfade

(Come to the park they say is dead, and view
The shimmer of the smiling shores beyond,
The stainless clouds with unexpected blue
Diffuse a light on motley path and pond.)

(Translation by Carol North Valhope and Ernst Morwitz, in the Kegan Paul
edition of Stefan George's *Poems*, London 1944)

7

I felt suddenly at peace. The peace continued. No further shell arrived. The Japanese battery had doubtless concluded that they were wasting valuable ammunition on an obscure target. So I hobbled back to the jeep and life unexpectedly continued.

In October 1946 I was flown home and demobilised. I took a train to Cambridge. My tutor welcomed me warmly. He had foreseen that I might find the shortage of food in England trying, so he had arranged for me to go into lodgings in Portugal Place, across the road from St John's. The landlady's husband was a baker, bread being in short supply. I might find other things in short supply, like eggs available for breakfast. There were some advantages, he said drily, in viewing things as an economist.

Cambridge, for someone returning from the war, was an odd place. Some things had not changed. Popping into the Baron of Beef the first evening I saw a horsy youth leaning heavily over the bar addressing one of the barmaids. 'You're simply gorgeous, Rita. Why don't we . . .?' Turning a fiery and lustful red his voice dropped annoyingly to a whisper I was unable to catch. Patting a dark curl and gazing approvingly at the mirror, Rita was quite unperturbed. 'Eow, Mr Trumpington-Fox,' she said, 'Yew do go on so.'

Other things had changed. Cambridge was divided between those who had come back from the war and those who had come straight up from school. The gulf varied between three years and six. Now it seems trivial. Then it seemed immense. The first person I saw at the Mill Lane lecture rooms was a friend from 100 Brigade, our Transport Officer. The last time I had seen him, he was being carried out from a party on a stretcher. The Brigadier was roaringly desirous of cross-examining him on our Brigade Headquarters' transport, but, not to put too fine a point on it, he was hardly, after five double gins, in a fit state to endure with lucidity prolonged questioning. I expressed my astonishment at finding him in these halls of learning. He replied with some hauteur that he had joined the Colonial Service, which had sent him to Cambridge for a year.

Reminiscence was not in short supply. There were cries along King's Parade of 'Last saw you in the box at Knightsbridge' (this was a reference to the desert war in North Africa). Old Burma hands, not to be outdone, would utter shouts of 'Good God, I never thought you'd make it across the Irrawaddy!' It was irksome after commanding troops in action to return to a regime which required you to be back in your rooms by ten every evening. On Guy Fawkes night a number of ex-sappers staged a protest. They organised in professional fashion, with long lead, detonator and plunger, a major bang. Several windows were blown in and an indignant letter followed from the Vice Chancellor to all those *in statu pupillari*. But those of us back from the war felt a blow had been struck in the right cause.

It was splendid to plunge into German again and the German part of the Modern Languages Faculty welcomed me with open arms. Indeed they made a suggestion about future employment. Subject to my continuing to do well, I might go as Lektor to the University of Freiburg im Breisgau for two years. Admittedly my diet would consist mainly of potato peelings. But then I should return to Cambridge as a lecturer.

In 1943 I would have been delighted. But three years in the wider world, fond though I still was of the language and the literature, made me hesitant. I consulted my tutor, Claude Guillebaud. He polished his glasses thoughtfully. He was sure, he said, that the Faculty would find me congenial. And there would be much that I would enjoy. But he advised against. He had a sense that I wanted to do something in the world. In ten years I would be bored. (More than forty years later, when Harvard was rash enough to invite me to teach there for a year, I told this story to a friendly professor. He looked at me with some amusement. 'You'd have been bored in two,' he said.)

9

But what other options were there? In those days the respectable choices for young men with intellectual pretensions were limited. I had no inclination for the law. The City was for the well born. Industry was hardly considered; the captains of industry seemed mostly to have started as apprentices on the shop floor. And did a fellow who had spent three years reading Aristotle or Goethe really want to spend his life as a glorified garage mechanic or selling ladies' underwear? The respectable alternative had traditionally been the higher ranks of the public service. The ICS (Indian Civil Service) had gone. So, in time, might the Colonial Service. But the Foreign Office and the Home Civil Service remained. Success in a stiff entrance examination in the world of that time could lead to a certain prestige and a chance, for those without money or family connections, of joining a well respected meritocracy advising on great affairs of state.

But my experience of Army bureaucracy left me with some doubts. After our Division had been disbanded in early 1946 I had been posted to what was, for all Indian Army men, the greatest bureaucracy of all, General Headquarters (India) in New Delhi.

Here I had found myself behind a comfortable desk on which had rained a constant stream of paper. A proposal for action anywhere in India would involve consultation with many interests. A scheme for example to set up a major training centre for amphibious warfare in Calcutta would start on its rounds. There were no files, the neat folders which I was later to know: there were bundles of what seemed like waste paper. Would finance be available? GFI S7 would add a sheet expressing doubt; this would depend on how much was spent that quarter on flood prevention in Bengal. The experts on Bengal in the Indian Political Service would add their views. The bundle of papers would grow. The provision of some radio sets would be required. Would D Sigs agree? If I were feeling under the weather, after carousing in the mess the night before, it was the work of a moment to send the bundle of papers on its way again, perhaps to D Ops (the Directorate of Operations), to enquire whether this deployment of resources in the Calcutta area was compatible with their latest planning?

Was this the best way to spend one's life? As it was, events propelled me to a decision. The events centred on my lodgings in Portugal Place.

Here things had gone as merrily as a wedding bell. The landlady was all smiles. Eggs were available in profusion. And mysteriously there were ample supplies of coal. Mysteriously because there was a general shortage. But keen to bask in the warmth of my fire, guests arrived for tea in increasing numbers. I reckoned that I was becoming one of the most popular men of my year – a just tribute, I thought, to my conversational talents. Admittedly there was the odd *froideur* with the landlady, such as when a number of friends climbed in through the front window late one night, laughing like hyenas and waking up the whole of Portugal Place. But as term started in January 1947 and the snow and ice began to thicken in the worst winter for years, I could only congratulate myself on my good fortune.

It was not to last. One morning I came down to a cold room and an empty grate. I summoned the landlady.

'No fire,' I said.

'That's it,' she said: 'No fire.'

I asked what had happened to the coal. It's all gone, was the reply. I began to speak of the husbanding of resources, prudent use of assets, tailoring supplies to fit a certain pattern of consumption.

'Don't know about that,' she said, sweeping out. 'There ain't no bleeding coal.'

She turned at the door and with the air of someone talking to a mentally defective child said: 'WE'VE USED IT ALL UP.'

It was snowing heavily at the time. The room was damnably cold and I felt depressed and not in the mood to write an essay on the early plays of Grillparzer. Suddenly I had an idea. I would go and buy an electric fire. Fighting my way through the snow, I found a shop opposite John's. A fire was produced. Money changed hands. I returned triumphant. As the plugged-in fire began to glow with warmth, I settled comfortably in my armchair, switched on the light and began to write. Suddenly the light – and the fire – went out. I had blown a fuse. Not only that, but looking through the window, I could see that the rest of Portugal Place was plunged into darkness. The electric fire must have packed the punch of a mule. A crowd gathered in Portugal Place. Through the snow I could see angry gestures and much shaking of fists. Gloomily putting on my Army greatcoat and lighting a candle, I turned to what light reading there was. I picked up a copy of the *New Statesman*. It had an article about conditions in Paris. It was some consolation to read that things were pretty much the same: little coal, frozen rooms and general misery. But the article continued with a paragraph which made me almost leap from my chair. The writer had been to visit various Ministries. There was apparently no shortage of fuel there. 'They were,' he wrote, 'as warm as reptile houses.' Like Paul on the road to Damascus a great light dawned. This, I thought, was the life for me.

To qualify one first had to pass a written examination, designed essentially to determine whether the applicant was literate. I hoped I was. But it did not prove as easy as I had thought to demonstrate this. Arithmetic had never been my strong point. I remember a group of us in 100 Brigade in Burma trying to figure out how many mules we would need for a minor expedition. We fixed on four mules. 'I say, old boy,' someone said, 'mules have got to eat, you know. What about forage?' We added another mule. 'But he'll want forage too,' someone said. We began to face a kind of mule chain reaction. We never figured it.

The essay was another problem. Three years earlier I would have been happy to let my callow thoughts spin in arabesques on the surface of everything known to man. But three years in the army had had a stultifying effect. My imagination found it difficult to rise above such practical statements as 'INTENTION. 100 Brigade will advance and occupy the village of DINGALONG. INFORMATION . . .'. So my performance was not an unmitigated triumph. But I was allowed as a borderline case go to the next stage, a weekend of interviews designed, it was rumoured, to ascertain whether candidates ate peas with a knife, but ostensibly at any rate as a substitute for the traditional written exams which those with years of wartime service would not be best qualified to face.

To prepare myself I read a hugely long book by some left-wing professor, whose name now escapes me, about the problems of the world. It was not that my sympathies were left-wing; indeed the reverse. But right-wing professors did not seem to be writing books as comprehensively ambitious, perceiving correctly, as I see now, that the problems which had baffled mankind for the last four thousand years were not to be solved by yet another turgid tome. But at the time, burrowing through this immense work, I was heartened by the volume of information it contained and the variety of solutions it proposed. As a result I was not at a loss in answering any imaginable question: inflation in Brazil, a failure of the wheat crop in Peru, electrification of the Urals – details and plans to deal with them came off my lips like the twittering of birds in springtime. At the country house weekend it was true that one or two of the other candidates were impertinent enough to question these views, but I reckoned I was able to put them briskly in their place.

I was then summoned to the final interview in Burlington Gardens, a stately hall near Piccadilly, where many had been before and many would come after. I had put down the Foreign Office and the Home Civil Service as alternative choices, with a preference for the former. An incident at Cambridge, however, was worrying. A slight acquaintance, who had not been fit for military service and who had spent some time in the Foreign Office, had firmly pronounced.

'You won't do for the Foreign Office, you're not the type.'

'What do you mean, I'm not the type?' I had asked indignantly.

'Difficult to explain,' he replied. 'What you ought to do is to practise saying "Frightfully good show, Nigel" three times a week.'

I reflected. 'That would be too high a price to pay.'

'Thought so,' he remarked, and pedalled away.

Still, confident that I had done pretty well at the country house, I entered the famous room in a spirit of reasonable optimism. The discussion turned out to be rather tougher than I expected. Some members of the interview Board seemed inexplicably well informed and disturbingly cynical about the views I was advancing. At least, as the interview was drawing to a close, I thought I had made a gallant attempt to enlighten these old fogeys. Then my attention was attracted by one particular Board member. London in 1947 was in the full grip of austerity. Among the men who were, almost without exception, wearing shabby apologies for sports coats and shapeless baggy trousers, he stood out like a firefly at dusk. He was exquisitely dressed. And on his bronzed and aquiline features there could be discerned a patina which can only come from many years of first-class travel, the comfort of softly padding domestics, and occasional snifters of rare old brandy. He was, he could only be, the Foreign Office representative.

'Tell me, Mr Denman,' he asked, 'how do you relate to people you consider less intelligent than yourself?'

This seemed to me a fair question and I thought it deserved a fair answer. The world, I said, was full of dimwits and dunderheads. From time to time they needed to be given a swift kick in the rear. A short silence followed this remark.

'Hmm,' said Glossypants loudly, and exchanged several insightful glances with other members of the Board. The Chairman told me with just the hint of a smile that they had no further questions.

A few weeks later the results came out. I passed comfortably into the Home Civil Service but my mark for the Foreign Office was just below the pass level. I got a letter saying I had been assigned to the Board of Trade. I was not displeased by this. Trade was bound to feature a lot in the post-war world and I was far from certain that I would have fitted into the Foreign Office. Although I was still due to remain at Cambridge for another two terms, under the wartime rules I had already qualified for a degree. There seemed little point in hanging around, so I said my farewells and left.

Back at home, a Civil Service friend of my father's was not entirely encouraging. First, he said, I would be spending a few years as in effect a cadet, an Assistant Principal. This might later, if I was lucky, include a year or so as Private Secretary to a Junior Minister. Then I would serve for some years in the basic grade, Principal. Only after that might I start a climb to higher things. I asked what the prospects would then be of dealing with Europe? I was mildly reproved. There were many more important questions than Europe, I was told. And it was not done to express enthusiasms about particular subjects. Mandarins dealt with things as they came along; that was trouble enough. And whatever I dealt with, I would first have to learn the trade. Brooding on this, I opened a letter which summoned me the following Tuesday to my future department.

As I stood meditatively that cold morning on the Millbank pavement, all this galloped through my mind, much as those drowning are reputed to see their previous life flashing by. But I suddenly remembered a snatch of dialogue in a play of J. B. Priestley. Someone was moving to Norwich. One of those present was not impressed. 'A cathedral town', he sneered. Another disagreed. 'There's a hell of a lot of fun to be had in cathedral towns.'

So I took my decision. I marched in and gave my summons to an imposing janitor-like figure in red and blue. I had crossed the great divide.

TWO

Apprentice

Respectfully I was conducted along winding corridors to what was clearly the anteroom of some Big Cheese. It turned out to be Mr Beer, the Principal Establishment Officer: what an industrial firm would have called the Chief Personnel Officer, or nowadays the Head of Human Resources. Mr Beer had a courtly air and a crumpled face. He looked like a time traveller from the world of Dickens, who had stopped at Moss Bros some time in the 1930s for a secondhand suit. He welcomed me formally to the Department. (I felt that I was being inducted into a little known religious order.) Mr Beer raised his eyebrows only a fraction when he looked at the piece of paper before him.

'A Modern Linguist,' he murmured with mild surprise. 'I thought we wanted economists these days.' Turning to his Assistant he essayed a joke. 'We'll be getting a zoologist next.'

'We are,' she said tartly – 'Next week.'

A faint tremor passed over Mr Beer's face. 'We're posting you to Statistics Division,' he said: 'That will give you a good grounding in things like the trade figures which you'll be coming across a lot in your time here. One of our Permanent Secretaries started in Stats. Best of luck. We'll be keeping an eye on you.'

I sought out the official to whom I was to report. He was, I discovered, an ex-Colonial Official from Malaysia who had served with the

Royal Navy during the war. A breezy extrovert, he made me extremely welcome. 'We could really do with another pair of hands,' he said. 'Jolly good of them to send us a bright young economist like you. Where incidentally did you read economics?' I suddenly had the feeling that I was in one of those situations encountered in nineteenth-century literature, where someone at a fateful gathering of the Gang of Seven or Ninety Nine is revealed as an impostor. I confessed in a small voice that I had read Modern Languages. My new Chief's eyes dilated in astonishment and his jaw fell so far it nearly clanged on the desk. He seemed momentarily bereft of speech. Recovering, he jerked open a hatch in the wall behind him.

'Charlie!' he sang out. 'The new lad.'

In a moment the grinning face of Charlie appeared, framed in the hatch, as if by some magic a painting of the neo-realistic school had been added to the wall.

'What's up, John? Has he got three eyes and two pairs of balls then?'

'They've sent us a bloody linguist!' cried John with deep emotion.

The grin on Charlie's face was replaced in a flash by a mixture of incredulity and alarm. 'Good God Almighty!'

Service in the Indian Army had taught me that adversity rarely lasted long. Inside a few weeks I was, if not accepted, at least toiling away in the Division. And I was better off than a notable economist from Hungary, whose import into the Department was regarded by the *cognoscenti* as a brilliant stroke. With this genius to advise us, it was said, the reputation of Statistics Division and the whole Department would shine in Whitehall like the sun. The Professor, on arrival, seemed every inch a guru. But there was one difficulty. His English was unintelligible and his writing incomprehensible. So his star, brightly heralded though it had been, waned. Looking back with memories of those other two eminent Hungarian economists, Balogh and Kaldor (known in Whitehall, not entirely with affection, as Buda

17

and Pest), I cannot help thinking that this was probably a blessing in disguise.

The Director of Statistics was Hector Leak, a stately official with a white moustache and a *pince nez*. To an irreverent junior like myself, he seemed to have stepped straight out of the 1920s. He would not, I think, have disagreed with this assessment; he once observed that things in the 1920s were a damned sight better run than in the 1940s. He had two favourite occupations. One was a close scrutiny of the monthly article on British external trade in the *Board of Trade Journal*, a publication with all the zest and zing of the *Prison Gazette*. This article was essentially a comment on the ebb and flow of trade in various commodities and by various regions. In preparation for this I had to examine closely long runs of figures. The way to Hector Leak's heart was to pen learned sentences such as 'Imports of iron ore from Sweden last month were the highest [or the lowest, as the case might be] since May 1926.' Reading this would make Leak as happy as a ferret. 'Very important,' he would say, stroking his white moustache with sage contentment, although I never understood why. But this was his quarterdeck and he was the Admiral.

His second favourite occupation was to watch, with the quiet but alert patience of someone stalking a tiger, for the seniors of the Department to trip over some statistical banana skin. When for example a figure for the growth of exports to Ruritania in a speech by the Minister was in blatant contradiction to the answer to a Parliamentary question, Leak's contentment would know no bounds. 'Had I been consulted on the figure used by the Minister,' he would write, 'the resources of my Division would have been able to prevent this regrettable incident, which can only have inflicted severe damage on the reputation of the Department.' Over the years a certain anti-Leak feeling had developed in the upper reaches of the Department and his retirement in 1948 was not regretted. His successor was an exlecturer in statistics at one of the more obscure red brick universities, who dressed rather like an out of work lumberjack. He was warmly received as much more in accord with the temper of the times.

One of Leak's Deputies was an Assistant Secretary – that is a fairly senior manager – who had been transferred from some other Department. Mr Bacon had a square jaw, keen blue eyes and dressed, unusually for those days, with a certain elegance. These unfortunately were his main qualifications for senior office. Before anyone from the outside world came to see him he would get his secretary to stack his desk high with files garnered from obscure cupboards in order to show how busy he was. With a weary sigh, a wave of his hand indicated to his visitor the crushing burden of administration which he daily bore. 'These are difficult times,' he would say in a resonant voice, which would have done credit to the late John Barrymore. 'But if we all pull together the country will get through.'

He gave me an early lesson in public administration. I had in a note described a certain course of action as simple. I was gravely reproved. To say something was simple would get me no thanks if it were accomplished. If on the other hand unexpected difficulties arose – as, my mentor sighed, they often did – I would seem an improvident, incautious booby. It was far wiser to describe any course of action as fraught with unimaginable difficulties. If then things worked, it would reflect my dogged genius. If not, then I would have accurately warned of the realities.

Then there was consultation, for which Mr Bacon had what could only be described as an unbridled passion. It brought back to me memories of New Delhi. For example, we would have consulted some thirty-four organisations about the design of a statistical enquiry, but the Assistant Secretary would still show signs of discontent. More consultations would postpone still further the dread moment of decision. So wider still and wider went our consultations. We would write to the Little Hogsnorton District Council, the Association of Retired Veterinary Officers, the Ships Chandlers Association. An NCO-like figure called Mr Root bore the brunt of this. As he trudged in and out of the Great Man's office we would hear those resonant tones, 'We must have the facts, Root, we must have the facts.' 'Silly old bugger,' Mr Root would mutter, *sotto*, but not so very *sotto*, *voce*. 'Be consulting the Masters in Lunacy and the Battersea Dogs Home next.'

I sympathised with Mr Root. In return, he would instruct me during the lunch hour on the history of the Department. Slowly chewing a sandwich, he would fulfil the function of those Company Sergeant Majors who teach young recruits the history of their regiment. Mr Root's version, however, was markedly more informal. One day a very senior – and, to me then, extremely elderly member of the Department, one of the world's leading experts on some branch of economic activity, had made a speech respectfully reported in the press. With this was his picture – donnish, grey and austere.

'Looks a bit dull,' I observed.

Mr Root shook with silent laughter. 'Cor, you oughter 'ave seen Mr— in action.'

'What do you mean in action?'

'Well,' said Mr Root, 'Flora [the queen of the local typing pool and one of the old stagers of the Department] told me once, "If I find myself in a taxi again with Mr— then he can pay for a new bra." And she wasn't the only one,' he added darkly. Whitehall was obviously not quite so colourless as it was made out to be.

Mr Root and I reached the stage of friendly banter. The Foreign Office once rang up to ask a question about the trade statistics. I answered in the brisk style I had learnt in the Indian Army. Mr Root was moved to comment. 'Listening to you', he said, 'would make a cat larf. You know bugger all really. But you sound like King Dick.'

Some days later there was a dock strike. It was assumed by the top brass of the Department that, with imports and exports brought to a halt, the trade figures would also fall to zero. This seemed to me crashingly obvious. Hector Leak's successor however, despite his academic background, had some feel for the outside world. He asked us to check with Customs. Mr Root threw me the note. 'You've got a fine line of classy chat,' he said. 'Why don't you ring them?'

In dealing with other Departments, Her Majesty's Customs and Excise combine a certain friendly informality with considerable professionalism. They consider that they are the ones in touch with day-to-day reality, while those in other economic Departments are simply skating grandly on the surface. I got on to one of our contacts.

'How's the week, Sid?' I asked.

'Going like a bomb,' said Sid. 'Up quite a lot on last week, particularly imports.'

I could hardly believe my ears. 'But there's a dock strike,' I expostulated. 'The Port of London is as quiet as the grave.'

'What's that got to do with it?' asked Sid. 'Our job's to take the Customs forms and enter them.'

'But is there still a pile of Customs forms?' I asked.

'Stacks and bloody stacks of them,' said Sid. A great light then dawned on me. Figures purporting to record trade may record movements of forms; they probably have little relation to movement of goods. No economic commentator should be allowed into the columns of the press without having digested this story.

Another of his departmental legends concerned a Higher Executive Officer (a higher-grade NCO) called Bumley, who had some separate duties and toiled away in a small room of his own with, mysteriously, a carpet (to which his grade was not normally entitled). His main interest in life was helping in the creation of some local Polytechnic (this was long before the days when they aspired to become universities). Occasionally when letters to him were opened in his absence they

21

were found to show growing irritation at the absence of any replies to previous correspondence. His superior, a dapper young bachelor who had discovered the pleasures of eating well at Oxford and was pursuing this in London, called in one morning on the way to his club, to enquire. Bumley assured him that all was well. 'Some people are far too impatient,' he said. His young superior was impressed by Bumley's surroundings. 'I say, Bummers,' he remarked (Mr Root gave a very creditable imitation of an Oxford drawl), 'jolly nice quarters you've got here. And the carpet's as deep as Quaglino's.' This remark must have stuck in the young man's mind, because the following week, when Bumley had started his annual leave and some further complaint arrived, he ordered Bumley's carpet taken up. Underneath were found some one thousand unanswered letters, the entire incoming correspondence of the previous year.

'But that was scandalous,' I observed. 'I assume Bumley was sacked.'

It was Mr Root's turn to be surprised.

'Sacked? Of course not. He was AN ESTABLISHED CIVIL SERVANT.'

I began to see that Whitehall was even odder than I had thought.

A year having passed, and having learnt much that was useful and some which was entertaining at the hands of Mr Root, I was moved to widen my experience. There was then a Raw Materials Department, which looked after the many commodities in which wartime had made it necessary to introduce state trading. I was posted to the section which dealt with timber. In charge of it was an Assistant Secretary of a very different kind from the stately pre-war variety I had come across in Statistics Division. His name was Ord Johnstone, known generally as OJ. He had been in advertising before the war, and had a habit of wearing sports coats of a striking yellow and ties of an electric blue. When he agreed with you or expressed approval, he would cry, 'Whacko!'

OJ taught me a lot. He observed once that the gap between what ministers wanted and what was possible was such that Whitehall's constant job was to 'madly squeeze a right-hand foot into a left-hand shoe.' And he could be quick, going through sloppy drafting and muddled argument like a fox through a hen coop. Massively cut about by OJ, a paper for the great of the Department would assume the readability and economy of advertising copy. And he was also kind to the young. I suggested to him once on some difficult problem that we take no action but watch the situation like a hawk, and decide in six months time whether to do anything. (I had in fact just succeeded in administrative terms in reinventing the wheel.) But OJ welcomed my suggestion warmly. Just the kind of line which goes down well in Whitehall, he said. I should go far in the Service. At the time I did not think so.

Unlike Statistics Division, the Raw Materials Department actually did things. It imported and sold as a monopoly the whole of Britain's timber supply. Its executive arm – because no one in his right mind would have entrusted the purchase of more than three pork pies to some of the more traditional characters I have mentioned – was Timber Control, staffed by those who had been in the timber trade before the war. Its head – the Controller – was Ted Monkhouse, later Sir Edward Monkhouse. Dark haired, dapper and in his mid fifties, Monkhouse at first sight gave the impression of an agreeable member of the Drones Club, who spent much of his time with a carnation in his buttonhole at the Savoy. He was invariably friendly, had an infectious laugh, was never without a funny story and was a mine of information on such fashionable subjects as tennis at Wimbledon and cricket at Lords. He could with reluctance be persuaded to talk about hardwood and softwood, but his essential interests were clearly elsewhere. And he had perpetually about him a look of almost childlike lack of guile. Monkhouse had made a great deal of money out of this act because it concealed an extremely astute and hardheaded businessman. Many were those who had taken him at face value and had in turn been taken to the cleaners.

Monkhouse (I was far too young to have dreamt of calling him Ted) personified the clash – acute in those days because of a semi-state economy, but always with us in some form – between town and gown, or the comprehension gap existing between those who wrestle with the rigours of the market place and the intellectuals of Whitehall.

An example was not long in coming. Sterling, as often, was in a state of crisis; cuts in foreign exchange expenditure were necessary. Yet our supplies of timber still had to be purchased. Monkhouse, together with a battery of experts, was summoned to be grilled by the Treasury. There was little argument about the quantities to be bought; these represented our minimum needs. Discussion turned on the price. With the air of an old countryman predicting that it would either rain or go dark before six o'clock the next morning, Monkhouse gave the Timber Control view. Seven-inch Swedish red battens should be obtainable, he opined, for sixty quid a standard.

There was a pause. The Treasury man seemed somewhat surprised by the brevity of this statement. What, he asked, was the reasoning behind it?

Monkhouse was genuinely puzzled. Reasoning, he asked, what did his interlocutor mean by reasoning?

The Treasury man raised his eyes momentarily to the ceiling. Surely, he said, with just a touch of acidity, the estimate Monkhouse had put forward must have been based on a series of assumptions. It was not difficult to see what he expected. He would have been agreeably lulled by a long disquisition putting forward a whole series of assumptions – of course of the most prudent copper-bottomed kind – about the growth of GNP per head in Sweden and the UK, adjusted naturally to take account of purchasing power parities, the growth of softwood consumption in the world, new plantings in the UK, the incidence of tree disease, the future of the US economy and say that of the Peruvian wheat crop, tides in the Baltic and the signs of the Zodiac. But this was far from the intentions or the ken of Monkhouse. Indeed that eminent man seemed taken between wind and water.

'Don't fully understand what you're saying,' he said. 'I've been in the timber trade thirty years and that's how I feel.' An impasse threatened. Then a thought occurred to Monkhouse. He brightened. He had clearly found an argument which would demolish the Treasury. 'As a matter of fact,' he confided, 'I was lunching at the Savoy today with Jesus Christ.' He added helpfully, 'They've got a very good Sancerre there these days.' The Treasury man gave the impression of having suddenly been confronted with a bibulous lunatic. Someone from the Raw Materials Department leant gravely forward. 'The Controller is referring to J. C. Larsen,' he explained, 'a very prominent Swedish exporter. They make a bit of a joke in the trade about his initials.'

'JC', continued Monkhouse unabashed, 'reckoned sixty three a standard. Mind you,' he added with an air of cunning, 'You've got to aim off for wind with JC. So that confirms what I thought – sixty.'

The meeting drew to an uneasy close. It took quite a lot of straightening out later. Looking back, I can only admire the patience Monkhouse showed in handling what he must have thought a bunch of mad professors.

It was interesting that few in the timber trade then were keen on reverting to the great days of free enterprise; Conservative cries of 'Set the people free' left them cold. Under the system prevailing they had, as OJ cogently put it, the security of the civil servant and the prosperity of the businessman. They did not have to sell; they did not have to bargain; they rationed out supplies which were virtually guaranteed at a guaranteed price. But the tide was turning against them. State trading had begun to wither on the vine. The Controller of Plywood, who had made a lot of money in one of the great Far Eastern trading houses before the war and who looked forward to making some more, summoned the plywood trade to tell them that the days of state control were over. 'Gentlemen,' he said with relish, 'the jungle starts here.' A shiver ran round the room.

Shortly afterwards I attended a course for Assistant Principals at the Treasury. This was a fortnight's course for all entrants into the administrative class – designed, it was hoped, to give us a wider view of Whitehall. I can remember little about it now. A singularly dreary lady from the Home Office had achieved a sort of fame by minuting on a Royal Commission Report that she agreed with it, rather like Carlyle's young lady who accepted the universe; she tended to carry on in the same vein. A lugubrious man, who later became Head of the Treasury, irreverently nicknamed by some on the course 'The Laughing Cavalier', declaimed to us at length on the 'Organisation of Government'. A much more amusing man, who later became Head of the Foreign Office, recounted how in pre-war days, instead of the automatic Whitehall distribution of telegrams we had become used to, he would have the job of practically taking a quill pen, and forwarding telegrams to departments 'By direction of the Secretary of State'. (This was generally thought to be an endearing glimpse of the past.)

At the end of the course I raised the question of contact with industry. I was going to spend most, if not all, of my professional life in a department dealing with industry. Would it not therefore be a good idea if some of us were seconded for a couple of years to an industrial firm to see what life was like on the other side of the hill? Indeed if a firm in, say, France or Germany could be found, we could at the same time learn something about Europe. The course was presided over in its more formal moments by some Sir Rumble Bumble. He promptly shuffled every kind of refuse on me from a great height. Why, he asked sarcastically, had I joined the Service at all if one of my first thoughts was to leave it? If I wanted to clear out to stuff myself with snails and garlic in some French café, I was welcome. Had I no concept of the austere loyalty and the lifetime of devoted service required of the mandarins of Whitehall? It seemed to him that I was a cuckoo in the nest. Why, he said crushingly, pursuing no doubt unconsciously a Stalinist line of thinking if people from Whitehall saw something of private industry, they might like it so much as not to want to come back. I returned to the Board of Trade with the uneasy feeling, that, if reports were issued, as in Whitehall they remorselessly were, I would be pretty well down the totem pole.

But damnation did not arrive. Summoned to Establishment Division to be told of my next move, I wondered whether I would suffer the fate of a War Office contemporary, who had made the same trip to enquire about his future. 'What makes you think', he was asked, 'that you have a future?' The Board of Trade's judgement was more favourable. I was to be transferred to the Minister's office with the title of Assistant Private Secretary to the President of the Board of Trade. I called on OJ to take my leave. 'Whacko,' he said.

I was partly flattered, partly awed. To be posted in one's twenties as a Private Secretary showed a young man or woman who had experienced a few years at the bottom of the ladder how life operated at the top. At this level one would work either as the Number Two in the Minister's Office (the Principal Private Secretary was someone in his mid thirties, virtually guaranteed a rise to the top), to work for one of the junior Ministers, or as Private Secretary to the top official in the Department. The appointments were widely prized.

My boss-to-be Victor Chapman, the Principal Private Secretary, struck me as friendly but austere. I was wheeled in to see Harold Wilson. He was small, plump, pipe-smoking and dapper in a Montague Burton sort of way. He was defiantly Yorkshire; he was the local lad who had become a political Brain of Britain and had scaled the heights of the Establishment. And he was frighteningly intelligent;

27

he spoke in a rapid flat staccato, scattering initials such as FST (Financial Secretary to the Treasury), SEC OT (Secretary for Overseas Trade) and DJ (dinner jacket). As I worked with him I was to find that his intelligence differed from that of anybody else I had ever met in the way a super-computer differs from an abacus. In any event or question he could in a fraction of a second see consequences, implications, dangers and possibilities by the hundred. Someone would be late for a meeting; a glance would be exchanged between two others. His computer would hum into action and multiple choices would be produced without end. Later some were to accuse him of being devious, suspicious, even paranoid. But when a traveller is guided not by a sextant and a single star, but by a massive computer and its flickering, dancing screen, his journey becomes a different one.

Yet I found him genial and kindly. His natural instinct was to have a friendly relationship with those who worked for him. The minor mishaps of the day he would bear with greater equanimity than most Ministers I have known. He had a well developed sense of humour and, on train and car journeys, an interesting line in reminiscence. He was not liked by the Conservative Opposition, nor do I think he greatly liked them. The social divide, ever present in British public life, was then even greater than it is today. On the well heeled, who had been brought up to regard a comfortable living as their birthright and a display of excessive zeal as bad form, he grated. This was compounded by the fact that, armed with a photographic memory of what had been said in Hansard and of every conceivable statistic, he could eat most of his opponents for breakfast. The aura of disapproval on the Conservative benches when this crunching of cornflakes took place was almost palpable.

I cannot recall being a great deal of use to Harold Wilson in my first few months. He would sound his buzzer; either Victor or I would enter. He would then fire with the rapidity of a machine gun some complicated questions about departmental business. Had he spoken in Sanskrit I would have found this almost as intelligible. But endeavouring to give an impression of owl-like wisdom I would sidle knowingly out of the room, and then frantically try and make sense of my notes, often with the help of the Juniors in the Department who seemed more approachable than the Great. After some research I would concoct a reply and saunter next door with the breezy self-confidence of someone who had known the answer all along but just wanted to check a minor detail. I would see a frown crossing Wilson's forehead. 'I knew that two weeks ago,' he would say, not unkindly. 'Indeed that is what I said on the 27 June, Hansard columns 1338 and 1339. What I wanted to know was . . . .' I left the room with what dignity I could muster and applied myself again to the telephone, which by now should have become red hot.

Beyond the operations of a far flung department it was necessary to get to know some of the tricks of the Private Secretary trade. Partly this meant knowing and working with my opposite numbers who served the other stars in the departmental firmament. The Permanent Secretary, the head Civil Servant in the Department, was Sir John Woods, known generally in Whitehall as John Henry. He looked rather like a cross between a prizefighter and a barfly, but as with Monkhouse, though on a higher intellectual plane, a sharp intellect was hidden underneath the misleading exterior. Serving him was Philip Brown, who did much to introduce me to the Private Secretary network. Philip had not had an easy start in the Department. His father had been before the war a celebrated Permanent Secretary, at a very early age. Extraordinary ability had apparently been combined as is often the case in life with mordant wit. By the then Juniors, now the Seniors, this was remembered. It is a tribute to Philip's talents that he nevertheless rose to one of the most senior posts in the Department and did a lot to smooth the very important, and for many years neglected, relationship with the City. We became life-long friends.

On my first evening he gave me a drink. Encouraged by this, I ventured a callow thought. 'I suppose one of our main jobs is to keep the great men of the Department together.'

'You will find', said Brown, 'that at times the best thing is to keep them apart.' An example was not long in coming.

At Oxford, Harold Wilson had been an economist of note and was bristling with ideas about developing partnership in many forms between government and industry. Rather than inflict these on the world without further ado, as more recently has been the custom, he would first discuss them privately with Sir John Woods. The two got on. The Secretary had lived through the depression years of the early 1930s in the Treasury and had a good deal to contribute about likely reactions from industry and the banking world. This Harold Wilson respected. But Sir John Woods was greatly averse to spending long evenings in rambling and inconclusive discussions with Wilson and some of his political cronies. Some hours before one such meeting had been scheduled, Brown telephoned. 'The Secretary has an early dinner with Sandy Maxwell [the Chairman of the Tourist Board and a cele-brated *bon viveur*]. So he's damned if he's going to be kept here chuntering away for hours this evening.'

'How do I explain this to the President?'

Brown indicated firmly but politely that this was my affair. He was quite right. A Private Secretary can expect help from others in the use of the bush telegraph and ensuring that their masters do not clash unnecessarily. But how any one of them explains this to his boss is a matter for him alone. After some alarmed and intensive thought I went next door. Assuming an appropriately funereal air, I explained to Harold Wilson that the Secretary was feeling rather ill and was thinking of going home early. Wilson was genuinely concerned. 'I do hope he's not overdoing it at his age. I'll give him a call in the morning.' He then prowled out after me into the Private Office and started looking at the incoming mail. At precisely this moment there tramped along the corridor outside a minor procession. Sir John Woods, eyes sparkling at the thought of a convivial evening with an old friend and some excellent wines, his driver, a messenger with a large parcel and Brown, clutching various files with the discreet but important air of a court chaplain.

Glimpsing this through the open door, Harold Wilson was immediately solicitous. 'Very sorry to hear you're unwell, John Henry. You ought to watch it, you know.'

'Unwell?' boomed Sir John Woods 'I've never felt better'. Wilson frowned. 'But Denman said . . . .'

I faded away as decently as I could.

But a few weeks later the other part of the Private Secretary compact was in evidence. One evening I went across to the House of Commons to check a draft speech in order to see whether there was anything to which Wilson might have objected. A debate – limited under the rules to half an hour – was about to take place on newsprint. Supplies were short. The Government maintained that this simply reflected our shortage of foreign exchange, in particular dollars. The press alleged that a Labour Government, which did not like the press, was deliberately limiting supplies. It had been arranged that a junior Board of Trade Minister would read out the departmental line. I glanced through the speech. It seemed, though dull, to be unobjectionable. Relieved, I packed it away and began to set out for home.

The door opened and a Labour MP whom I knew slightly entered as if pursued by lions and tigers. 'Where's Harold?' he cried frantically. 'It's newsprint!'

'The President's in Newcastle,' I said, somewhat puzzled. 'But X, the junior Minister, is handling it. I've seen the brief. It's all right.' The

MP gave a maniacal laugh. 'And I've seen him,' he said, 'in the bar. Brother, he's so drunk he'd have to be carried into the Chamber.' He left. I wondered what to do. Wilson was between destinations in Newcastle and there were then no telephones in cars.

I rang up Brown. 'Try the Treasury,' he said. 'Someone like Douglas Jay [who was then a Treasury junior Minister].'

I went along and got Douglas Jay out of a dinner party in the House of Commons. He thanked me courteously, and said I had been quite right to disturb him. He would see to it. He did. Another junior Minister was found half an hour before the debate. He read out the brief with a slightly wondering air as if he had just come across some rather puzzling inscriptions on Assyrian tablets. So, in a way, the situation was saved. But the *Daily Express* had the last laugh. Its headline the next day read: 'NEWSPRINT: SITUATION TIGHT'.

Of the other stars in the firmament the most unusual was the Parliamentary Secretary, the junior Minister who dealt with domestic affairs. Hervey Rhodes had started life as a Yorkshire factory hand, had joined the Royal Flying Corps in the First World War, and with his gratuity of a few hundred pounds had set himself up in the wool business. He became a prosperous manufacturer and much later a Labour MP. He was someone of powerful personality and intelligence and it was unfortunate that these had never been disciplined by a university education. I acted once as a note taker at a meeting between him and another Minister, Dick Stokes. What Stokes said made little sense but was perfectly comprehensible. What Hervey Rhodes said made, I felt instinctively, good sense, but was largely incomprehensible. Racking my brains over what I should record, I thought the only solution was to put down what Hervey Rhodes, such as I knew him, was probably trying to say. The minutes of the meeting were never challenged, a fact which only increased my scepticism about the accuracy of historical documentary evidence.

Hervey Rhodes found it difficult, after the breezy informality of the North of England and the rough and tumble of the House of Commons, to adjust to the stately minuet of Whitehall. In his first meeting with officials someone had mentioned a wool top. Smoothly one of the seniors leant forward. 'A wool top, Parliamentary Secretary,' he explained 'is . . .' Hervey Rhodes held up a fist like a mutton chop. 'Nay,' he said, 'Ah have some knowledge of these matters.' He had a genuine sense of democracy and found no difficulty in talking to anyone, whether Prime Minister or messenger. Once a Registry Clerk burst into his room, comparable in industrial terms to a doorkeeper forcing his way into the presence of a Vice Chairman of ICI (whose former offices we were now occupying). The Registry Clerk, a new recruit, had been asked for a file, and looking up the docket found it had been marked out to a Mr H. Rhodes. Looking up the room number of H. Rhodes he had marched straight up, ignoring the Private Office, and accused him of having had the file for a week. Hervey Rhodes promised to send the file down the next day, hoped that no one would be too inconvenienced, gave the Registry Clerk a cup of tea, and asked about life in the Registry.

Hervey Rhodes complained about one of the Deputy Secretaries, George Calder (Deputy Secretaries were the level immediately below the top official). Hervey Rhodes thought Calder supercilious. 'If he takes that hoity-toity line with me again,' said Hervey, 'I'll dot him on the snout.' This prospect of a scene so dramatic as to enter the history of the Department with drums beating and banners flying had me hanging around for quite some time hoping that Calder would turn up. I was disappointed.

I also, but at a vastly more junior level, found Calder trying. He had a habit of calling on the Private Office in the evening. Gazing at me in a stern and owlish way and swinging his spectacles menacingly, he would ask about one of the submissions to the Minister. Had I consulted the National Gallery or the Association of Birdseed Manufacturers? I had to admit that I had not. 'Unfortunate,' Calder would intone, 'most unfortunate.' I had failed to grasp that the essence of democratic Government was full consultation with all the interests affected.

Fortunately a year or so later he was sacked. He had made the mistake of the clown who wanted to play Hamlet. He had coveted and then taken the Deputy Secretary job dealing with overseas affairs. Calder had a certain instinct for the domestic scene. But the world beyond our shores was for him *terra incognita*, and no amount of spectacle-swinging could disguise the fact. He was appointed Commissioner of Phosphates. Brown and I rejoiced.

The senior Deputy Secretary was a very different type. A few years earlier the film *In Which We Serve* had shown Noel Coward in the role of a dashing destroyer captain. It was generally agreed that if Noel Coward had not been available James Helmore would have been a convincing substitute. He was a mercurial personality. Brilliant and quick-witted, he could at one moment display a terrifying rage and at the next a charm which could fetch birds from trees. He had the benefit of long experience in the Department and knew the traps and pitfalls far better than the more recent recruits. And he had the gift of leadership. By Whitehall standards we all worked pretty hard in those days. I would get to the office at about half past eight, earlier if a speech had to be checked and sent somewhere first thing. It was difficult to get away before eight or nine at night. One evening at about half past eight the door swung open and Helmore appeared with a sandwich. It was getting late, he said, and I had had nothing to eat all day. (In some remarkable way Helmore knew everything that went on in the Department from the momentous to the trivial.) My gastric juices, he said, were eating the walls of my stomach, and if I kept on like this I would be a case for the sickbed. Personally he did not give a damn if

I were a case for the graveyard. But my absence, whether temporary or permanent, would be a slight inconvenience since someone else would have rapidly to be trained to replace me and the smooth functioning of the Private Office would suffer an interruption. I was therefore in future to look after myself. And if late one evening I felt suicidal a drink was always available in his office. He left as suddenly as he had come. I felt henceforth that for Helmore I would if necessary work all night. He became in due course a Permanent Secretary. Disillusioned with Whitehall, he left early for banking. This did not work out as well as he had hoped. But he never changed. Years later I went to the Travellers Club to dine with a friend. My host was late. I met Helmore. 'Who the hell'. he asked 'let you in?' Then he chuckled, gave me a drink and we talked happily about old times.

These instances of talent at the top helped generate the feeling of marked optimism with which I regarded the world from the anteroom of what had been the Chairman's office of Imperial Chemical Industries. We had an energetic and immensely able Minister who would be one of the movers and shakers in changing Britain. We had a top-rank Civil Service in which the Firsts of Oxbridge could rise to the top without political influence or the patronage of the rich. And we had in British industry firms which, as the press never ceased reminding us, had pioneered radar, the jet engine, polyethelene and God knows what else.

But my confidence was admittedly sometimes challenged. Harold Wilson was once bidden to a small lunch at the opening of the annual British Industries Fair (long since abandoned in favour of specialised exhibitions). He took me along. The Prime Minister, Clem Attlee, was in the chair. The reputation of Attlee in the press was not high. Small, mild, bespectacled and balding, he had nothing of the charisma of Churchill. One joke about him was that he took a taxi to No. 10, Downing Street, and when the door was opened nobody was there to get out. So I looked forward with only minor interest to seeing him in the flesh. I was sure that the demigod for whom I worked would dominate the discussion and I hoped mildly that he would treat his nominal boss with tolerance and tact. It did not work out like that. Mr Attlee in no way corresponded to the popular perception of him. There was instead an air of laconic asperity and command. I realised instantly that I was in a situation familiar from my Army days. Mr Attlee was a testy and very senior battalion commander; Harold Wilson, who had suddenly become rather nervous, was a young subaltern. The Prime Minister removed his pipe from his mouth. 'So you want to go to America, Harold. Think it'll do any good?' I began to see that Harold Wilson was not going to find it as easy as I had thought to transform England.

Captains of industry called on Harold Wilson. As a respectful attendant and note taker I regarded these great men, on whose talents our export drive depended, with awe. Unfortunately they seemed to vary between the mediocre and unmitigated dolts. The Chairman of a major textile firm, for example, looked like a cavalry colonel whose grasp of the problems of the textile industry would have been less than that of his horse. The heads of the major motor manufacturing firms had had no scientific training but had picked up what they knew as apprentices on the shop floor. I remembered from reading the German press that in that country the great of industry all seemed to have at least a doctorate in engineering and occasionally the title of professor. One boardroom where Wilson and I were asked to lunch was adorned with pictures of hunting and shooting; I gathered that conversation was normally limited to prospects for salmon and grouse. In another when I ventured to ask at the end of the table whether business details were ever discussed, I was loftily told that they preferred to concentrate on the big picture. Only the previous week they had had a long and difficult discussion. It had ended in agreement. Henceforth, as an alternative after lunch to brandy or port, only cointreau would be served.

I found that the Board of Trade had an industrial adviser, the Chairman of a major paint firm in Birmingham. He was reputed to be wise and kindly. I asked him how seriously scientific training was taken in industry. He smiled. 'Let me tell you a story,' he said. 'I joined my firm from Oxford, where I had read chemistry, in the 1920s. On my first day in the works I found a foreman pouring some acetone into a vat. I asked him what the formula was. He was dumbfounded. "Formula, Guv, wot's that?" I asked him how much acetone he was pouring in. "Twenty glugs" was the reply.'

'But that must have been twenty-five years ago.'

'Things haven't changed much.'

From time to time Wilson and I ventured out of London. Visits abroad were considered a perk and so the senior Private Secretary went on these, while I would gloomily fear that government business would never take me abroad. Of domestic visits I remember three. The first was to Harrogate for a Cotton Board Conference. At Manchester we had to change trains. Scooping up the red boxes which had surrounded us in our reserved compartment, I followed Wilson on to the platform. It was some way to our connection; in fact it turned out to be a separate station. There seemed a distinct shortage of porters. Seizing a trolley, I piled on the red boxes and set off. The way seemed long; the time was short; we broke into a trot. Some curious glances turned in our direction as this odd procession rushed along the cobbled streets. At the other station we reached the top of a bridge, fortunately smooth so that the trolley could manoeuvre up to it, though with dreadful exertions on my part. Below our train was about to depart. 'HOLD THE TRAIN!' I bellowed, 'CABINET MINISTER!' The Guard – about to wave his flag – stood transfixed with curiosity. Throughout the train heads poked out of windows. As well they might have done. Because propelled by gravity and with myself clinging on for dear life, the trolley rattled down the incline with increasing speed, a noise like thunder and Harold Wilson in hot pursuit. Breathlessly arriving at an empty compartment, I flung open the door and loaded in the boxes. Harold Wilson bounded in beside me. The train began to move. At this moment porters, who had so far been conspicuous by their absence, appeared in profusion. They applauded in a somewhat half-hearted way, indicating with that meaningful gesture which is comprehensible world wide, that they expected their palms to be crossed with silver. Rather crossly I threw a couple of half crowns to this unde-serving throng. Wilson was enthusiastic. 'Nice work, catching the train,' he cried. 'Give them more. More.' I could see no connection between the two, but emptied my pocket. It took me most of the journey to Harrogate to recover.

The second journey – to Torquay – will remain even longer in my mind. Torquay had been chosen as the seat of the second major post-war tariff cutting conference. The first had been at Geneva in 1947. A second minor one had been held in Annecy in 1949. But Torquay was designed, like Geneva, to be a major attempt at reducing international trade barriers. Late in 1950, a month or so after the Torquay Conference had started, it seemed right for the President of the Board of Trade to visit the conference, inspire his troops and generally check things out. I was detailed as escort. It was thought useful for my education for me to arrive a day early and stay on a couple of days. Seizing with alacrity this first chance of venturing on to the interna-tional stage, I went down with the Head of our Press Section. Arriving at the hotel we took our seats for dinner. We gave our orders to a grave and stately looking waiter and congratulated ourselves on the fact that, while the food might not be up to much, at least Britain was still able, through its traditions of impeccable service, to show foreigners a thing or two. After a few minutes the grave and stately waiter appeared again with a slightly apologetic air. He was frightfully sorry but he had forgotten our order. We repeated it with some emphasis. A few minutes later he appeared again. It was now clear that he was hopelessly tight. Somehow we got some food, although after attempting to eat it I wondered whether the effort had been worth it. We then joined the British Delegation who were having a friendly discussion with the Dutch. Heading the Delegation was a considerable potentate called Sir Stephen Holmes. He had spent most of his career with the Dominions Office, later the Commonwealth Relations Office. I can see now with the wisdom of hindsight that a lifetime spent in discussion of 'Trends in liberal Canadian thinking' or 'The influence of aborigines on Australian cultural development' had not fully prepared him for the sordid task of negotiating the level of customs tariffs on dried goatskins. But he had a curious sort of imperturbability. If informed for example that the British Empire was near collapse, he would not be in the least put out. Blandly puffing his pipe, he would utter such sentiments as 'Not to worry, dear boy, things will turn out all right in the end.' On the other hand, if he saw the words 'United Kingdom' shortened to the uncouth abbreviation 'UK' he would zoom round the room like an enraged bluebottle. This particular evening he was in fine form. Puffing his pipe contentedly and with the air of a man who had arrived at the perfect – the only – solution to the problem of his guests, he suggested that the Netherlands should join the British Commonwealth. 'Just the thing for you fellas,' he said with an air of finality.

The next day I encountered the American Delegation. I was anxious to meet them, because they were clearly playing a pivotal role in the conference. I listened at length to a man from Alabama. I found it as difficult to understand him as – I later assumed – he found it difficult to understand me. He would refer dolefully in discussion to some mysterious entity called 'Kahngess'. I found it difficult to figure out what this mysterious, apparently all powerful and malevolent thing was. 'Wait till Kahngess gets at it,' he would say and would give a wolfish and mirthless laugh. After much reflection the conclusion I came to was that Kahngess was some sort of savage beast, kept chained up in Washington, but from time to time apt to break loose from its chains, run amok, and bite various eminent citizens in tender portions of their anatomy. This explanation fitted like a glove all the doleful references of our friend from Alabama. So discreetly, after a couple of days, I tried this explanation on another member of the US Delegation. He was a friendly soul with a slow burning sense of humour but said little; he came from some place called Vermont. A slow smile came over his face. 'That's it, boy,' he said. 'You've got it.' That night I entered in my diary: 'The high ups in our Delegation do not seem to know much about the United States. But I am making quite some progress. Good there, Denman!' Years later on a visit to Washington, and now better able to appreciate what a fool I had made of myself, I tried to get in touch with my informant. But he had retired to his beloved Vermont.

The third journey to Great Yarmouth presaged the end of the Wilson reign. It was the spring of 1951. Wilson was making a speech at the local Chamber of Commerce. We were conscious in Private Office that the ice under the Labour Government was beginning to crack up. A great dispute had broken out between Nye Bevan, the Minister of Health and the leader of the Left, and Gaitskell, the Chancellor of the Exchequer, on whether expenditure on the National Health Service should be restrained. Wilson, we knew, was in the Bevan camp. He hoped for high office if Bevan achieved his ambition of becoming Prime Minister. Having dined comfortably, I was listening to Wilson's speech, when someone gave me a message. I was wanted on the telephone. I thought I could figure what it was. An excitable Under Secretary had rung up just before we had left. There was nothing I could do about it now. Nor did it seem courteous to get up and go out during the speech of my boss. I waved the message aside. A second even more insistent message arrived. Reluctantly I went out. In the Mayor's Parlour I was given a telephone number to ring. I recognised it. It was Nye Bevan's. Telephoned, he was suspicious. I might have been the *Daily Express* in disguise. I gathered that he wanted urgently to speak to Harold Wilson. I explained that he was at that moment making a speech. I would get him as soon as I could. After the speech I approached Harold Wilson. He was in that mood of relief which comes to politicians after a successful speech. Laughing and joking with a number of the locals, he waved me away. It did not seem advisable with the press around to bellow the name of the man who wanted to speak to him. So I wrote him a little note and after some urgent sign language got him to read it. We withdrew to the Mayor's Parlour. I got Nye Bevan on the telephone. Curious, people started to enter the Parlour. I barricaded the door against a protesting throng. It was clear that Bevan was resigning. Wilson promised to do the same. A few days later he did. As Victor and I took our leave, he said with a trace of melancholy that he would probably be out for a long time. I remarked that since I had no longer anything to gain from flattery, I could decently venture the view that he might come back as Prime Minister. He would have liked to have believed it. I do not think he did. But thirteen years later he did indeed enter No. 10 Downing Street.

Wilson was succeeded at the Board of Trade by Hartley Shawcross. He was an imposing figure, one of the outstanding lawyers of his day. It was said of him rather unkindly that if he were a Socialist his Socialism was of the gold-plated variety. But while I shall never be a Socialist, it does not seem to me that if you are, you necessarily need to wear a hair shirt. And of his ability there could be no question. He had an appearance and an imposingly modulated voice which could on their own have got him a role as a leading man on the London stage.

With that came a forensic skill which had made him a sizeable fortune at the pre-war bar. Of the legal world he had some interesting tales to tell. He specialised in libel cases. But he explained to me once on a train journey that he always advised potential clients against starting proceedings. Puzzled, I asked why? So much mud is splashed around, said Shawcross. But how on earth had he done so well if he advised his clients not to go to law? Shawcross observed in a kindly fashion that I was as yet unfamiliar with all aspects of human nature.

Like a number of eminent lawyers, who seem to feel some aversion to the Whitehall bureaucracy, he did not find it easy to accustom himself to its ways. Shortly after his arrival he held a large meeting on consumer protection. The running was made by someone very low down in the hierarchy – a Principal, Alan Neale. Although junior, he dominated the meeting by knowledge and cogency of exposition. The next day I found in the Ministerial box a hand written note for typing. 'Mr Neale,' wrote Shawcross, 'I was interested in the points you made at today's meeting, and would like your views on the following . . .'. I approached Shawcross deferentially. It was somewhat unusual for an enquiry from a Minister to be launched directly at someone so far down the hierarchy. Shawcross would have none of this. Neale made more sense than everyone else in the meeting combined. So he wanted Neale's opinion. I withdrew. I sent out the minute. The Department was loudly resentful. I was told that I had not done my job in alerting Shawcross to the ways of Whitehall. Various embryo Sir Rumble Bumbles were offended at being bypassed.

The Labour Government continued to fragment. Signs of grace, including invitations from eminent City figures to the President of the Board of Trade, became less frequent. The election came. The Conservatives were back. We got ready to welcome our third Minister in six months. Peter Thorneycroft appeared. He was then in his forties. He made an immediate impression. He was a patrician. He had served before and during the war as a gunner and had been elected just before the war to a Birmingham seat. He lived in some comfort in Eaton Square. But he was not a Drone. He displayed an air of friendly self-deprecatory informality which concealed a good deal of hard work. Going to Cabinet, he would saunter through the Private Office, his hat on the back of his head, hoping loudly that the briefs the Department had prepared for him would make up for his gross ignorance of economics. He told me shortly after his arrival that he had been somewhat surprised by his appointment. He had, it was true, taken a vigorous role on the back benches. This had started with a summons to speak from the Opposition Front Bench on a motion attacking Herbert Morrison, one of the great figures of the Labour Party, who was then in the running to succeed Attlee as leader (and was to lose out to Gaitskell in 1955). Thorneycroft, then a junior back bencher, was elated. His elation was short lived. Churchill summoned him. 'I want you quite clearly to understand,' the great man said, 'that you have been put up to speak on this motion as an insult to Morrison.' Not many politicians would tell such a story against themselves.

In keeping with this shrewd and realistic assessment of the world and his position in it, Thorneycroft deputed me to write his speeches. Wilson and Shawcross had written their own. Thorneycroft thought his time better spent on mastering the details of his Department and taking major decisions. The banalities of after-dinner speeches could be produced by someone else. A twelve-hour day left me little time for this. So frequently, late at night in the suburban home of my parents, I would find myself in bed, surrounded by newspaper cuttings, notes from the Department, and a compendium of jokes entitled *Fifty Ways of Setting the Table on a Roar*.

To begin with all went well. A speech urging the United States to open up its market got a leading article in *The Times*, I think mainly because there just was not much to write about that day. A fortnight later I drafted a speech on the need to control expenditure. I quoted Micawber: 'Income twenty pounds per annum; expenditure nineteen pounds nineteen shillings and sixpence: result happiness; expenditure twenty pounds and sixpence: result misery.' One of the Sunday newspapers gave this an approving reference. Thorneycroft was distinctly pleased. He was getting, he was kind enough to say, a reputation for oratory.

Then a cold wind began to blow from the East. Labour MPs became indignant. Micawber, they cried, what kind of model is he? The word Fascist was not used, but it was made clear that limiting expenditure to income was a mean-minded, benighted, destructive policy worthy only of the Gradgrinds of the 1920s.

Several Labour MPs put down questions. The traditional Parliamentary way of attacking a Ministerial statement is for an Opposition Member to ask the Prime Minister, 'Whether the speech of the Right Honourable Gentleman . . . represents the policy of her Majesty's Government?' I was mildly alarmed when I saw these questions. Thorneycroft was even more alarmed. He conveyed in clear and cogent terms that I had landed him in the mire. I was to go straight away to the Prime Minister's Office and check on the reply. I did so. To my relief the Private Secretary on duty in the Prime Minister's Office in the House of Commons assured me that there was no trouble.

'Sound speech,' said Peter Oates. 'PM sees nothing wrong in curbing socialist extravagance.'

At that moment the door to the inner sanctum opened and Jove, in the form of Winston Churchill, appeared. He looked as though he had just woken up from a post-prandial sleep, and did not seem in the best of tempers. Gazing at me with evident distaste, he enquired grumpily and loudly of Oates: 'Who's he?'

'The President of the Board of Trade's Private Secretary, Sir,' replied Oates.

The great man was by then pretty deaf. 'Who?,' he repeated.

'THE PRESIDENT OF THE BOARD OF TRADE'S PRIVATE SECRETARY!', bellowed Oates.

'Huh,' said Churchill scornfully: 'Tell him to bugger off.'

I did.

Drafting after-dinner speeches was not an easy task. There tended to be in the audience after dinner a clinking of brandy glasses and a mood of conviviality hardly conducive to the scaling of lofty pinnacles of thought. So I penned such sentences as 'We must not falter in seeking to export more than we import.' Such basic and hardly brain-taxing sentiments received warm support. 'There's an old head on young shoulders there,' people would whisper to me, gesturing towards Thorneycroft. I felt gratified. But it was even more necessary, given the sparse nature of the pabulum, to embellish it with a few jokes. It got about after a bit that there were too many jokes. It began to be said that this merely illustrated a well known fact – that the young Denman was too much imbued with frivolity and irreverence.

I could see that Thorneycroft was again concerned. This time I was rescued by the Danish Ambassador. He had been in London for years, was immensely respected, and knew our country as well as he did his own, even if he still had an unashamedly Danish accent. He called to see Thorneycroft on some bilateral matter, but in traditional fashion started off with a few minutes of general chat. He wanted, he said, to congratulate Thornycroft on his speeches. There had been, he knew, some criticism of an undue element of humour. But he disagreed. As a Dane he felt there was a lot to be said for some 'yolly yokes'.

Thorneycroft was delighted. 'Yolly yokes,' he said to me afterwards, laughing heartily. 'You're saved, Denman. Write me some more.'

Increasingly I began to find my time taken up with Parliamentary questions. This is not easy to explain to anyone outside Whitehall. Surely a question about the quantity of oranges imported last year is straightforward enough? This view would be naive. The exchange of questions and answers in the House of Commons has little to do with earnest enquirers after truth and benevolent purveyors of information. A government department, to start with, is not desirous of conveying more than the bare minimum of information. To go further would simply encourage the Opposition and *hoi polloi* generally to harass still further those patiently conducting the nation's business. The questioner, for his part, does not usually want a simple answer to his question. He is trying to bait a trap for the Minister. In one of the first Question Times after the Conservatives had came into office, Thorneycroft answered a Parliamentary question with the reply which the Department had submitted. With a triumphant leer, his questioner rose with a supplementary.

'But is not the Right Honourable Gentleman aware', he asked, 'that I have in my hand' – he waved it about – 'a circular from his Department which says precisely the opposite?'

Uproar followed. My blood froze. I had a chilly few minutes with Thorneycroft afterwards.

So the first difficulty was to anticipate the supplementary. With the draft answer from the Department come what are called 'Notes for Supplementaries'. These may for example read: 'What Sir Rupert Snitchum may well be after is to ask about X. If so the answer is Y' or 'The Minister should be aware that the Minister for . . . said on . . . Z. This is quite compatible with the answer given because . . .' So Parliamentary questions resemble a steeplechase. The question is asked; the answer given. The Private Secretary in the Box awaits with bated breath the supplementaries. If they are covered by the notes, particularly when added by the Private Secretary himself, he will feel elated. If not he will feel alarmed. Then it is up to the Minister. Some in my experience have taken the view that, if stumped, it was best to stick to the piece of information nearest to the question: thus persistent questioning about imports of oranges could be met by dogged references to imports of apples. One post-war Labour politician, Manny Shinwell, on the other hand, would follow a policy of saying something so insulting to the Opposition as to provoke an uproar, in the course of which the original question would be forgotten.

The second difficulty was the draft answer itself. Every Department has for its questions one particular day of the week. The previous afternoon thirty to forty draft replies would begin to arrive in the Private Office. I would scan these with some foreboding. The trouble was that, while factually correct, they were often grossly at variance with the general line Ministers were following. The Churchill administration, while keen to support free enterprise, was anxious to avoid any impression that it was hankering after the pre-war days of top hats for the rich and soup kitchens for the poor. Unfortunately, imagination not being one of the main qualities of Whitehall, the answers prepared were rarely sympathetic. To a question, for example, about the tragic level of unemployment in Little Hogsnorton and what the Government was proposing to do about it, the reply, as if drafted by Scrooge himself, would take the line that traditional remedies were available, and what pray was wrong with that? The workhouse and the treadmill were not mentioned by name, but their shadow loomed heavily over the answer. Perceiving that, while factually correct, this reply would create uproar in the House of Commons, I would prepare an alternative draft. I would then show Thorneycroft both. Blanching slightly at the Departmental draft, he would usually opt for the more emollient version. This then had to be telephoned back to the Department for approval. The Parliamentary Clerk charged with this was an elderly man who had been dealing with Parliamentary questions from time immemorial. One evening I was in his cubby hole with a stack of rewrites. Listening on the other telephone to him putting one of these to a very senior and testy Under Secretary, I heard him finish his standard urbane spiel, 'So, Mr Snodgrass, while the President was grateful for your draft, he would really much prefer the answer I have just read out.' There was a moment of heavy breathing. 'Do you mean,' asked Snodgrass menacingly, 'that the President wants this redraft, or is it that young sod Denman?' I began to feel that it was time for me to leave.

There had also been some momentous changes in the scenery. John Henry, the Permanent Secretary, had left; he was near retirement and had accepted an offer to join the board of English Electric. Philip Brown escorted him down to the entrance and saw him picked up by one of the largest and most opulent limousines Brown had ever seen. As he drove off, the Great Man (who had known his father) wound down the window. 'The best of luck in your chosen profession, Mr Brown,' he cried cheerfully.

The new Permanent Secretary, Sir Frank Lee, was of a very different stamp. He was small, ugly and bespectacled, with a voice like a corncrake. He was not long on social graces. And he would misuse French words in a way which even Churchill could hardly have rivalled. A minor change in organisation or staffing somewhere, he would refer to as a *'bouleversement'* (an upheaval). This became known to Brown and myself as a 'boule'. He would arrive in the office at some ungodly hour and Brown, arriving later, would find him rifling through Brown's intray. Philip inserted a sign once, halfway down the tray, with the words 'KEEP OFF. THIS MEANS YOU'. Entering the office the following morning he saw Frank Lee encountering this in his rummaging through Brown's papers. Wordlessly he put the notice aside. Brown and I christened him 'Monster'.

To ease the tribulations of life under this new regime, Brown and I would lunch more than occasionally at his club, which he helped me to join. Arriving back at the office in due course, after a generous interval, Brown might find Monster pacing impatiently up and down.

'Where have you been? I have been back some time,' he would ask in a voice of rusty old iron. But at the same time he had a not unkindly perception of human failings. I was told that one evening, leaving the building, he passed by the Private Office. I was engaged in an animated conversation with Brown. Hearing a loud hyena-like laugh, Monster turned to his aide. 'I assume,' he said, 'that Roy has encountered some new human folly.'

He was without doubt one of the great Permanent Secretaries of Whitehall. His advice was never evasive or uncertain: it had that ring of authority which the great proconsuls must have had. And his advice was always courageous. The final decision is always with Ministers. But he and his generation told it as it was. The present day Whitehall world, where Ministers are told what they want to hear by timeservers pathetically anxious to please, and disasters like the poll tax follow, would not have been for him. He went on to be Permanent Secretary of the Treasury, and there played a notable part in persuading Harold Macmillan to apply for membership of the European Community. I called on him nearly twenty years later. He was then Master of a Cambridge college. He had had a heart attack and a stroke. But he was much the same. He told some ribald stories of Whitehall, and gave several lurid but accurate assessments of the leading personalities. He died a year or so later. I was sorry not to have had a chance to work more closely with him.

The last time I escorted Thorneycroft was on a visit to Birmingham for a banquet where the great and the good from the business world of the Midlands were to gather. The event did not start auspiciously. I had packed my white tie and tails. Unfortunately I had not made it clear to him that it was to be a white tie occasion. Discovering this on the train journey, only a frantic telephone call and a dash by his driver saved the situation. In Birmingham it was clear that this was not the only hurdle. An eminent industrialist – a rather nasty piece of work –

was, we were warned, going to make a slashing attack on the Government and its policy towards industry. Fortunately it was clear that the man was not universally popular; and Thorneycroft as a former Birmingham MP was not without friends. I reminded him of a crack by Joe Chamberlain, one of the old-time heroes of the city, 'The allegation's wrong, and the allegator knows it.' The industrialist spoke and, got only a modicum of applause. Thorneycroft made a rattling good speech and with that sense of the audience which good politicians and actors have, he introduced the Chamberlain reference with perfect timing. He got a considerable ovation.

The time came for me to leave the Private Office and return to the body of the Department. I called on Thorneycroft to take my leave. He was in bed in Eaton Square with an injured back. Ushering me in respectfully, a butler returned with an enormous tray of drinks and at Thorneycroft's insistence mixed me a large one. 'What are you going to do?' he asked. I said I was going to be a Principal. 'That,' said my host, 'sounds extremely important.' I assured him it was not. We gossiped. I confessed that with all the criticisms Conservatives had made of Whitehall I had been somewhat alarmed when he had been appointed President of the Board of Trade. Thorneycroft was amused. 'Not half so alarmed as I was,' he said.

In the two and a half years in Private Office I was fortunate in my three Ministers. They were very different. But all were considerable figures on the political scene, and they treated me more kindly than I deserved.

I had hoped, on leaving Private Office, to be posted to what was called CRE (Commercial Relations and Exports), the overseas relations part of the Department. It was considered the Brigade of Guards of the Department, and Brown had already gone there. I longed for the chance to deal with European trade questions. But it was not to be. I was given to understand that after the rather high-handed line I had taken with my seniors, a period in the salt mines would be good for my soul. I was posted to a Division dealing with the chemical industry. Those few of the Great of the Department with whom I was still on speaking terms commiserated with me in terms appropriate to a death in the family.

In those days when physical controls, building licences, import licences, Government controls of every kind proliferated, it was thought necessary to have a series of so-called Production Divisions, which would ensure that, in the continual struggle for scarce resources, the industries which they sponsored would get a fair share. Among these the Textiles Division, dealing with one of the great traditional industries very much in Ministers' minds, had great prestige. The Division dealing with chemicals rarely seemed to attract Ministerial attention, so it was way down the totem pole. This situation was not improved by its Head, an elderly Assistant Secretary, who had risen from the ranks, and was not considered by the Oxbridge mandarins to be of the intellectual level appropriate to the senior ranks of the Department.

Somewhat gloomily I reported to Mr H. A. Cork CBE, Corky, as he was generally known. He was a short, neatly dressed man with a small moustache, an alert air and a style which betrayed a military past; he had in fact served with distinction as a Company Commander in the First World War. The support troops of the Division were not reassuring. The equivalent of my old friend Mr Root was a lacklustre, potbellied fellow, who had, I was to find, a habit of falling after lunch into a sleep which only the Last Trump would have disturbed, and whose main occupation when awake was a line by line scrutiny of the *Budgerigars Journal*. My gloom was temporarily abated by a kindly afterthought of Corky. The next day he was having lunch with a chemical firm. I might as well come along. His secretary said that we were expected at 12.30 at Grosvenor House, so I made a mental note to drop in on Corky at 12.15.

The next morning, at 11.20, I was summoned to Corky. He spoke with a hoarse croak, like a man slowly dying of thirst in the desert but who has sighted in the distance an oasis. 'Think we'd better be on our way,' he said. I pointed out that it was only 11.20. We were due at 12.30. 'Traffic'll be heavy though,' croaked Corky. Looking out of the window I could see no evidence of this. But it seemed to me at that stage inadvisable, as a character in one of Barrie's plays once remarked, 'to dam the flowing tide.' As we hailed a taxi Corky's spirits rose measurably. They rose even more when we entered Grosvenor House. 'Guests of Monsanto,' said Corky, 'two large gins and tonic, please.' 'Certainly, Mr Cork,' said a respectful waiter. 'And how are you today?' The drinks arrived with record speed. There was a restrained gurgling noise and in two shakes of a lamb's tail Corky's glass was empty. Without a word the waiter took it and returned with another. After a time the Monsanto men arrived. Discussion was more businesslike than I had expected. We left in fine form, though arriving back at the office I did encounter a moment of difficulty, when for some unaccountable reason I confused the ash tray in the door of the taxi for the opening catch. The following day we lunched with the Canadian exporter of a chemical which Monsanto had discussed with us. The day after that we lunched with Canada House. I began to see that life in the Chemical Division, while obscure, was not without its advantages.

I also began to see why Ministers had been bothered little by the chemical industry. Not only was it even more highly protected than most of British industry; it did not have the hazards of changing styles or consumer taste; it supplied a steady flow of vital but unglamorous goods such as pthalic anhydride and acetone and in return was no doubt well remunerated. Also quite simply Corky was king. In a period of large scale Government control he wielded massive authority. The industry knew that if they had to go to Government with a request he would give them a fair and well informed hearing. If they had what

Corky considered a case, he would see them right. If Corky thought their case undeserving, he would tell them so. In the years I worked with him his authority was never questioned.

Corky was not a man for penning memoranda explaining at elegant length: 'On the one hand . . . and on the other'. Nor did he shine in long meetings. He would remain brisk, down to earth and monosyllabic. So radiance from on high did not fall on him, nor did he rise high in the Whitehall hierarchy. But he probably had a more amusing time than many of those who did.

When for example he was not lunching with the chemical industry, he would lunch at his club. It was not one of the grander clubs, but a small military one, quartered together with a number of other clubs, either eccentric or decaying or both, in Whitehall Court, across the road from where the Department then was. Corky did not believe, after many years of meritorious service to Queen and country, that he needed to stint himself at lunch, but as an old campaigner he knew that precautions needed to be taken. When therefore in early afternoon the steps of the Department were thronged with those returning to work, he would from time to time rise from his chair near the bar and move to the window, colliding at intervals with such pieces of furniture as had been incautious enough to station themselves in his path. His eyes would then look for a window to the right of the main entrance. If the window were blank the coast was clear, and he could happily return to the bar. If the window featured a white blotter, the message was: 'Various telephone calls have been received. The situation is not urgent but we suggest return reasonably soon.' If a calendar of garish red were in the window the message was: 'Balloon rising. Someone high in the hierarchy wants to see you. GET BACK QUICK.'

The stories told of Corky took on the quality of legends. He always attended the annual meeting that a firm held with its major customers at its plant in North Wales. The emphasis was on good fellowship and loyalty to the customer rather than intellectual discourse. Drink flowed in generous quantities. After one particularly boisterous evening, Corky stepped on to his balcony for a breath of fresh air before retiring to bed. The hotel faced a river and immediately in view were some rocks, round which the current whirled and swirled. For some reason best known to himself, Corky thought that he could discern in the swirling water someone drowning. Being a man of decisive action he seized with his remaining strength a nearby lifebelt and threw it towards the rocks. He then tottered to bed. The bright light of morning revealed that what he had done was to throw into the river the second 'O' of the sign 'Ruabon Hotel.' Of anyone drowning nothing was heard. The firm quietly settled the bill. For a new legend they probably thought it worth the money.

But overshadowing an industry rich in personalities was the Beaverbrook-like figure of Lord McGowan, originally Harry McGowan, a Glasgow lab boy, who by sheer force of character and acumen had bludgeoned his way before the war to the Chairmanship of ICI. He had come to see Harold Wilson when I was still in the Private Office. Enormous briefs had been prepared by both sides. The briefing for Wilson had resembled a minor telephone directory. The size of ICI and the vast scope of its interests meant that from regional policy to the freezing of Icelandic fish pretty well every interest of the Department was covered. The briefing on the Board of Trade side had been masterminded by an officious lady, whom Brown and I christened the Termagant or the T. If the T rang me once she must have rung me twenty times. Had I any intimation from ICI of what Lord McGowan wanted to discuss? Did I think the President would want to raise X or Y or Z? Would he want a press statement prepared summarising the discussion; in this case the T would gladly sit in and help with the drafting, a suggestion which, with a shudder, I repelled.

The great day arrived. The two men greeted each other with a certain wary respect. One was much older than the other. But both had come from humble origins, and had made a considerable dent on a world not predisposed to welcome them. They both put their briefing books aside, and spent the allotted half hour telling each other the bawdiest stories I had ever heard. They laughed. They roared. They became weak with laughter. So did I. And I had the comforting feeling that never again would I have to buy books with such titles as 'Fifty ways of setting the table in a roar': I had been given free of charge the means of setting the whole table on fire. Leaving the President's office, still shaking with laughter, I found the T on the telephone. 'How was it?' she cried excitedly. 'The discussion,' I said in a strangled voice, 'was largely social.'

A year or so afterwards Lord McGowan retired. He was a man accustomed, in the ICI he ruled, to an expense account which would have done credit to a mediaeval monarch. One of his retirement jobs was to advise Oppenheimers, the South African diamond kings. They had annoyed him by insisting in his contract on only 'reasonable expenses'. A week after his retirement he was due to embark at Southampton for a visit to South Africa. He chartered a special train and invited the ICI Board. An imperial lunch was served: champagne cocktails were followed by caviar and vodka, several fine wines, numerous courses and a very fine old brandy. At Southampton he was given the bill, which must have been the size of a small country's national debt. He signed it with a flourish. 'Send it to Oppenheimers,' he cried, 'That'll teach the buggers what reasonable expenses are.'

My worm's eye view of the chemical industry was about to take on an international dimension. One morning Corky summoned me and asked if I could do him a considerable personal favour. At least that was how he put it; behind the neat moustache and the soldierly gaze there lurked a considerable sense of humour. The OEEC (the Organisation for European Economic Cooperation, set up originally to parcel out Marshall Aid) had among its committees one dealing with the European chemical industry. A meeting was due in Paris the following week. Corky usually attended. But friends had got him a ticket to a boxing match, and, as a keen follower of sporting events, he wondered if I could replace him.

I accepted with the speed of a striking snake. I had been to Paris several time before to stay with a French family to improve my French. Going to Paris was always a delight; to go on official business a double delight. This turned out to be the first in a series of meetings I went to for the Department.

Round the conference table the two languages I had so laboriously learnt were in full flood. I felt like a wine buff given the run of a considerable cellar. For a neophyte the interplay of nationalities was fascinating to watch. There was an ebullient Belgian, who would occasionally arrive at lunch imperially tight. The German was a chemist, whose inclination was to insist on any report of the Committee being drafted in terms of chemical formulae; this was hardly acceptable to the majority of diplomats and generalists present. The French Chairman, a comfortably rotund Monsieur Bouchon, was apt to make long and eloquent speeches about various initiatives of dubious practicability, while my Swiss neighbour, a delightful Swiss German from Zürich, with whom I used to share the cartoons from the German illustrated weeklies, would ask short and direct questions after these interventions such as 'Will it work?' and 'What will it cost?' Monsieur Bouchon would refer darkly in the corridors to men of limited vision. He was however a kindly and well intentioned man. He prevailed once upon the French chemical industry to give us lunch. We started with champagne, and then progressed through five courses and three wines, all rounded off by a generous supply of brandy. When we took our leave, I went, sweating slightly, to thank Monsieur Bouchon. Looking as though his waistcoat buttons were about to fly off at any moment, he told me proudly that he had insisted with his friends on a simple lunch. He was glad he had been able to restrain them.

But activity was not entirely social. After talking to a number of industrialists, both from Britain and the Continent, I thought the most useful direction in which to move the Chemical Products Committee was to exchange information on investment. A lot of investment was taking place; duplication would be an expensive mistake. The industrialists were reluctant to exchange details of their plans among themselves but found useful the circulation by governments of total investment figures, scrambled so that the details of individual firms were not apparent. The industrialists got on well among themselves, indeed rather better than the national civil servants. (Sometimes they threatened to get on too well. I recall one preliminary meeting in the British Delegation, when the representative of a Midlands chemical firm said, 'What about a little quiet price fixing, chaps. I suggest a reasonable price for ethylene glycol is . . .'.)

Whitehall's view of the Committee's work in Europe was more jaundiced. Being the Delegate to one of the OEEC committees involved attending occasional meetings in the Department, where European affairs were discussed. The general mood was in marked contrast to that of my friends across the Channel. In Paris it was clear that the war had been one of the great divides in European history. On the Continent, as opposed to Britain, frontiers had been devalued. Everyone in turn had been defeated and occupied. Continental Europe had emerged from the war a shambles. Their economies had to be rebuilt from the bottom up. And increasingly there was talk of Europe in some way getting together. Germany had to come in from the cold. People still shivered when they remembered the Germans in the war. Some means had to be found of binding them safely in a uniting Europe. In 1951 the Coal and Steel Community had been founded with this fundamental aim. On the Continent it was clear that the adventure would not end there.

The attitude in Whitehall was fundamentally different. There was a lot of fog in the Channel. Paris was all very well as a place to go for a decent meal. But these Continental Johnnies were frightfully unreliable. They were always starting wars and losing them. Britain had won the war; we were a great power and the centre of a great Empire; it was Britain which had the special relationship with the United States. To get mixed up in all this European flummery was unthinkable. Britain would lose its vastly privileged status, and just become a province of Wogland, with gendarmes patrolling the streets, and fish and chips replaced by decree with snails and garlic. So the conclusion of any Whitehall meeting on Europe was that of the Victorian mother who instructed her nanny to find out what the children were doing and tell them to stop it.

But the children did not stop. With every year their impertinence increased. The Coal and Steel Community was followed by an attempt to create a European Defence Community; this failed when the French Assembly refused ratification (it was too soon after the Second Great European Civil War). But a desire for further integration gathered pace. Unable now to deny that a tiger was coming down the track, the Whitehall view was that it was only a paper tiger. At Messina in 1955 the Six set up a conference to work out a detailed plan for taking integration beyond coal and steel. The British, still profoundly sceptical, sent an observer, one Russell Bretherton of the Board of Trade.

This man had had the heavy responsibility of teaching Harold Wilson economics at Oxford before the war. He was quiet and pipe-smoking. I had worked for him for a while on timber in the Raw Materials Department. Periodically he used to summon large meetings. As the junior my task was to take a note. Opening the meeting, he would remove his pipe and summarise not only the problem but the only sensible solution to it. He would then look round like a gargoyle and ask menacingly for any comments. After a few seconds of cowed silence I was able gratefully to sum up that 'there was general agreement with the Chairman's approach'. To his juniors he was polite, but no one could have described him as a barrel of laughs. From the few conversations I had with him about the external world it was clear that he regarded Commonwealth men and Americans with great respect, Continentals with grave suspicion.

So I was not greatly surprised when news came that he had walked out of Messina. Someone I knew had been to a meeting of the Great which had discussed this. I asked what the reaction had been? 'General approval,' my friend said. 'We can't become a province of Wogland. Bretherton played it with a straight bat.'

After five years in the Chemical Division it was more than time for a change. Expecting a call from our Establishments Division, I was told that the Permanent Secretary wished to see me at 10 a.m. on Monday. This was highly unusual. I consulted Brown. He pulled a long face. 'There are only two reasons why Monster would wish to see anyone of our lowly rank,' he said. 'The first is promotion. There is no conceivable chance of that.' 'The other reason?' I asked. 'The sack,' said Brown. I spent an uneasy weekend.

Appearing at the Great Man's office on Monday, my knees shaking slightly, Monster greeted me, to my relief, in a friendly fashion. 'I want you to go to our Embassy in Bonn,' he said. 'We've been having an argument with the Foreign Office. We need to get some of our people seconded there. Tried for the Minister (Commercial) job, but the FO won't have it. So we've settled for a First Secretary job there. Thought of you. You were always hanging around Private Office reading those foreign newspapers.' A fearful doubt suddenly gripped him. His knuckles went white. 'I hope German is one of your languages,' he said. 'You're not into Tibetan or Sanskrit or anything like that? If so, I've made a bloody fool of myself.' I reassured him. His relief was visible. 'Don't know what the allowances are,' he said. 'But you should be able

59

to afford a bottle of Rhine wine now and again. Har Har. Might even come and drink some myself.' He asked me to reflect on the offer and let him know. I said I could let him know there and then. If it were possible to go to Bonn that afternoon, I would be gone. I was to learn later that it is a great mistake to accept any offer of employment with undue alacrity. A twinge of doubt crossed Monster's features. 'Do hope we'll see you again,' he said. 'Anyway fix up the details and come and see me before you go.'

I went down to the Department light of heart. I had finished my apprenticeship. In the hierarchy of the mediaeval guilds I was now to become a Journeyman. I began to plan my departure. Negotiations with the Foreign Office and with the Embassy in Bonn would be necessary. But first I put the finishing touches to an operation long planned.

The other Departments with which the Chemical Division corresponded were legion. The Treasury, because without it any inter-departmental correspondence is a version of Hamlet without the Prince. The FO, because of the OEEC. The Colonial Office, because of a long standing argument about synthetic versus natural rubber. The Scottish and Welsh Offices and Town and Country Planning (as it then was) because of regional plans and the wide geographical spread of the chemical industry. So it continued. My long cherished plan was to write some pabulum to the Treasury about the importance of the Board of Trade in Whitehall planning, given its responsibility for an industry as large as the chemical industry. I would conclude by copying the letter to the other Departments adding 'and finally a copy to the Brown Trout Research Laboratory'. Only those who have served in Whitehall can appreciate the diabolical subtlety of this ploy. Throughout Whitehall there would be furrowed brows. What exactly was the Board of Trade up to? Was this a warning that they wanted to take over a piece of maritime research? Did it mean that the old ambitions of the Board of Trade (once responsible for the shipping industry) had been revived? It was of course true that my correspondence was one between minnows. But every Whitehall man knows that minnows can herald the movements of whales. And I speculated with much pleasure on the fate of the Superintendent of the Brown Trout Research Laboratory. One moment he would be sitting in his office, drinking a mug of tea and gazing at the placid rustic scene before him: a pool, pleasantly shaded by trees no doubt, in which brown trout would be happily disporting themselves. The next moment strange and sinister telephone calls would be coming from Whitehall. Had he received a copy of a letter from the Board of Trade? What contacts had he had with that Department? Could he take a train to London that afternoon? The Treasury wished urgently to see him. Happily I put the finishing touches to my draft and marked it for issue on the day on which I left.

Then I turned my attention to my new post. I had had some brief contacts with the European world. Now, for some years at least, I was going to live there. Part of a dream was coming true.

THREE

Journeyman

---

1. GERMANY

The Embassy wrote to say that I had been allocated a flat in a building which belonged to them. The basic furniture was there – beds, tables and chairs. The rest I would have to provide myself. I was living at home. My worldly belongings amounted to an empty magnum of champagne (bought one December in Paris and extravagantly drained on Christmas day) and a wooden bear, which my brother had brought back for me from his honeymoon in Lucerne. But I had from my Army days saved a few hundred pounds. So I bought a Ford, some china and glasses and a quite revolting picture of a rural landscape.

I arrived in Bonn in July 1957, steering my Ford car somewhat uncertainly, since I had not driven since Army days. I reported to the Ambassador, Sir Christopher Steel. He looked rather like a bluff cavalry General and gazed at me with a certain disdain. 'From the Board of Trade, eh?' he said.

My French supervisor at Cambridge used to say that English like Chinese is a tone language. This is true; in tone and emphasis you can in English convey a sense which in French would need a different grammatical construction. In Sir C. Steel's intonation 'Board of Trade' sounded like 'Bawd of Trayed' – with an ending like a sad autumn wind.

'Don't suppose you know a word of German,' he said resignedly. I pointed out that I had got a First in German in the Modern Languages Tripos at Cambridge. This was exactly the wrong thing to have said. Had I laughed apologetically – 'Oh, just a few words, Sir. Mustn't give those Krauts the feeling one's liking them too much. Har Har!' – I would have been well received. As it was the curl in the lip increased.

'Good God,' he said. 'One doesn't study a language. One just picks it up.'

He did in fact suffer from the illusion that he spoke German. That in itself for an Ambassador was serious enough; what was even more serious was that he was apt to use it on official occasions. In the three years I spent there it would be a gross exaggeration to say that we developed a warm relationship. He did not think, to start with, that gentlemen dealt with trade. I thought him an old Bumble. He thought me a young man with far too much to say for himself. I cannot quarrel with either assessment.

My next call was on the Ambassador's Deputy, Michael Williams, the Minister (Political). He concealed a basically kindly disposition under an exterior of freezing austerity. He simply did not like people. At lunch at the Ambassador's shortly after I arrived he found himself sitting between two British journalists. One of them asked about a recent decision by Professor Erhard, the German Minister of Economics. 'Can't comment on that,' said Michael Williams. 'That's an internal German matter.' Later the other journalist asked a similar question. He got the same reply. Afterwards on the balcony even Michael Williams thought he had overdone it. Approaching one of the journalists with the uneasy jocularity of a bishop essaying a song and dance act, he remarked, 'Jolly nice view of the Rhine from here, what?'

'Can't comment on that,' came the reply: 'That's an internal German matter.'

My boss, James Marjoribanks, had been appointed to Bonn as Minister (Economic), the junior of the two deputies to the Ambassador. He had started as a Probationer Vice Consul in Peking; his first three years were devoted to learning the language. It was difficult, he remarked, to remain entirely sane when one had spent an afternoon memorising various ideograms and then on the way home had seen a tree which looked exactly like the character for 'Devil'. He told me of his first night in Peking. The First Secretary in the Legation was giving a party. James arrived early to see what he could do to help. The host disappeared to change. 'Be a good fellow, James, and mix a cocktail,' he drawled languidly. James was left to his own devices. Brought up in Edinburgh in the 1920s, where the words 'Noel Coward' and 'cocktails' had about them the whiff of sulphur, he was momentarily nonplussed. But a Scot is seldom nonplussed for long. Seizing all the bottles round the table he emptied them in turn into a large porcelain bowl. The party was a great success. The next morning his host congratulated him. 'Devilish good cocktail, James,' he said. 'Haven't got the recipe by any chance, have you?' James, with a straight face, said it was an old family secret.

Had it not been for the war – and the amalgamation afterwards of the Consular and Diplomatic Services – he might have ended his days as Consul General in Shanghai, a pillar of the local business community. In fact he soldiered in a great variety of places – from Marseilles to Jacksonville, Florida. He ended up as Ambassador in Brussels to the European Community. I shall always be much in the debt of James and Sonya. Integrating a young outsider into an Embassy is not an easy task, but they took me under their wing. They made me feel a member of their family. They gave me a lot of wise advice, cheered me up when I was down, and did their best – not, I can see now, all that easy a task – to keep me tethered to the ground when I was heading for the blue yonder.

I moved into the flat. It was in Bad Godesberg, just outside Bonn, and looked on the Rhine. Things perked up. In London, living as a bachelor with my parents, I had not been impoverished in the same way as my married contemporaries. But the price of a gin and tonic was still enough to make one think. In Bonn G&T seemed to flow like water. I went to the NAAFI (the Army institute which sold drink free of duty to Government employees) and brought back an armful of bottles. Installing them in a cupboard in the drawing room, I observed them with satisfaction. They seemed to me to make one of the most attractive and soothing still life pictures I had ever seen. My allowances began to roll in at what seemed to me a princely rate. I acquired a maid and began to give dinner parties. I felt like a million Deutsche Mark. Had I been a little older and wiser, I would have realised that this is usually a precursor to life giving one several kicks on the bottom.

These were not long in coming.

I had taken over the flat from the Assistant Military Attaché, an agreeable Major from the Royal Tank Regiment, who was known as Hawk. Dining happily with Hawk on one of my first evenings, I interrogated him closely – since German military history was one of my enthusiasms – about Wehrmacht tactics and their use of armour in the closing stages of the war. Checking in the course of this on my German, Hawk grew thoughtful. As we took our leave he said something which surprised me. 'So you say you're from the Board of Trade? Huh.'

At the time I was blithely ignorant of the fact that those in embassies who belonged to the shadowy John Le Carré world of espionage were not of course identified as such, but were featured in the Embassy list under a standard diplomatic rank, First Secretary or Counsellor or whatever was appropriate. It was easy to identify from the Diplomatic List the regular diplomats (Entered Diplomatic

Service 1949, Third Secretary Jeddah 1950-53, Second Secretary Paris 1953-56 etc). Among those who did not have this pedigree, such as for example anyone seconded from the Brown Trout Research Laboratory, there could arise a suspicion that they were what the Americans called members of the 'Company' or the British called 'Friends'.

A couple of days later someone in Chancery (the political section of the Embassy) drew me aside. 'Tell me,' he said confidentially, 'Are you a friend?' 'Friend of whom?' I asked. My questioner's eyes narrowed. 'Don't try and play silly buggers with me,' he said frostily and stalked off. A cloud of suspicion seemed to envelop me. It was only dispelled as a result of an incident a few weeks later.

There had been posted to the Embassy in the evening of his years an Assistant Secretary from some Home Department, called Mr Potts. His duties were fairly menial; indeed I wondered why it was worth while giving a Counsellor (for such was the equivalent diplomatic rank) such a job. I was not the only one to whom this question had occurred. At every National Day party – which tended to happen in Bonn twice a week – Mr Potts would find himself surrounded by an interested array of Soviet bloc diplomats. 'Vot do you tink, Mr Potts,' someone would ask, 'should be British policy towards Egypt?' Gratified that at long last his views on world events were being given the attention which they deserved, Mr Potts would happily enlighten them. Fortified by more than several dark brown whiskies and soda, he would voice such sentiments as 'Wot I'd do with those geezers is to stick a bayonet up their backside, and then cut their balls off. That'd get their attention orl right, make no mistake.' Busily noting all this down, the Soviet bloc men would then exit, doubtless to the telegraph rooms of their Embassies. But one day they did not appear. Control in Moscow had obviously made some enquiries. Potts – in the jargon of the trade – was blown. He retired shortly afterwards, a disappointed man.

Enlightened by this episode, I explained the position to my colleagues. Relations improved. There were, after all, misunderstandings which arose because of organisational differences between Embassy and Whitehall life.

The differences in the way life was lived were almost as great. The contrast between life in a London club and selling soap in Bootle was no greater. A few weeks after I arrived, the German chemical industry gave a large party in Frankfurt. Distinguished people such as Ambassadors were asked; for old times sake they also asked me. I was greatly pleased at the prospect of showing off before the Ambassador my knowledge of the chemical industry. I was even more pleased, shortly after arriving at the party, to get an urgent summons to see the Ambassador. With the air of a man who had foreseen everything, I retired momentarily behind a potted palm and took from my pocket a summary of the main figures relating to the German chemical industry – exports, investment and expenditure on R & D. I had a gut feeling that it was the latter that Sir C. Steel would be interested in – there had been several articles about this recently in the German press. Suitably primed, I reported to the Ambassador. His face changed in a flash from friendly urbanity to a scowl of rage. 'Get me a drink, damn you,' he cried. 'What do you think you're here for?'

Relations were not greatly improved by an incident a few weeks later. The Treaty of Rome setting up the European Community had been signed in March 1957. The European press began to speculate that Britain, surely not wanting to be left behind, would join. The Foreign Office decided to quash this irresponsible talk. A circular instruction to all European posts, somewhat in the style of a Papal encyclical, invited all Her Majesty's Representatives to take whatever measures they thought appropriate to set the record straight. A meeting was held in the Embassy. It was decided, since the matter was commercial and the young Denman could talk to the natives in their own tongue, that he should be sent to various newspaper offices to explain why Britain could not join this new fangled Common Market. So I set out in my Ford car and drove far and wide. I went to Hamburg, to Düsseldorf, to Frankfurt and Munich. I explained that while Britain generously wished the new venture well, it could not join because of its links with the Commonwealth, and its special relationship with the United States. My German hosts were kindly and hospitable.

Much white wine was consumed. But they were puzzled. Did I not think that my ideas were somewhat out of date? The Commonwealth was now fading. The United States were realistic. They would deal with power. And a uniting Europe would far outrank an isolated Britain. After a fortnight I became convinced. In a moment of folly I went back and told the Ambassador. He flew into such a rage that I was uncertain whether he would bite the desk, the carpet or me. 'You bloody young fool,' he cried. 'That's not what you were sent out to say.' He drew himself up to his full height. 'Her Majesty's Government could never join this Continental cockalorum', he intoned. 'But it was damned impertinent of them to go it on their own.' He was setting out what was to become British policy towards Europe ever since. I was almost sent home on the spot.

Back at the Embassy in a mood of some gloom I found that life, while exalted by the standards of London suburbia, nevertheless had clearly defined compartments, and that I was in one near the bottom. This perception was given added force a few weeks later. Before I left London it had been put to me from all sides that I would soon be enjoying a social life beyond anything I had previously experienced. The diplomatic life, I was told, was a never ending series of cocktail parties, dinners and dances. My main concern would be to remain awake during my morning's work. Admittedly the stream of elegantly embossed invitations did not exactly pour in during my first few weeks. But this was after all the end of July; the social season had drawn to a close; it would get going again in September. So when I returned from a few weeks in Italy it was with a pleasant sense of anticipation. I was not then grand enough to have a secretary of my own and to find incoming mail or missives from other parts of the Embassy I would go to the Registry, where my name was on one of the boxes on the wall. I saw that my box was virtually empty. This cheered me considerably. Clearly there had been so many invitations that it would have been impossible to stuff them in the box. They must be in a sack in the adjoining room. There was no sack.

Thus for a variety of reasons my entry into Embassy life had some rough patches. And in my first month or so I did feel rather lonely. But I began to circulate. More and more people began to come to the flat. In this I was helped by two things. The first was a quite fortuitous introduction to the world of journalism. Shortly after my arrival, it had been put to me that the transformation of a dull chrysalis to a splendidly coloured diplomatic moth could in the case of Denman best be achieved by attending weekly lunches of a club of young diplomats. In the American club for the first, and for me the last, of these dreadful socially minded occasions, I saw a number of men sitting purposefully round the bar. I asked. It was the daily gathering of the foreign press – following an old tradition of the 1930s when they would gather in Berlin at midday at the bar of the Adlon. I joined the group. They made me welcome, though they were surprised to find in their midst anyone from an Embassy who was not condemned to official dealings with the press. They were intensely professional, knew everything that was going on in Germany, and told many diverting stories. They started coming along to drinks and dinner at the flat. Many an uproarious and informative evening followed.

The other factor which helped was the baggage of the mind which I had brought with me. In a month or so I was comfortably bilingual. And what I had learnt about the history and the literature of the country proved invaluable in breaking the ice, and in being able to learn more. I found myself in the position of a student of mediaeval history who by some magic was able to talk with those of his period. I came across the General who had been Rommel's Chief of Staff in Africa, people who had known Hitler when he was an obscure agitator in Munich in the 1920s, and men who had served in the Freikorps in the Baltic. I told an American. 'You must feel,' he said, 'like a kid in a candy store.'

All this was not entirely well received by the Embassy. They seemed to prefer entertaining other diplomats. And besides a good Whitehall man, when he sees a journalist, will run a mile. 'Better watch it, Denman,' I was told. 'Hear you're entertaining press wallahs – and lots of Krauts.' I was unrepentant.

A couple of months after my arrival I was asked by the Board of Trade for help in a case where the higher of two import duties was to be levied on a sizeable export from the UK. I looked up the papers. As far as the Germans were concerned the case was evenly balanced, depending on which internal interests they wanted to placate. But our case was weak. The Germans had the perfect right in this case to opt for whatever alternative was legally possible. I got in my car and drove to the Economics Ministry, housed in a converted artillery barracks near Bonn. The Ministerialrat (Assistant Secretary) had the bearing and the clipped tones of a Prussian. He did not exude warmth and my case was clearly lost before it could be put. Nevertheless in duty bound I explained my problem. He shrugged his shoulders.

As I began to take my leave I noticed a picture behind him. It was of a small German village, Gieselwerder. I remembered it because it featured in a very widely read German novel of the 1920s *Volk ohne Raum* (A Nation Cramped for Space) – a plea for the return of the German colonies. I had taken it with me to Burma. It was not one of the greatest German novels. But it had some very moving passages.

One, at the beginning, imagined bells ringing across Germany. First in the cathedral of Lippoldsberg, then in village after village – Gieselwerder, Odelsheim, Gottestreu, wonderfully evocative, sonorous names – and then across the sandy plains of Prussia, church after church, right until the Gedächtniskirche in Berlin, would follow – and the bells would ring out across the German land.

The Ministerialrat was interested. He had been born in Potsdam. But his wife had come from Gieselwerder. His father had served in German South West Africa. Had I read any of the other novels of Hans Grimm? I had read them all. We briefly reviewed some of them. The Ministerialrat got up and went to a wooden cupboard. Opening it, he produced a bottle of Schnapps and two glasses. I proposed a toast to Gieselwerder, happily on this side of the border and saved from the Bolsheviks.

We spoke about the great traditions of Prussia, of duty, loyalty, service and honour. We drank a toast to Prussia. The sun began to set, but the Ministerialrat did not switch on the light. He talked of his own past, the struggles of the Freikorps after the First World War, the folly of Hitler's attack on Russia, of how much had been lost. After what must have been a good hour the bottle was empty. We got somewhat uncertainly to our feet. He shook me warmly by the hand.

'If you have any other problems,' he said, 'don't hesitate to come to me. And by the way,' he added, fortunately since the object of my visit had now completely escaped my mind, 'that matter you mentioned. *Ist in Ordnung* (That'll be all right). The next morning, still somewhat incredulous, I checked with his office. 'Yes, yes,' they said. The Herr Ministerialrat had given instructions. I rang up the Board of Trade. They were also incredulous. Had I offered some unauthorised concession?, I was asked suspiciously. No, I said, I had offered nothing except some memories of old times.

I began to travel and talk to all sorts of people about the prospects for British exports. Some in London thought that the efficiency of German industry was so legendary that there could be little scope for sales of British goods outside the traditional specialities such as marmalade and Shetland pullovers. The level of technical education and the dedication of German industry – then as now – were impressive. I stayed once in Düsseldorf with a man who had done business in steel in China before 1914. He had gone out as the first of a German sales team from one of the great Ruhr companies. The British were surprised by his arrival. They were mortified by his activities. For the British led a fine and leisurely life. They had large houses, many servants, played polo, did one hour's work a day, and lingered long and comfortably at the Club. My German friend took a small apartment and worked from early in the morning until late at night. He achieved much success and was violently unpopular. 'We really ruined life for you,' he said. (*Wir haben Euch das Leben richtig versaut.*) I was often reminded of this when trying to get hold of a British company director in London at say 4 p.m. on Friday.

But of course there were possibilities for British exports. At a machine tool exhibition in Hanover, British and German experts agreed unanimously on the machine tools which would sell and those which would not. I went to Cologne to talk to the buying director of one of the big chain stores. He had spent some time in England after the war. Why, he asked, did we not get some of the German buyers to see what was available in stores like Harrods or Hamleys? Germans liked going to Paris where the buyers were always extremely well looked after. Maybe we should do the same. So I hit on the idea of inviting fifteen or so of the main buyers of the German chain stores to England for a week. To make a splash and attract publicity I proposed that James Marjoribanks should at the same time write to some three hundred British machine tool manufacturers with a detailed assessment of the possibilities in the

German market. We would take some modest advertising space in the German press. And the Ambassador could introduce the campaign by a rousing speech.

With the somewhat reluctant agreement of the Board of Trade, preparations were put in hand. A co-plotter was the representative in Germany of British industry (then the Federation of British Industry, not yet the CBI), Lt. Col. Leslie Parkin – one of the minor but legendary figures thrown up by the British Empire. He had once commanded a battalion of the Gurkhas, had stirring tales to relate from the marches of the Empire, had done mysterious and secret things in Berlin in the 1930s, and for some years had been based in Cologne. He had made a considerable impression on the Germans. Going out of his office one evening I could not help overhearing two German businessmen. They agreed that run-of-the-mill characters like Denman one met every day. But, as one of them said, 'This old English Colonel who shot tigers in India before 1914. There's somebody.' (*Dieser alte englische Oberst, der Tiger in Indien vor 1914 geschossen hat. Das ist ein Kerl.*) Not unnaturally Leslie became known as Tiger.

The launching of the operation did not go smoothly. We had to figure out how the goods could be displayed for which we wanted the Germans to place large orders. Toys were a particular difficulty. Racking my brains one afternoon, I called Tiger. He was reassuring. One of his oldest friends had had an unrivalled experience of the toy trade in Germany and England – immensely successful businessman, bilingual, man of great charm and resourcefulness . . .

A weight fell from my mind. I whipped out a pad.

'His telephone number?' I cried excitedly.

'He died five years ago,' said Tiger. I felt like throwing the telephone out of the window.

But somehow we set up the arrangements and D-day finally arrived. The Ambassador made a speech in Frankfurt. James Marjoribanks gave a press conference at the Embassy. My friends from the press turned up in force. They told me in the bar of the American Club afterwards that they had given the news the full treatment. 'Ring-a-ding-ding!' someone cried.

Unfortunately London was not in a ring-a-ding-ding mood. Those in the Board of Trade who had given their reluctant assent to the scheme, doubtless thinking that nothing would come of it, had not told their seniors, who were in turn astounded to read newspaper headlines about 'BIG NEW BRITISH EXPORT DRIVE IN GERMANY'. The seniors were not pleased.

Tiger was the first to hear. He telephoned that afternoon.

'Just been speaking to London,' he said.

'Oh yes?'

'Stormy weathah,' said Tiger.

Since I was accompanying the mission this was hardly encouraging news. The situation was hardly improved when we arrived at London airport and one of the Germans announced, I am sure with the best of intentions, that what they wanted to do was to hoist us up by our boot-straps. This hit the British popular press in no uncertain manner. I was told later, when I had returned to Bonn, that a friend of mine in the Embassy had encountered James Marjoribanks. He looked gloomy. 'I do hope', he said, 'that Roy doesn't get me into any more scrapes.'

But suddenly official opinion began to change. David Eccles, the President of the Board of Trade, was delighted. 'A bit of salesmanship at last,' he cried. The German buyers were friendly and cooperative and muttered about substantial orders. Comments in the British press began to verge on the enthusiastic. At last the stuffed shirts in our Embassies abroad were doing something to help exports. James Marjoribanks greeted me warmly on my return. Germany as an export market, he said, was now on the map.

This was not lost on the British Establishment. The eminent came to visit, among them David Eccles, then President of the Board of Trade. In Bonn some of the British press thought he had been haughty with them, so they followed him with malevolence to the Hanover Fair. There he made a speech in which he said that he was glad that the Royal Family had German blood. This got a headline the next day in the *Daily Express* and a cartoon of Eccles in a spiked helmet with the caption 'Herr von Smartyboots'. As the Ambassador wrote a fortnight later to Eccles, the only consolation he could offer was that shortly afterwards the *Daily Express* office in Bonn had been totally consumed by fire.

Eccles may have affected pleasure at the Royal Family having German blood, but he was not an easy guest in Germany. His father had been a successful doctor and the son had been suitably expensively educated. This had somehow produced airs and graces fully appropriate to a thirteenth Duke. To the Germans of this day and age his attitude was one of ill concealed contempt. On arrival he told me with regal grandeur that he had been at Winchester at the time of the First World War. So he had not been brought up 'to think much of this lot'.

Professor Erhard, the Economics Minister who made possible the German post-war boom, the 'Economic Miracle', came to Hanover. It was natural that he should come to the opening of the biggest German fair, but as a courtesy to the British (Hanover was in the British zone of occupation) he made a point of arranging to see the British Minister attending. Eccles met him at the airport and I was in attendance. As they strolled away from the plane some bystanders clapped. Erhard beamed. 'You see,' he remarked to Eccles, 'I am the most popular man in Germany.' This was not admittedly the kind of remark that a conventionally brought up Englishman would have made, but Erhard was an honest, decent man who was proud of his achievements. When I translated what he had said, Eccles, who had already demeaned himself by having to consort with this Bavarian peasant, gave a creditable imitation of a man about to vomit.

Things did not greatly improve over lunch. Erhard was worried about British attacks in Geneva (the base of the General Agreement on Tariffs and Trade which administered the international trading rules) on German agricultural restrictions. Eccles, who was by now well into the champagne, waved this aside. I could see another great cultural gap opening up.

'My dear Professor Erhard,' he cried, 'you don't have to worry about things like that. When I was young I drove fast cars and was had up before the beaks. Didn't give a damn. Har har.'

With a heavy heart I translated this. Erhard gave me a wondering look as though I had just given him a message from another planet. In a way he was right.

Reginald Maudling, then Paymaster General – in charge of negotiations on a European free trade area, and later Chancellor of the Exchequer – was another visitor. He was also from another planet. But his world was one of jolly weekends in the country with cries of 'Anyone for tennis?' and rounds of gin and tonic. He came to speak at a large gathering in Frankfurt, at which Walter Hallstein, the first President of the European Commission, was also present. The two did not get on. Germans have a respect for age; the more urbane British politicians a considerable line in small talk. Hallstein seemed to Maudling an elderly Teutonic bore; Maudling seemed to Hallstein a young chatterbox.

I was in attendance when they clashed. Maudling accused Hallstein of splitting Europe with the six nations' customs union. Hallstein, as a Commission man, owed allegiance to no nationality. He was polite. 'My dear young friend,' he replied, 'it is not Germany which is splitting Europe, but you and your Swiss and Scandinavian friends. We want to create a united Europe to banish for ever the terrible memories of the past.' (I could see that the reference to the past baffled Maudling. For him the recent past was a glorious one. Spitfires over Dover, Vera Lynn singing 'Forever England' and the sinking of the *Bismarck*.) 'So a first step is a customs union. We would very much like to have you in. But if you do not wish to accept the obligations, then that is your choice. After all, Mr Maudling, England is the country of clubs. If, in London, you do not wish to join a club, you have no right to march in and alter the menu.'

Nevertheless, this apart, the evening was long and convivial. The next morning I suggested to Maudling that we should call on the chemical baron who had presided, to thank him for the evening. 'Do I really have to?' asked Maudling. I said it would be wise.

We set off. The chemical baron was proud of his English. He wanted to display this and also convey that he had a considerable hangover. The colloquial word in German for hangover is '*Kater*', literally a tomcat. So he greeted Maudling with the words, 'I haf a heavy tomcat.'

Maudling was strikingly quick on the uptake. He waved aside my attempted explanation. His face showed that he had instantaneously grasped the situation (a young man had been introduced to him as from the Embassy; he was in fact an impostor and a dangerous lunatic, with equally lunatic friends). We extricated ourselves as quickly as we decently could and made for the airport. The Germans had organised a private plane. I enquired casually who it belonged to. 'Krupps,' said my beaming informant. I nearly had a heart attack. The *Daily Express* would have run out of newsprint. 'BRITISH MINISTER FLIES WITH MERCHANTS OF DEATH', it might have thundered. But fortunately the press were sleeping off their hangovers and never found out.

If Germany was on another planet as far as British Ministers were concerned, much the same was true for Home Department officials. The two who featured most in our lives were from the Board of Trade and the Treasury, the two Departments steadfastly in favour of a multi-lateral world run by us and the Americans, and against any entangle-ment with Europe. One was Russell Bretherton of the Board of Trade, for whom I had once worked in London and who in 1956 had walked out of the committee of the Six which was drafting the Treaty of Rome. The other was his opposite number at the Treasury, Frank Figgures, later Secretary General of the European Free Trade Association. Bretherton was terse and terrier-like, Figgures Pickwickian and expansive. While it was easy to detect from which the telegram to Bonn had originated, the message was always the same. The Germans were an errant tribe and must forthwith change their ways.

On receipt of such a message in my capacity as District Officer I would climb into my Ford and drive out to the Economics Ministry, housed in a former artillery barracks on the outskirts of Bonn. There I would convey what I decently and plausibly could before driving back, cursing Whitehall.

One day these two great men came on a joint visit. At the end, the Embassy having rapidly tired of them, I was deputed to take them out to dinner. Bretherton was quiet and sardonic. Figgures eloquent. He had heard that I was dangerously drawn to this 'Community business'. It was not for us. I replied that in the long term we might have little choice. His eyes flashing and his voice booming, Figgures gave every appearance of a barrister reaching the climax in a long harangue of the jury: 'Look here, young Denman, can you imagine – can you possibly imagine – the United Kingdom leaving its trade relations with New Zealand to be handled by this anonymous Commission?'

Twenty years later, as the Commission's Director General for External Relations, I was to find myself in Wellington explaining to the New Zealand Prime Minister why what he wanted in the British market could best be achieved by a method other than the one he was putting forward. I have often thought that whoever shapes the future has an impish sense of humour.

The most amusing visitor was Sir Frank Lee (Monster), still Permanent Secretary of the Board of Trade. Sometime in my last year he fulfilled his promise to come and drink a glass of Rhine wine. He differed from all the other visitors in being curious. On the way from the airport he bombarded me with questions. Why did the Germans want a united Europe? Would they seek to dominate it? Why had they voted into office that sinister Charlie Chaplin-like clown Adolf Hitler? Would the Common Market last? Would it ever develop into a United States of Europe?

On the Embassy Monster made an immediate impression. They might not have expected anyone quite as sleek as a professional diplomat. But they did expect a Permanent Secretary to have a certain stately air. Instead there darted into the room a singularly ill favoured troll, with a voice like the tearing of calico, clad in something that had once been a suit but now seemed more like dungarees, who had clearly been sent to fix the radiators. Once Monster began to expound though, everything changed. All were bewitched. It brought to mind one of the classic captions of the 1930s, advertising a piano playing course guaranteed to produce enthusiastic applause: 'They laughed when I sat down to play.'

The Ambassador gave a dinner for him and I was allowed to give him lunch – with the rest of the Economic Department of the Embassy. On the preparations for this I spent most of my monthly allowance in, I thought, a good cause. Monster was in excellent form. The news had just been announced that he was to fulfil his life long ambition and go as Permanent Secretary to the Treasury. After some searching questions about our export drive, the excellent Rhine wine which the housekeeper was unstintingly serving began to have on all a pleasantly mellowing effect. Monster's thoughts, I knew, were moving in favour of Britain's membership of the European Community. (In just over a year's time in his Treasury role he was to play a key part in persuading Harold Macmillan, as Prime Minister, to apply.) He did not speak of that on this occasion. But it was clear, he said, that the younger generation in Whitehall would have far more to do with Europe than his contemporaries. He would gladly see a system introduced in the Home Departments under which officials – as in the Foreign Office – could get an allowance for proficiency in a European language. And there was room for improvement, he added darkly, on the part of Ministers.

He recounted an incident when Dick Stokes, a Labour Minister, was reporting to Attlee and a small group of Ministers and officials during the Abadan crisis of 1951. Stokes had gone out to Teheran to reason with the Persian Prime Minister, Mossadeq, who had just nationalised the oil refineries of the then Anglo–Iranian Oil Company, and to persuade him of the folly of his action.

Stokes, who had a brisk manner half way between that of a school prefect and Captain of the Greyfriars First Eleven, recounted the dialogue. He had explained to Mossadeq the disastrous consequences of nationalisation.

'*Tant pis,*' Mossadeq had replied.

Stokes had explained that further disasters loomed. The answer was the same. Stokes had then gone into overdrive with a picture of fire and brimstone which would have scared the pants off any normal man.

'*Tant pis,*' Mossadeq had said.

Attlee removed his pipe. 'Tompee,' he asked. 'Is that a Persian expression?'

The mood at lunch now verged on the hilarious. Monster told stories of Lord Keynes, who had gone to Washington in 1946 to negotiate for the American loan which was to be the lifeline extended to a victorious but bankrupt Britain. As Treasury Minister in the Embassy he had been the principal aide to Keynes, who was having a difficult time with instructions from London which seemed to take no account of reality. Dalton was then Chancellor of the Exchequer. Twenty-five years before, after the Versailles Peace Conference, Keynes had made his name with a savage attack on the Treasury called 'The Economic Consequences of the Peace'. When he read with growing disquiet the telegrams of instruction from London he was reminded of this feud.

'My dear Frank,' he would cry, 'there is no need to stop talking sense simply because London is talking nonsense.' Later he would exclaim, reading some incoming telegram, 'If I get any further insanities from London, I shall write "The economic consequences of Dr Dalton". Fetch me a shorthand writer. I am going to send a telegram.'

The young Frank Lee would then rush out and ring up the Treasury.

'Our next outgoing telegram, No. 103,' he would say urgently. 'You'll want to give it a very restricted circulation.'

Further reminiscences followed. At the end of the lunch a colleague of mine was sitting at the table laughing until the tears ran down his face.

I picked up Monster the next morning and drove him to the train.

'We can't do much about your promotion,' he said. 'There's a logjam. But you'll be looked after.'

Getting out of the car and seeing him into the train, I affected a certain weary nonchalance. 'Yes,' I said. 'Nice guys always finish last.'

Monster's gargoyle-like features suddenly appeared in the open train window, convulsed with laughter. 'Whoever said you were a nice guy?' the corncrake voice cried. 'That should be the least of your worries.' And with a cheery wave he was gone.

And in a few months so was I. After three happy years in Bonn the Board of Trade thought that a halt to champagne and caviar (as they saw it) was overdue. I tried to get my tour extended. For a short time it seemed that even the Ambassador might intervene on my behalf. Monster's visit had cast on me some minor reflected glory; my relationship with the Ambassador had momentarily thawed. But fate – or more precisely my blundering – soon put paid to this.

Dick Stratton – a bachelor and one of the most jovial and hospitable men in the Embassy – rang up. 'You doing anything on Sunday?' he asked. I had an immediate vision of one of Dick's memorable parties. I remembered too late that he was also a pillar of the local English church.

'Not a thing,' I replied cheerily. 'Free as a bird.'

'Good,' said Dick. 'So you can come and read the lesson in church.'

This was austere news. Suitably coached, since my acquaintance with the intricacies of Sunday morning service was regrettably limited, I got up at the right moment and strode purposefully forward. The lesson was that sonorous passage in Chapter 19 of the Gospel according to Saint Matthew. I remember reciting it with increasing gusto, waving my right arm like some demented orchestra conductor. 'But many that are first shall be last,' I thundered, fixing with a meaningful gaze the increasingly empurpled countenance of Sir C. Steel, who as the senior of the flock was directly below me. 'AND THE LAST SHALL BE FIRST.'

Going out, carefully avoiding the Ambassador, I ran into Dick. He was shaking with laughter. 'You've blown it this time,' he said. 'Come and have a drink.'

Two weeks later I was back in London

I returned with two convictions about Germany, which the years have only strengthened. The first: that Adolf Hitler could never come again. Hitler's success was a chemical explosion. Two elements had come together. One was a sinister oratorical genius. No one who remembers the 1930s can forget the voice, hoarse, persuasive, ironical, taunting, satirical, defiant, ranting and triumphant, capturing the heart of a nation and echoing round the four corners of the world. The other was the temper of the times – the deliberate humiliation of the Treaty of Versailles, the six million German unemployed of 1932, the feeling of democratic impotence before cataclysmic economic forces, the strident nationalism. Hitler's achievement was to mobilise with Wagnerian thunder all the hopes and fears of a great, defeated, bankrupt, starving nation. But if Hitler were to return today he would find his props had gone. A country prosperous beyond the dreams of 1932, a youth internationally minded and anti-militaristic beyond the comprehension of the 1930s, would neither understand nor listen. A few thousand skinheads can still ape the past. But the shining eyed millions of the 1930s, with one faith, one voice, and one leader have gone for ever. Jean Monnet's greatest achievement was not creating the European Community, it was busting the ghost of Adolf Hitler.

My second conviction was that something was basically wrong about the attitude of Britain to Germany. The British attitude to an emerging, unifying Europe was bad enough. But the attitude to Germany had distinct undertones of something worse. One strand was the attitude expected of an educated Englishman. He was supposed to speak some French – though not too well – and perhaps a few words of Italian. But German was a joke language, full of seventeen-syllable nouns and people crying *'Donner und Blitzen'*. And an interest in German history was regarded as about as eccentric as joining the Society of Rope Worshippers.

Another strand was the war. I had served in a war. Passions can run high. But it did not take me long afterwards to come to terms with the Japanese. The atrocities of the concentration camps were another matter. But most European countries have something ugly in the closet. Cromwell butchered whole townships in Ireland, right down to the women and children. British blew Indians apart across the muzzles of cannon. The French revolution was not a vicarage tea party – nor the Spanish Civil War. And Stalin was responsible for the death of at least twenty million of his compatriots. So holier-than-thou attitudes in Europe have more than a whiff of hypocrisy.

Yet the British have maintained for half a century a phobia about Germany. British television ran time and time again films about the sinking of the *Bismarck*, Spitfires in the Battle of Britain, and prison camps with humourless German warders. I visited the Nuremberg Toy Fair every year in my time in Germany, and would call in at the British stands to see if I could help. One year I came across someone displaying kits of model aeroplanes. One was of a Spitfire. The picture on the package showed a Spitfire shooting down single-handed four Messerschmitts, their pilots cowering with simian, terrified faces in their cockpits.

I approached the exhibitor and introduced myself. Assuming my most polite and correct manner, I asked whether he really thought this was quite the way in 1958 to sell his goods in Germany.

The man was mystified and scratched his head. Then a great light dawned on him. 'I see what you mean, Sir,' he said gratefully. 'I suppose shooting down four of the buggers in one go is a bit much. I'll make it two.' I took my leave politely, feeling that I could do no more.

The attitude was bound to change. Yet more than thirty years later a British Cabinet Minister, Nicholas Ridley, had to resign because of some violently Germanophobe remarks. It was common knowledge that many in Britain, although they would have expressed their views a shade differently, shared his sentiments. The young will be wiser. But the change is taking place too slowly for Britain to play its full part in an integrating Europe.

2. GENEVA

In London I did not find my reception at the Board of Trade erring on the side of exaggerated warmth. 'So you're back at last, are you?', a senior said to me. 'About time you got down to some real work after all those cocktail parties.'

Paradoxically the work was abroad again. It was another world trade negotiation, like the one I had briefly glimpsed in Torquay in 1951. This time it was to be held in Geneva at the headquarters of the General Agreement on Tariffs and Trade (GATT). It had a double importance. Not only did we want, as a major exporter, to continue the success of the first two negotiations and open up markets to our goods. We also faced for the first time the six-nation Common Market. This had amalgamated the national tariffs into one Common Tariff, which meant new duties on some of our exports. Moreover, the six members were beginning to abolish tariffs between themselves, which meant discrimination against British goods. So we really needed to get what reductions we could in the Common Market tariff.

Nevertheless, the distaste felt in Whitehall for the newfangled Common Market ensured that a suitably senior official was sent out in due course to deal with US Delegation. Someone as junior as I was would do for the Continental ragtail and bobtail. I was elated. My elation even survived some sobering administrative details. Geneva was not abroad; it was GATTland. And a Board of Trade Delegation was nothing fancy like an Embassy with a champagne fountain in the courtyard. The few of us posted out there would live in a hotel for however long the negotiations would take, our allowances would be miserable, and we would be under strict Board of Trade control. It was hinted that this would be good for my soul.

In August 1960, armed with this information, and after a couple of weeks poring over files on the GATT, I took a train to Geneva. After moving into an attic in the hotel Beau Rivage, which was where the British always stayed, I reported to the Delegation. The Head of Delegation was Sir Edgar Cohen – formerly the Deputy Secretary in the Department who dealt with overseas affairs. He was a very unusual bureaucrat. Portly, bespectacled and then in his early fifties, he looked like a cross between a Professor of Economics and major-domo. He had had an unusual Civil Service career. In his first job he was considered so bad as to provoke serious discussion about whether he should be sacked. Promoted one grade he was passable. Promoted to Assistant Secretary he began to be considered promising. One grade more and he was considered brilliant. As Deputy Secretary, one grade from the top, he was so brilliant, particularly in pointing out the follies of others, that after a time it was felt that posting him to Geneva would ensure a quieter life for those at the top of the Department.

Edgar had a mind like quicksilver and a ruthless logic. Sitting behind him at a GATT meeting was an experience. He never spoke on the basis of a text; drafts he would brush aside. He would embellish the UK case with eloquence and impeccable logic, and then turn to some of the arguments which had been produced against it. He would tear at these like a dog at a fox; in a moment their follies would be analysed, parodied and destroyed. His eyes flashing through his spectacles, his voice would rise and become shrill. Words would tumble after each other with increasing speed; quotations would follow like a machine gun – *Alice in Wonderland*, Edward Lear, Macaulay and the great writers of Greece and Rome; the interpreters would finally give up, throwing their hands in the air; one third of the room would be laughing, one third cheering, one third in bewildered silence. The bureaucratic world is not as uniformly gray as it is painted. But birds of paradise are rare.

Yet he was an immensely kindly man. If he had some bad news to impart his first act would be to offer you a chocolate. This in his eyes was the equivalent of a stiff whisky and soda. I once asked him, when I had got to know him better, what he would do if his doctors advised him that he could no longer eat chocolate. 'Get a second opinion,' said Edgar shrewdly. It followed that Edgar was not a drinking man. His hospitality was both generous and impeccable. Yet behind the spectacles there would be a slight air of puzzlement that people would prefer wines and brandy and roast pheasant to a glass of Perrier and a few chocolate creams. Logic also came into play. Edgar once discovered that his French housekeeper had been using a Chambolle Musigny 1954 for cooking while only serving at table a Chambolle Musigny 1959. I was told that the altercation had been deafening.

My immediate boss was Henry Heinemann, a shrewd and friendly man from the Board of Trade who had developed great expertise on the GATT. Even Edgar would say from time to time, 'But Henry, you know about Article XXIII. What about X?' Heinemann's other assistant was an austere girl who had much time for the GATT and little for anything else. On long walks on Sunday mornings, which Henry thought a good thing to organise for our well-being, the austere girl would pass the time in long theological discussions on the GATT. (In a splendid sunlit autumn in the Geneva countryside this seemed rather dull.)

At work, after the formal opening statements had been made, negotiations finally started. Unifying the customs tariffs of the Six in a Common Tariff meant that some tariffs (previously charged separately by its members) would go up and some would go down. Our job was to get compensation for the tariffs which would go up against the UK.

There came the first formal meeting between the British and the European Commission Delegation which would negotiate for the Six. Edgar appeared with Henry and myself. A formidable phalanx of Commission men was ranged before us. Monsieur Donne, the French Head of the EEC Delegation, courteously introduced all his experts. And very impressive they seemed.

Edgar began to fidget and to look increasingly uncomfortable. He turned to me and said in a hoarse whisper, 'I can't tell them you're going to do the negotiation. They'll take it as an insult.'

Privately I thought he was on to a good point. But I whispered back that there was nothing else we could do at this late stage. Let Denman be tried on the dog and if the dog refused to eat Denman, then alternatives could be considered. Edgar with a sigh and a certain gloomy reluctance agreed. He and Henry must devote their time to other GATT matters and relations with our partners in the European Free Trade Association (EFTA). I would have to deal with the Commission and report to them from time to time.

So two days later I turned up with a couple of helpers to start our negotiations. Facing us was the Commission team headed by a tough but agreeable Italian, Fizzarotti, Donne's Deputy. While the Commission negotiated, the eventual result would have to be approved by the Council of Ministers, i.e. a meeting of the Foreign Ministers of the Six. So representatives of the Governments of the Six attended as observers, three on each side of the table. Separately seated was a representative of the Secretariat of the Council of Ministers. This was my introduction to the complexities of the Community world where I was to spend nearly thirty years of my life.

The Commission line was to argue that we were entitled to no compensation at all since the increases we faced on tariffs in the low tariff countries were balanced by reductions in tariffs elsewhere. We naturally contested this. So week after week we went through interminable lists of tariff rates. I would wring my hands at the havoc our exports would face in Holland, Belgium and Germany, and profess myself quite unmoved by reductions of tariffs in the French and Italian markets.

In between these sessions we had periodic meetings with our Commonwealth colleagues and with our counterparts from the countries of the European Free Trade Association. They were also in negotiation with the Six. With the Commonwealth in particular, as old comrades in arms, we sought to establish a common front on the grounds that a massive coordinated assault on the Community tariff would achieve more than separate isolated efforts. But it rapidly became clear that the Commonwealth resembled the expanding universe; each country was out for its own interests; the last thing they wanted was to be marshalled by London for London's ends. An Australian spoke up. 'If you blokes think we're going to get your bloody chestnuts out of the fire, you can go and screw yourselves.' This view received general assent. Any idea of a cohesive Commonwealth battling for British interests, a dream for years of British Ministers, was and would remain claptrap.

Our EFTA colleagues were in their own way no less colourful, though generally more polite. A Portuguese told the story of his father's chauffeur. Out driving one day some way out of Lisbon, his father asked, 'Mario, where are we?'

'Sir,' came the reply, 'I am lost. But I am confident.'

This struck us all as a general-purpose definition of government policy in any country.

The Austrian was slightly eccentric and had an unusual gift for language. He would utter such sentiments as 'Vee must take zee bull by zee corns.' The fierce internal struggle – in the interests of international courtesy – to keep even a relatively straight face is something I shall never forget.

Pleasant and intelligent though the EFTA colleagues were, I found the Community men much more interesting. EFTA seemed stuck in the past – no yielding of sovereignty, no progress foreshadowed towards a closer union. The Community was different. The references which the Founding Fathers had made to a federal union were discreet but clear. A new wind was blowing in Europe, rattling the windows throughout an old Continent. I hoped it would blow away the fog in the Channel.

The two Community men I got to know best were the representatives of France and Germany. They were both of Counsellor rank and, I was to find, carried some weight in their capitals. The Frenchman was saturnine, with tinted glasses and a figure which did not indicate any aversion to the pleasures of the table. He had served with the Free French in London during the war and retained despite all our eccentricities a certain affection for the British. He gave me lunch after our first negotiating session. Towards the end, in the interval between an excellent Burgundy and a Courvoisier, he wondered politely if he could offer me some advice. I had started that morning by rejecting the whole Community approach – an approach, he said modestly, to which the French had made a major contribution. A Frenchman would have taken a different tack. He would have said that in principle he agreed with the paper and would have congratulated its authors on the elegance of their exposition and the good sense of their conclusions. But then he would have gone on to say that he did have a few points of detail which he would like to see featured in the fine print. A lot, Monsieur Balensi said, depended in the Community on the tone of voice.

The German was tall and ramrod straight. He had commanded an artillery battery on the Eastern front and had fought his guns all the way to Moscow and most of the way back. I called on him when we arrived and he was glad, he said, to hear a friendly German voice. At our first lunch together I mentioned that I had been reading the latest novel by Hans Helmut Kirst. This was one of a series of light and rather funny novels satirising the blockheads of the German military establishment. The hero was always some corporal who managed by ingenuity and resourcefulness to get the better of his dimwitted superiors. This mention was a mistake. Dr Born erupted with a noise like an artillery salvo. Kirst, he cried, was '*ein verdammter Simulant*' (a damned shirker). Some people had fought for the Fatherland. Others had sat on their bottoms sniggering. Calmed by a large slug of brandy, Dr Born agreed with a certain melancholy that a lot of good men had gone in a bad cause. That was why he believed in the Community.

With the Community the terrible things of the past – in one nation – would no longer be possible. He hoped one day Britain would join. In the meantime we must do what we could to get down trade barriers. The negotiation in which we were engaged must succeed. He kept his word. We saw each other often. Dr Born would report over the lunch table on the deliberations of the Six in a parade ground voice which would at times bring conversation throughout the restaurant to a standstill. When he had amusing moments to report his laugh was like a seal barking. But he was always straight and to the point. When we, the British, had put forward something which seemed outrageous to the Six, he would explain rather more frankly than the Commission why they could not accept it, or might be able to with some variations. I shall always be grateful to him for his friendship and his advice.

The end of the year came and went. In the first few months of 1961 I had a feeling that things were beginning to move. It was becoming increasingly clear that the Commission line – no concessions – was not politically sustainable. There were clearly no great victories to be had. But if we shook the tree hard enough, some apples – in the form of tariff concessions – would fall off. One day Dr Born arrived for lunch with the air of a man who had just witnessed a great change in world affairs. What had happened, he cried, was a sensation of the first order. THE COMMISSION HAD DISAGREED WITH THE FRENCH! I was as electrified as he was. It was as if someone in the Politburo had risen and denounced Stalin. For in those days – and for years afterwards – the French dominated the Community like a snake a group of rabbits. The French were the founder members; they had the vision; they had the intellectual horse power; and they had De Gaulle. But dissension in the ranks had broken out.

Brooding on this I encountered in the street our Commission inter-locutor, Fizzarotti. The bush telegraph had reported that there was going to be a critical meeting in Brussels later that week of the Council

91

of Ministers. They were going to take decisions, perhaps the final decisions on our negotiations. On the spur of the moment I said that if we could have reductions in tariffs on three key items we would settle. Two days later my Italian friend reappeared. He had fought in Brussels like a tiger. He had succeeded. We had our concessions. Could we now settle? Taking a deep breath I saw my superiors. Henry was aghast. I had no authority for my offer. I was far too junior to engage in ploys of this kind. London might not agree. I – and more importantly the Delegation – would be in disgrace.

Gloomily we went to see Edgar. Henry told his tale. I expected to be sent back on the next train. But Edgar was delighted. 'Splendid!' he cried. 'He won't get any more. Let's settle now.'

Telegrams were despatched. London was not exactly keen. But Edgar got on the telephone. Edgar on the telephone in full flood had something of the quality of the Niagara Falls. London agreed. The United Kingdom was the first major trading partner of the Community to settle. Some in Geneva were miffed. But the Commission men were delighted. So was I.

Tidying up the deal took a few weeks. I successfully concealed from my superiors the fact that by much thumping of the table and an eloquent description of the plight of the British carpet industry I had obtained a tariff reduction which, on closer inspection, only benefited imports of hand-woven carpets from Iran. But we closed the books. Spring came to Geneva. By no means all the compensation negotiations between the Community and its trading partners were completed; the USA in particular had not settled. But the Director General of the GATT, a Pickwickian Englishman, Eric Wyndham White, suggested – with the ingenuity which was his trade mark – that we should all move to the next stage, a multilateral negotiation to reduce world trade barriers, and subsume in this whatever the provisional results had been of the compensation negotiations.

For this next negotiation – the Dillon Round, called after an eminent American banker and Secretary of the Treasury – reinforcements arrived from London. Henry left for home in the spring of 1961; he had been away from his wife and family for six months and felt, not unreasonably, that it was time to end his nomadic life. The new seniors were Fred Budd – plump, bald, late fiftyish and decidedly middlebrow – and Stewart Edwards – ten years younger, an able and cultivated man who spoke impeccable French and was a great wine buff. The circle for dinner at the bistro round the corner widened. On one of the first evenings Stewart produced with a slight air of melodrama a bottle of *vin jaune* – a much prized speciality of the Haute Savoie. Glasses were reverentially poured. Unfortunately something had gone wrong with the bottle. Fred, who greatly disliked what he regarded as affected lifemanship, took his first sip. Ill concealed delight illuminated his features. 'Tastes like cat's piss!' he cried. The evening was not a success.

Summer came. Bored with endless hotel life I rented for two months a flat in the old town. It was extremely comfortable, the view breathtaking and the rent surprisingly low. Moving in on a Sunday evening I had a leisurely drink on the balcony. Below me in the sunlight the old town was at peace. I congratulated myself on a minor real estate coup. At seven o'clock the next morning I was woken by a shattering, continuous uproar which nearly rattled every picture off the walls. A road was being taken up and a bridge rebuilt. I discovered that the work was scheduled to take exactly two months. It is always a great mistake to underestimate the shrewdness of the Swiss.

Sobered by loosening Commonwealth ties, the debacle of Suez, and uneasy about the success of the Six, Britain applied to join the Community. To be more precise it asked for negotiations with the Six to ascertain if Britain could get terms on which it could then decide to join. This was hardly a passionate declaration of faith; in fact the application from start to finish had all the quality of an alcoholic applying in a bemused moment to join the Band of Hope. Britain was just not ready to embark on the remorseless process of European integration. And General De Gaulle a year and a half later was right to veto our entry. Had we then entered I have little doubt that the Labour Government that came to power in 1964 would have insisted on a renegotiations of the terms so fundamental as to be unacceptable to our partners. And then, having agreed to a divorce, remarriage later would have been considerably more difficult than our entry in 1973 – and that was far from easy.

At any rate the tariff negotiations between the British and the Six in Geneva became somewhat desultory because most top level attention in Brussels had switched to the negotiations for British entry. What depressed me most was that I was not present at that scene of action. I pictured the rest of my life being spent in hearing others tell how they shaped the entry of Britain into the Community.

But two things moved me very much during this time. The first was a funeral. The Leader of the Commission Delegation died in the autumn. He was not – and would not have claimed to be – one of the great men of the Community. As Edgar once tartly remarked, he was 'a Customs man, a bit out of his depth in the GATT'. But he was an honest, likeable, decent Frenchman. At his funeral the representatives of the Six in effect stood guard at his coffin. Here were my friends with whom I had talked, gossiped, and argued for a year. They had fought each other in the greatest and the bloodiest of all the European civil wars. But now they were united, in death, as in life, in one cause.

Jean Rey, the Commissioner for External Affairs, had come down for the occasion to pay his last respects. I ran into him later at a reception. He drew me aside. 'In Brussels now,' he said, 'your people are talking all the time about exceptions and derogations and amendments. I can see why you need some. But look at it another way. You

94

remember Churchill talking of the old and famous states of Europe. If we could add to our ranks 'Old England' with all its traditions, its wisdom and its knowledge of the four corners of the world, what could we not do together?'

I was moved. I have often remembered his words.

In 1961 the sun smiled on Geneva and on UK–EEC relations. In fact I asked whether it was really useful to continue our tariff negotiations, if in a year or so we were going to join the EEC? But it was felt that to pull out now would undermine the worldwide negotiations in the GATT. And it was not yet certain that we would be joining. Edgar hated the idea; he confided in me that he thought London had gone off its rocker.

Doubtless thinking that Britain might soon join their ranks, the Six, while they had settled with us on the compensation question, were not yet willing to agree to a broader deal on a reciprocal reduction in trade barriers. So towards the end of 1961 the Dillon Round in Geneva became bogged down. An agreement had been reached with the Americans, but, as with any multilateral deal, this could not be finalised until the UK deal with the Community fell into place. It was decided to return the officials to London. I packed my belongings into my car and set off home. My path led me across the snow-covered Jura and I nearly got stuck. At length I safely reached a Channel port. My father who had friendly dealings with HM Customs was kind enough to alert them at Dover to my arrival. I had a moment of anxiety on the cross-Channel journey remembering suddenly the tale of the young man who had joined Customs and had asked smugly on his scheduled return from the Continent for 'special treatment'. 'Ah,' said the Customs man with a glint in his eye, 'Mr Grimshaw. Special treatment, eh? Come this way, Sir.' He was then stripped to the buff, various indignities visited on his insides, and his belongings gone through with a toothcomb. But this time it worked. I was waved through with friendly greetings and was home – out of the trenches – by Christmas.

Soon though I was back in the trenches. By February 1962 twitterings were heard from Geneva. The Americans wanted – for reasons of legislation and the Congressional timetable – to settle. The Six were ready to move. It was decided that the young Denman should be sent out to tie up the various loose ends.

I then began a steerage class shuttle to Geneva and back. I remember one morning trudging in a snowstorm from my hotel – considerably down market from the Beau Rivage – to the office. What a hell of a way to spend one's life, I thought. The Americans were no problem. The deal was mostly in place. And when it was necessary to meet a Congressional timetable almost anything was possible. The Six were more of a problem. But after much argument we finally reached agreement on the details.

Then a great theological row broke out on the form of the agreement and its compatibility with various provisions of the GATT. Back in London I was summoned by my seniors. 'Edgar is being quite impossible,' I was told. ' This is the telegram we are sending him; you must catch a plane tomorrow and reason with him.' The telegram seemed highly plausible. At the airport in Geneva the next morning it seemed somehow less plausible. The roaring and shouting when I entered Edgar's office bore out the accuracy of this foreboding. Chastened, I sat down to write a reply to the London telegram. I caught the evening plane.

In the office in London the next morning I underwent the process in reverse. 'What on earth is this nonsense?' my seniors cried. 'Were you mad? Were you drunk? The telegram does not stand up.'

I wrote another and with a heavy heart took a plane back to Geneva. The reception was even stormier. I endured three goes of this process and then threatened to go sick. Somehow the problem was solved. In

April 1962 the Dillon Round agreement was signed in Geneva. It was praised on all sides as one of the most successful of the periodic post-war negotiations to reduce trade barriers worldwide. The UK was represented at the ceremony by the Foreign Office Counsellor in the Delegation who had taken no part in these proceedings. I was glad to hear later that he had been made in the next Honours List a Companion of the Order of St Michael and St George. Distinction in the public service often follows a curious path.

Back in the Board of Trade I was posted to Tariff Division. This was run by an extremely senior and irascible Under Secretary, known generally as the Patriarch. My job could not be called wildly exciting. It was an extension of the work on tariffs I had been doing in Geneva, together with such tariff questions as emerged from the Common Market negotiations. I was at last in contact with these but at a far from exalted level. Monster's words in Bonn came back to me. The promotion block was large; advancement was not yet.

Some old friends were on the scene. Henry, who had returned from Geneva the previous year, headed the GATT Division. Philip Brown was my opposite number on the overseas side. His immediate boss, who supplied a good deal of the horse power, was a formidable lady, Nancy Fisher, who later became Head of an Oxford College. Her office was at all times crackling with telephone calls, clacking type-writers, vigorous argument and generally constructive uproar. Next to hers was the office of a colleague less enamoured of the work ethic. Here there reigned a deep peace, broken only by the occasional clink of a tea cup or the rustle of a page being turned in *The Times*.

The supremo, as far as the Board of Trade was concerned, was the Deputy Secretary who was a member of our negotiating team with the European Community. A short and stocky Yorkshireman with a rolling gait, he was described in one of the Sunday newspapers as 'brilliant, bilingual and looks like a grocer'. The last attribute could not convincingly be denied. The middle was plain wrong. On the first there was some doubt. But he was for the young and irreverent known thereafter as the BBG. When the negotiations collapsed he was knighted and made Permanent Secretary elsewhere. Some thought this verged on the odd. But the BBG redeemed himself at the farewell dinner the Department gave for him.

He had been asked, he said, what incident he remembered most in his years in the service. Gliding painlessly over the Common Market negotiations, he went back to his early years in the Patent Office. There was an Examiner (I am sure a soulmate of my old friend Mr Root) who could distinguish blindfold between various forms by chewing them. 'Nice bit of 0278,' he would say masticating ruminatively. 'Now what's this?' And like a seasoned wine-taster happening on a Chateauneuf du Pape 1958 he would say with solid satisfaction, 'Really nice bit of P38 that. Let me think. Yes, it's the new printing they brought out in '35.' Of such remarkable talents has the British Civil Service been composed.

I cannot say that my contributions to the Board of Trade end of our negotiations to enter the Community were either distinctive or well received. What I had learnt in eighteen months in negotiation with the Commission and the Six in Geneva seemed strange and unwelcome to the insular orthodoxy of Whitehall. What struck me most was that London and the friends I had made in the Six were living in two different worlds. The French talked about *l'adhésion de la Grande Bretagne aux Communautés Européennes.*' The British talked of 'joining the Common Market.' Forty years later the gap remains.

Someone produced at one stage a Whitehall paper on the glittering prospects in the Common Market for the British motor industry. I pointed out that unless the industry pulled itself together it would have no future. The only reason why British cars were bought in the UK was that a prohibitive tariff prevented imports, that nearly two thirds of

British cars were given away by British companies to their executives as a perk, and of the remainder many were exported to Commonwealth countries which had no production and where British exports were protected by Commonwealth Preference. Given a really free European market and the disappearance of Commonwealth Preference, the Germans would eat us for breakfast. This was not well received. Even less well received was a criticism I launched of some draft instructions for our negotiators dealing with a visiting Commission team. 'Taking a line like that,' I said, 'would be like feeding mice to cats.'

A rather plain girl, not noted for her subtlety or sense of humour, intervened helpfully. 'The Head of the Commission team', she said, 'is Herr Katz.'

At the end of 1962 the hope began to spread that the negotiations to join the EEC would succeed. I teamed up with a friend and colleague in Tariff Division, one Robert Goldsmith. Goldsmith had a straightforward, unvarnished Yorkshireman's approach to the problems of the world, but was no great admirer of his fellow Yorkshireman, the BBG. I shall always remember him on a visit to Brussels. Discreet and sober-suited Foreign Office and Treasury men were chatting quietly. Goldsmith had come to deal with a problem on rules of origin – that is, determining where an import comes from, important because on this often depends the tariff to be charged. Putting on his trench coat before leaving, he voiced his discontent in clarion Yorkshire tones. Referring to the august members of the negotiating team – the BBG and his colleagues – he informed a shocked audience that, 'In matters of origin these eminent sods don't know a bee from a bull's foot.'

Between us we sketched out a plan which we thought would be saleable. We looked forward to the time when Britain would be a full member of the EEC. There would be a good deal of work involved in our adjusting to the Common Tariff. I would transfer to the Commission on promotion, I hoped, as a Head of Division (Counsellor rank). Bob would take over an equivalent job at home. We began to lick our chops. We soon had to unlick them. Going home one evening I saw a newspaper headline 'THE GENERAL SAYS NO'. I hoped this was simply a one day sensation. It was not. I felt that if the bottom had not fallen out of my world a good part had. The dreary grind resumed. I began to get depressed about lack of promotion. At thirty-nine I was still only on the basic rung of the ladder. My contemporaries, when I rang them up, all had imposing sounding secretaries. The wife of one friend actually told me not to ring her husband up at the office that morning. He was expecting a call from someone important.

The Government did its best to put a brave front on the failure of the Brussels negotiations. There was coming, they said, a major new trade negotiation in the GATT – the Kennedy Round. Its objective would be to reduce tariffs by 50 per cent. So what we had lost on the Common Market swings we stood to gain on the Kennedy round-about. The leader of the American Delegation to the Kennedy Round came to London. He was, I gathered, well dined at the Savoy. I was allowed to creep in at the back of the meeting the next morning.

A week later the Permanent Secretary sent for me. He was in an affable mood. 'You're promoted,' he said. 'I want you to do the Kennedy Round.' Later Henry rang up. He had been transferred elsewhere. 'It's all yours now,' he said. I felt like a man who had won the pools. I had a monumental lunch with Brown and inherited a comfortable office with a secretary. Admittedly she took dictation at the speed of a snail and gazed at her notes afterwards with the air of someone deciphering cuneiform. But things were on the move.

One problem had to be tackled at the start of the Kennedy Round. The French had shown their habitual cunning. They argued that the 50 per cent cut all round in tariffs proposed was unfair; the low Common Market tariff would almost disappear; the many high American tariffs – even if halved – would still remain a substantial obstacle to trade. The French argument made waves. Rab Butler, Foreign Secretary in the Douglas-Home administration, wrote on one of his briefs before a meeting with Chancellor Erhard of West Germany, 'Have I after forty years of public life been reduced to discussing tariff disparities?'

But they had to be discussed. The subject was a bureaucrat's dream. It was so obscure, so complicated but suddenly so important that even a minor official could become one of the priests of the temple. I revelled in it. I wrote a paper for the relevant Whitehall committee recommending a solution based on isolating the cases where the disparity mattered statistically. If the problem was obscure so also was my paper. It was accepted mainly, I assume, because no one could understand it. I was not entirely sure I did. Armed with it I went back to Geneva to see Edgar. My reception was rather kinder than three years before. I got the impression that, while I was still far from being a member of the GATT Club, I had passed some of the apprenticeship tests. 'How', asked Edgar, 'are we going to deal with this question of tariff disparities? It's a pity Henry's gone. He was always so good at this kind of thing. And X and Y' – he mentioned two senior officials – 'haven't the time.'

I mentioned that there was a paper and that it had been approved by the GATT Policy Committee. Edgar expressed disbelief.

'Written by whom?' he asked sardonically.

'By me,' I said. 'Here it is. Read it.'

Grudgingly he agreed that it might be worth trying on the Six. We did. It became a basis for discussion. Then it was agreed. Before long it became submerged in many other currents. But we had made a start.

I began to commute to Geneva again. I would do a week there and then a week back in Whitehall. In the interests of economy I bought some nylon shirts and washed them in my hotel room. One day, as I was emerging from the Department it began to rain. I slipped from my briefcase a plastic raincoat. Unfortunately a small bag of detergent had leaked. I found myself walking along in a cloud of soap suds. Several told me that it was a remarkable sight.

There was in fact quite a lot going on both in Whitehall and Geneva, because the Kennedy Round was a much more ambitious undertaking than its predecessor. Agriculture, which I have never fully succeeded in understanding, began to loom large in our discussions. The Commission produced an agriculturist called Malvé, who expounded a new doctrine – the '*montant de soutien*' (the level of support). The important thing, he explained, was to attack not particular protective devices but the general level of aids to agricultural production.

The difficulty with the new doctrine was that it left out of account the remorselessly increasing productivity of agriculture – four ears of corn were being grown where three had grown only a few years before. Thus freezing agricultural support would not eliminate surpluses. But Malvé was not to be gainsayed. To packed and spellbound audiences in the Palais des Nations he would declaim in the manner of the great preachers of the Middle Ages.

Life in Geneva looked up. I inherited Henry's suite in the Beau Rivage. Our old friends from the Six were glad to see us again. I continued to lunch with Dr Born, and his parade ground voice still issued like a trumpet over the lunching throng in the 'Au Fin Bec'. I also spent a good deal of time with the French. The French appealed to Edgar and he to the French. They were delighted by the flash and outbreak of his intellect and his mocking wit. In return they were not only brilliant and witty but very frank. One evening one of the small band who advised De Gaulle on economic matters came to Edgar's for dinner. Kojève was known in the international fraternity of trade officials as someone of legendary resourcefulness. One day in 1948 France had been under heavy attack from all sides in the Organisation for European Economic Cooperation for its restrictive import quotas.

Kojève had to defend them. The task was hopeless; the noise deafening. He asked for the floor. The jeering throng gave him a moment, the better to tear him to pieces after they had drawn their breath. Kojève modestly asked a question. The base period for the French quotas was 1936–8. Would France's trading partners prefer as a base for future, naturally enlarged quotas, 1936, 1937 or 1938? Uproar broke out again. But this time it was between France's trading partners. '1936', cried some. 'Nonsense,' cried others. 'That does us down. 1937 must be the key.' 'No,' cried others, equally passionately, '1938 is the only fair basis.' Kojève sat quietly, smiling like a cat.

In Geneva at Edgar's house we discussed the French opposition to our bid to join the Community. Edgar asked why the French had chosen one particular argument.

'To keep you out,' said Kojève. 'If that hadn't worked, we would have chosen something else.'

He laughed merrily. He was so outrageous and so engaging that we all laughed. Edgar had an eminent career in the British service. But the very qualities that made him an uncomfortable companion in the cosy, enclosed British world would have made him a pillar of the French establishment. Some people are born in the wrong country. Edgar was one.

My Commission opposite number was Theo Hijzen, from whom years later I was to take over as Director General for External Relations. He was a stolid and friendly Dutchman. He was not an intellectual heavyweight. But he was straight and he talked sense; we became friends. The Americans had seen a changing of the guard. A new star had appeared. Michael Blumenthal was a first generation American. His family had emigrated from Berlin to Shanghai after 1933. He had emigrated to the United States immediately after the war, had worked his way through Princeton and had started in business. His job in the State Department was later to prove a stepping

103

stone – as often in the United States – to a very successful business career. He was a brilliant man, easy to talk to and with an irony, sometimes gentle, sometimes savage. I once said to him that Edgar would have made a very distinguished banker but, with austere tastes, would not have known what to do with the money. Mike removed a cigar from his mouth. 'Guess he could always hang some gold bars on the walls,' he observed.

Hijzen and Blumenthal did not get on. Sir Richard Powell, the then Board of Trade Permanent Secretary, came out to Geneva to see how the Kennedy Round was faring. I gave a cocktail party. At both ends of the room Hijzen and Blumenthal held court like mediæval kings. People would attend one court and then move to the other. But the two kings did not meet. Afterwards Richard Powell remarked, 'Blumenthal came up to me and said that he liked Geneva and seemed to get on with you, but there was one fly in the ointment and that was a frightful fellow called Hijzen. I said that I was not surprised. Then Hijzen came up and said that he liked Geneva and seemed to get on with you, but there was one fly in the ointment and that was a frightful fellow called Blumenthal. It seems', he said thoughtfully, 'that you have quite a job on your hands.'

The job – like all the major GATT negotiations – took time, and the more the scope of the negotiations widened and the number of participants increased, the longer the process took. After just over a year a Labour Government came in. I said to Edgar that I assumed there would be no change in policy. 'Don't you believe it,' said Edgar shrewdly. 'They won't be as keen as the last lot. They'll all see lower tariffs as a threat to wages and jobs.' And sure enough Thomas Balogh, a new economic adviser to Harold Wilson, now Prime Minister, would have been glad to see the negotiations fail for the reasons Edgar gave. Perceiving that this was hardly practicable, he fell back on a major attack on our conduct of the trade negotiations. 'We were economically illiterate,' he cried, 'a lot of dolts.' Fortunately my Whitehall boss, Alan Neale, no mean economist himself was a tower of strength. So the attack was beaten off. But this was the time of the New Men, of the white heat of technology and of the hour of the economist. Droves of them arrived in Whitehall, determined to put an end to government by illiterate Tory squires and generalist administrators. Our affairs needless to say prospered no more under the new regime than under the old. This is not to say that there is anything wrong with using economists. But a large scale import of meteorologists does not in itself guarantee a period of fine weather.

The negotiations intensified. The point approached when it was decided that a small team would have to set up shop in Geneva for the two or three years the negotiations still had to run. I enquired about allowances. I was told that our team would get a minimum per diem on the lines paid to War Office clerical staff in Cyprus. I said that in that case we would not be going. Alan Neale was reproachful. I could hardly refuse to go, he said. I said that I had every intention of refusing. The job in Geneva was no different in kind from other jobs where Board of Trade people had been attached to Foreign Office missions and paid the going rate for Foreign Office personnel. I had no intention of spending three years in Geneva in a bedsit on a diet of potato peelings. After occasional displays of thunder and lightning our point was conceded just before Christmas 1964.

In Geneva early in 1965 I looked for somewhere to live and found a very pleasant villa about a quarter of an hour away from the city. It was fully furnished and had a swimming pool. I moved in at the beginning of March. On my way I called in on some neighbouring friends for a drink and was told of a Spanish couple who wanted a job. Consuela appeared the next day and I promptly signed her on. Consuela was a character reminiscent of one of the bit players in Italian opera. The syntax of her French was uncertain. '*Moi dis à vous,*' she would shout.

She had a heart of gold and with it a shrewd eye for the foibles of mankind. Before my first dinner party I expressed anxiety to Consuela about the non-arrival from the village of an elaborate iced pudding.

Consuela shrieked with laughter. 'At the price you're paying for it, they'd bring it on their hands and knees,' she said. Brown came to stay and remarked with a certain gloom that I seemed even better installed than in Bonn. He conveyed that, while trade negotiations in the GATT might involve late nights and much hard work, the rewards did not seem inconsiderable. Gazing that summer from the veranda at the lake and the mountains and hearing with satisfaction the clink of Consuela busy in the kitchen, I thought he had a point.

Edgar took his leave. He had been offered as his last post the Head of the British Delegation to the Organisation for European Economic Development in Paris and, accepting this, opted to transfer formally to the Foreign Office. Someone rang up to acquaint him with the details of his allowances. Edgar was told that at his age and rank he was to be credited with a notional child. 'A notional child!' he cried, his voice rising to a shriek at this apparent illogicality. 'Am I supposed to be harbouring a Peter Pan?'

I missed him. His successor summoned me on his arrival. 'I do not intend to get involved in this trade negotiation of yours. If it works I shall of course take the credit. If it does not I shall simply say "You know what these fellows from the Board of Trade are like. He insisted on doing his own thing and never showed me anything".' This struck me as commendably frank.

Installed in Geneva it was possible to get to know a wider circle. From the Commission I began to have a lot to do with Fernand Braun, a calm and congenial Luxembourger who is the wisest of men. On any point of dispute he would explain rationally and dispassionately the view he thought sensible. He was also a fund of useful advice on the intricacies of the Commission. He knew not only what everyone was doing but why they were doing it. I depended on him a lot in Geneva, in Brussels, when later we came to negotiate our entry into the Community and later still as a close colleague in the Commission. If Fernand ever advised against a particular course of action I would have thought long and hard before undertaking it.

But the most important new face was that of my wife, met just before leaving for Geneva at a party given in the Foreign Office by Ken Scott, my neighbour in Bonn, who was now *en route* to Washington. In April 1966 we got married. Moya took over what had been for a year a bachelor household with a firm and expert hand. She was somewhat surprised to find several hundred empty bottles in the cellar, but I explained that in our line of business we needed to have friends in for a drink now and again. A friendly gardener took them away. Moya remarked on his willingness. I pointed out that at ten centimes a bottle it must have been worth his while. One of the bizarre results of getting married on (temporary) Foreign Office allowances was that these virtually doubled while household costs (iced puddings being hence-forth made at home at a fraction of the cost) fell. But our entertain-ment increased. In our first fortnight a number of chemical friends came to dinner. I pointed out to Moya in advance that this would be a very dreary affair. Moya took the hint and retired for the evening with a boiled egg on a tray. But the next morning she was puzzled. 'I thought this was billed as a very technical discussion,' she said. I replied that it largely was. 'Then why,' she asked, 'when I woke up for a moment at midnight, did I hear you laughing like a hyena and crying, "Have you fellows heard the story of the dog that could play the violin?"' She added for good measure that the noise was like Barnum's Circus.

In the spring of 1967 the end began to approach. Negotiations need a deadline for their conclusion. American legislation ran out at the end of June. This prospect at last got things moving. Sir Richard Powell came out periodically from London to supervise the dealing of the cards. He wrote his own reports for the Cabinet. With the arrogance of comparative youth I wondered how much of the complicated Geneva scene he understood. Reading his reports I found that there was not a nuance he had missed. And in what he wrote there was a balance and brevity which I would have found hard to match.

The end of the negotiation was not without its anxious moments. We had offered much more in terms of concessions than the Six, and for several years had basked in the sunshine which beams on liberal traders. But in the Dillon Round I had learnt that at the end one could always pull back a large chunk of one's offer on the grounds that this had not been reciprocated by others. We did just that. There was uproar. We were accused of wrecking the negotiation. But we battened down the hatches and the storm blew over – with a politically accept-able deal at the end of it.

We were not the only ones with anxious moments. At the end the Commission found that they would not be able to settle within their instructions, i.e. the mandate approved by the Council of Ministers. There was no time to call another meeting. So Jean Rey, the Member of the European Commission responsible for external trade, rang up Bonn and Paris. From Bonn he got an indeterminate reply. In Paris he spoke to Couve de Murville, the Foreign Minister of General De Gaulle. With a certain icy majesty Couve replied, '*Est ce que vous voulez vraiment une réponse?*' (Do you really want a reply?) Over the words hung the shadow of the General. Asking the General would be like scaling a mountain and putting the question to one of the gods of old. The answer would come with a clap of thunder, awesome and irre-versible. It might well be No. Rey understood. He promptly exceeded his instructions. The Kennedy Round was saved. Wyndham White, the GATT Director General, announced its success to a packed late-night meeting of negotiators with the air of an alchemist who had at last succeeded in transmuting lead into gold. A major cut in trade barriers across the world had been agreed; the prosperity of the West would continue to advance.

The time had come for me to change track. For a short while the Community seemed to beckon. George Brown had become Foreign Secretary. He was intent on restarting our negotiations for entry; he was a man of dash and vision. Unfortunately this was combined with a temperament so mercurial that the result was often a vaudeville act *sans pareil.*

A friend of mine, who had once been his Private Secretary, encountered him near the Foreign Office one morning shortly after he had moved in.

'Hullo there, Tom!' he cried in a stentorian voice. 'See what's happened to me, don't you?' He gave a little hop, skip and a jump. 'They're trying to make a proper little gentleman out of me.' The expressions on the faces of the Foreign Office flying wedge behind beggared description.

From friends in Brussels there reached us the tale of Harold Wilson and George Brown attending a dinner at the residence of the British Ambassador to the Community. Several Commissioners were present, anxious to size up the new Labour Government. At a certain point Wilson excused himself for a call of nature. Scarcely had he left the room when George Brown bounded after him. Turning at the door with fine theatrical timing he cried, 'What I say is, you can't trust that little bugger if he's out of your sight, even if he's in the men's room.' This, a Dutch friend told me, was 'what you call knockabout theatre at its best or – I cannot really decide – at its worst.'

Knockabout theatre or not, not even George Brown was able to unblock the General's opposition to negotiations over Britain's entry into the EEC. So Moya and I packed up and drove back to London having said goodbye, we thought for ever, to the international circuit where I had happily been for most of ten years.

FOUR

Master

BRITAIN INTO EUROPE

Back in London some things were good; others not so good. We found a small modern house in Chelsea, looking over some gardens and a stone's throw from the King's Road. Early in 1968 we moved in. James arrived in July; Julia two and a half years later. The family settled down to London life.

I was promoted to Under Secretary. Tony Crosland was the Secretary of State for Trade in the Labour Government, a Cavalier among the Roundheads and fun to work for. While his political views were not ones which I could ever endorse, he was miles away from the Loony Land of the Far Left. He was courteous, except when he thought he was dealing with a fool, and would listen to any advice providing he thought it intelligent and honestly meant. I saw him only once nearly burst a blood vessel. That was at a memorable meeting when one of the Seniors, not the brightest of the Department, was holding forth on the future of our merchant marine.

'We must', he intoned solemnly, 'have a large merchant marine.'

'Why?', asked Crosland.

The Senior seemed shocked by the irreverence of this question.

'Because otherwise,' he said, 'we shall have a small one.'

110

Working for Crosland was also fun because he liked a certain amount of argument in the Department. Most submissions (memoranda submitted to Ministers) had to be copied to the Division which I now headed because it had a roving brief to advise on pretty well anything. So it was open to me to fire off a note challenging the submission from the point of view of the general interests of the Department or Whitehall or both. This would normally – and understandably – get an irate reply from the Under Secretary concerned inviting me to go and boil my head. But Crosland would listen. It was not that he thought I was necessarily – or even usually – right, but he had a horror of the sanitised unanimity of a formal departmental presentation. He liked to hear opposing points of view argued out. So back would come a note. 'The Secretary of State thinks that Mr Denman has raised an interesting point. Please let me have a note on it. Then a meeting to discuss.'

Other things were less good. With De Gaulle continuing to block British entry into the Community, dealing with European affairs would be years away. But as a colleague pointed out, I could hardly expect the history of Europe to adapt itself to my wishes. And it was about time I had a change of scene. It was not the new job which was depressing but the view from it. For Britain had lost its way both at home and abroad. Gloom eddied through the corridors of Whitehall like one of the London fogs of old.

We were cursed with a state educational system gone to ruin, a vindictive egalitarianism, and despotic trade union power. A glossy minority regarded industry with disdain; a sullen majority thought that life had been tilted unfairly against them. These problems could not be tackled because they were real and dogma does not easily adapt to reality. Instead there was a desperate Micawber-like hope that somehow something one day would turn up.

So much time was spent gazing hopefully into the mists of the future. Three times a year a massive economic forecast was drawn up. As Crosland once sagely remarked, any fool could see it was wrong; what was not clear was how wrong and in what direction. But never were entrails so closely examined. The economic gurus of Whitehall assembled to approve the final version. Someone, puffing a pipe, would say, 'There's an interesting anomaly here, Fred. I see no sensible correlation between the number of housing starts in the third quarter and the issue of dog licences.'

This hare would run round the track in splendid form for a good quarter of an hour. Another hare would then be let loose. Finally the forecast would be approved. The gurus would walk to their clubs, feeling with some pride that they had done a solid week's work. Yet the forecast proved about as much use as trying to foretell the weather in six months' time. I used to console myself in the evenings by reading *The Forsyte Saga* and thinking of how much better off Victorians had been with more money and fewer figures.

The effort expended on forecasting paled compared with the attempt to find the Philosopher's Stone of economic well-being. How could we become more prosperous without changing anything or working harder? Anyone who could find such a solution would be in power for ever. To the search for it some of the best brains of Whitehall devoted an enormous and continuing effort. But travel to any other European country would have shown that all this was a search for fairy gold. The rest of Europe had found prosperity by picking themselves out of defeat and rubble after the war and rebuilding on the basis of a social consensus and simple hard work. I remarked to a colleague one day that the only way to salvation was to blow up the British established order and start again. Hardly a solution likely to be acceptable to Ministers, he said.

The other fundamental problem was external. How was Britain, in its altered circumstance since 1945, to relate to the outside world? For long Britain had seemed a major world power – one of the victors of the Second World War, centre of a great empire, ally of the United States. Churchill proudly proclaimed the doctrine of the three circles. Britain would have its own relationship with the Commonwealth. It would of course have a special relationship with the United States. And it would also have a relationship – of a friendly but rather distant kind – with the rest of Europe. Britain was too grand – was the implication – to have an exclusive relationship with anyone. It bestrode the waves with a friendly clasp of the hand to clean-limbed men from the United States and the Empire and a rather disdainful smile for the wicked Hun and the unreliable French.

Two of the three circles did not take long to reveal themselves as illusions. The Commonwealth expanded to a mini United Nations of much talk, much hypocrisy about imperialism from dictators who threw their opponents into jail, and harboured unlimited expectations about aid.

The Anglo–American special relationship was equally illusory. In some ways it resembled the Cheshire Cat – sometimes there and smiling, more often a memory on an empty branch. There are certain Anglo–American links from history. But some of them are on the dark side – the burning down of Washington in 1814, the Anglo–American dispute over Venezuela in 1895 and the calls in the United States for war against Britain, not to mention President's Wilson's cold rebuff at a victory dinner in Buckingham Palace in December 1918: 'You must not speak of us who come over here as cousins, still less as brothers; we are neither. Neither must you think of us as Anglo-Saxons, for that term can no longer be rightly applied to the people of the United States. Nor must too much importance in this connection be attached to the fact that English is our common language ... No, there are only two things which can establish and maintain closer relations between your country and mine; they are community of ideals and interests.'

Churchill thought he had restored the situation with his Second World War alliance with President Roosevelt. He painted a picture of himself and Roosevelt on some elevated plateau deciding in common the affairs of the world. It was a romantic story of the United States always eyeing us with fraternal affection, riding to our aid whenever danger threatened, looking to us as their most faithful ally and grateful for our wise and experienced counsel in world affairs. But this was part of the post-war British dream world.

As the Americans saw it, the relationship was from the beginning a business deal. When it was in their interest to support Britain as their first line of defence against Hitler and then as an unsinkable aircraft carrier in the Cold War, then American support was forthcoming. But the United States saw no reason to provide an open-ended subsidy for our post-war imperial and socialist ambitions, or to forgo any opportunity to use aid as a means of securing concessions. During the war they pressed us hard on subjects as various as territorial concessions in return for out-of-date destroyers, the ending of imperial preference in return for Lend Lease, American access to Empire air routes and Middle East oil and cutting our desperately needed meat imports from Argentina to further American policy towards Latin America.

After the war Churchill's proposals for a 'fraternal association' of the English speaking peoples got nowhere. In January 1952, shortly after he had returned to power, he made an impassioned plea to Truman for Anglo–American cooperation 'in the great tradition'. Truman dismissed it by suggesting that 'We might pass this to our advisers for further consideration.' A few weeks later Churchill made the same plea to the newly elected President Eisenhower. Privately Churchill was peeved to find this one-time military subordinate and late entrant to politics now outranking him. He thought Eisenhower an over-promoted Brigadier. He exerted all his charm. It availed him little. Eisenhower thought Churchill at nearly eighty was past it and, while perfectly courteous, considered Churchill's desire to relive the days of the Second World War grotesque.

And so it went on. Britain's sabre-rattling Suez adventure under Anthony Eden was brutally cut short by Eisenhower. Eden's successor, Harold Macmillan, made much of his friendship with President Kennedy. But this ended badly; at their last meeting at Macmillan's house at Birch Grove in 1963 President Kennedy was reported as 'resentful and disappointed at Macmillan's lack of grip on international affairs.' When I got back to Whitehall in 1967 Harold Wilson was Prime Minister and ensconced in an Anglo–American dream world as exotic as that of any of his predecessors. The plain fact is that it was and always will be folly for the British to imagine that, because of a historical relationship which the British eye with sentiment and Americans often with resentment, the Americans will be prepared to go against their own interests. As a shrewd American diplomat once said, when I asked him whether there really was an Anglo–American special relationship: 'Yes, but the British have never understood it.'

The third circle was rapidly changed by one of the great revolutions of the second half of the twentieth century – the unification of Europe. Britain in the late 1940s could have had the leadership of Europe for a song. But it threw it away. In 1950 it rebuffed the Schuman Plan. In 1955 it refused to go along with the drafting of the Treaty of Rome, signed two years later. The prosperity of the Six began to rise sharply; the comparative prosperity of Britain declined. But the more it declined the more British Ministers, and particularly the Prime Minister of the day, travelled the world. So many of them streamed through Washington that one of the wittier post-war British Ambassadors coined the memorable phrase: 'We can change the sheets but we can't cool the mattresses.' British television screens were filled with pictures of British Ministers getting on planes, getting off planes, speaking at length to seemingly admiring crowds, and making an allegedly triumphant return. And the more events, in particular the growing unification of Europe, exposed this as an illusion, the more British politicians clung to it. Their attitude to Europe getting together was to wish fervently that Europe would just go away.

It was true that Macmillan had made a half-hearted attempt to join the European Community in 1961, and that Wilson had applied in May 1967. But Macmillan's memoirs reveal him as an Edwardian who, at least until a late conversion, regarded the Community as a reincarnation of Napoleon's Continental blockade. He was one of the great jetters round the world in search of the top table. A story which is part of Community folklore tells of him once encountering in London, on a visit from Brussels, Walter Hallstein, the first President of the Commission. Macmillan was languidly condescending. '*Ah, la Commission,*' he said: '*On mange bien à Paris, n'est ce pas?*'

But in 1969 things began to look up; the roadblock against British entry into the Community began to crumble. In April 1969 General De Gaulle lost a plebiscite he had called on the reform of the regions and the Senate. On 28 April he resigned. One Sunday evening I heard on my old German radio the haughty voice of Couve de Murville, De Gaulle's Foreign Minister. The country had decided, he said; it would now have to take the consequences. I looked out at the lights beyond the gardens and wondered about the consequences.

At the beginning of December a summit of the Six at the Hague decided that new members could now be admitted. It was agreed that the negotiations should start on 30 June 1970. Preparations in Whitehall got under way. But I was told informally that I was out. The Deputy Secretary who dealt with international trade was very experienced. Although he was near retirement, it had apparently been agreed that his term would be extended to the end of the negotiations. The choice could not be faulted, but I was depressed. I had spent seven years in negotiation on trade matters with the Community, more than anyone else in the Department.

Then something odd happened. I went in the spring of 1970 to a course at Cambridge – by chance at my old college – run to pool experience between executives from a number of international companies and some officials from Whitehall. The businessmen were a lively lot and I think we (at least the civil servants) learned a good deal. The final session was attended by the Permanent Secretary of the Ministry of Technology, Otto Clarke. One creep from the Whitehall contingent, hoping doubtless to ingratiate himself, made a passionate plea for Government intervention in industry. I intervened to say that I did not believe in intervention. If my years in the Department of Trade had taught me anything it was that Government officials simply did not know enough to decree that for example the production of acetone should rise next year by 8.3 per cent; that was for the market to determine. To the surprise and chagrin of the creep, Otto Clarke agreed. At the final dinner that evening I was asked to speak. I told the more respectable of a number of stories given me by an entertaining man from Shell; this seemed to go down well. After dinner Otto Clarke made some friendly comments. 'I'd like to have you in our Department,' he said, 'but I gather you're going off on this European thing.' I left deep in thought.

Early next week I was summoned by Antony Part, who had succeeded Richard Powell as our Permanent Secretary. He offered me a drink and then came to the point. I was to be promoted Deputy Secretary and be part of the team which would negotiate our entry into the Community. Feeling like someone who had won heavily on the pools, I listened while Part explained that there had been a change of plan. No. 10 and the Cabinet Office had taken the view that the Deputy Secretary we had proposed was too near retirement. They wanted someone younger who would be able to use the experience of the negotiation in later dealings with the Community. My name had been put forward and accepted. I had at last reached in the guild the rank of Master. But far more important was the long sought chance to take a hand in Britain's entry into Europe. In a happy daze I went out, bought a bottle of champagne and celebrated with Moya.

The negotiating team was announced shortly afterwards. The Head, at official level, was Sir Con O'Neill from the Foreign Office. I did not take to him. He had a curious pallor, as though he had just stepped out of a grave. His manner was cold and formal and on the rare moments when he smiled it was like the proverbial gleam of moonlight on a coffin. His voice was richly canonical; the more irreverent on the team began to refer to him as the Archbishop or the Arch.

I discovered later that this was a badly mistaken judgement. Underneath the cold exterior there was a warm and lively spirit struggling to get out. Con O'Neill was simply a shy, rather austere man. He was an outstanding diplomat of the old school with a stately caution in communication reminiscent of a vintage Rolls Royce. Beneath the surface lay a delightful sense of humour and a variety of Irish stories. And he was a man – like Edgar Cohen – of passionate honesty. A Foreign Office friend told me of a discussion once between Harold Wilson, then Prime Minister, and George Brown, his Foreign Secretary. Con O'Neill was present. Wilson and Brown disagreed. O'Neill opined that the Prime Minister's point was the sounder of the two. After Wilson had left George Brown erupted in fury. Why had his adviser let him down? Con was quite unmoved. He had concluded that one particular argument was valid and another not. The fact that he was in disagreement with his own Minister did not disturb him. He was out to give the best advice he could, regardless of who would be pleased or annoyed by it.

Con called the first meeting of his team, the negotiating Delegation. His principal Foreign Office adviser was John Robinson, who had spent

118

many years in the British Delegation to the European Community in Brussels; his knowledge of the Community was encyclopaedic; his ability unchallenged. He was a believer; he had believed in the Community in good times and in bad; there was never a moment of hesitation or a scintilla of doubt; in the relentless fixity of his approach there was something of the Recording Angel. He did more than anyone else, except Edward Heath, to make our entry possible. The Treasury man was Raymond Bell. Raymond's features look out of countless medieval pictures of advisers to kings and princes: austere, shrewd, quizzical, cautious – with ever watchful eyes. He only spoke when he had something to say, a quality which disturbed some and astonished many. Freddy Kearns from the Ministry of Agriculture was a miniature Falstaff – happiest with a large cigar and a glass in his hand – cheerful, voluble and with a flow of language which would have made a brothel keeper blush. Patrick Shovelton, who was to deal with coal and steel, added a touch of twentieth-century normality. It was a good team.

There was throughout the negotiations much talk of the 'terms' – the terms of entry we could secure. In one sense the terms were irrelevant. No sensible traveller on the sinking *Titanic* would have said, 'I will only enter a lifeboat if it is well scrubbed, well painted and equipped with suitable supplies of food and drink.' Our historic task was to repair the mistakes of the past and to restore our position at the centre of European affairs. If when we entered we found any particular feature of Community arrangements intolerable then our problems would have to be dealt with as part of the family. As the Community assured us, 'if unacceptable situations arose the very survival of the Community would demand that the institutions find equitable solutions.'

Yet, politics being politics, solutions to two problems in particular had to be found before our negotiations could be presented as successful to a sceptical public and a strongly entrenched and bitter opposition. One was the treatment of New Zealand – continued access for a reasonable portion of their traditional exports to the UK. The other was the British contribution to the Community budget. Of the two the New Zealand problem was politically the more important. In two world wars they had been the most impeccably loyal of all the Commonwealth and they would be hardest hit by our joining the Community. If John Marshall, their Deputy Prime Minister who had been deputed to watch over these negotiations, were to denounce the results as unacceptable, then it would quite simply have been impossible to get the approval of the House of Commons. Thus New Zealand had a virtual right of veto over the negotiations.

The question of the British contribution to the Community budget, while major, was less of an immediate political danger. Our contribution would have to be on a sliding scale. We needed to get a low figure for the early years. The position in later years could not be forecast with any accuracy. But it was clear that trouble would be bound to come. The economic structure of the UK was different in two respects from those of our Continental neighbours. With the repeal of the Corn Laws in 1846 British agriculture had declined to a fraction of that on the Continent where protection had continued. And Britain imported much more than the Continental countries from outside the Community. So a Community budget derived largely from customs duties and levies charged by Member States on imports from third countries and devoted largely to agriculture would be no great deal for Britain. Our receipts would be much less than our contribution. Could we have done something about this in the negotiations? I am clear that we could not. The Commission argued that expenditure on agriculture as a proportion of the Community budget would fall and that the dynamics of entry would bring us major but unquantifiable advantages. Our bargaining position was weak. Had we joined the Community at the outset the Common Agricultural Policy and the financial arrangements would have been different. But we had not. And to the reluctance of the existing members to change the rules for a new entrant was added a tactical link which the French astutely established between the New Zealand problem and the budgetary one. The more we got on one the less we would get on the other. It was to be years later when Mrs Thatcher swung her handbag and forced a satisfactory solution to the British budgetary problem – thereby demonstrating the validity of the Community's assurance that equitable solutions would have to be found when problems became unacceptable.

Other subjects abounded. One, inevitably for a British Government, was Ireland. This time it was a free trade agreement we had signed with Ireland some years ago; somehow this would have to be subsumed into a wider customs union agreement with the Six. Con O'Neill and I flew to Dublin to sound out the Irish before the negotiations in Brussels got under way. It was a sunny May day; the Irish were hospitable and charming; wine at the Gresham flowed with the abundance of a spring in an Irish fable.

Seeking to inform myself about a country of which I knew little, I asked about Irish politics. I would have been much wiser to have held my tongue. What was the difference, I asked, between the two main Irish political parties? Was it essentially economic?

'It depended', I was told, 'whether you were for or against the Treaty in '23.'

My ignorance of Irish history and (as I later found) of the long and bitter struggle between those who accepted the partition of Ireland and the hardliners who did not, was such that this meant nothing to me. '1923?' I replied. 'That was rather a long time ago.'

There was a stunned silence. My neighbour rolled his eyes. I knew that somehow I had put my feet right in it. Someone finally broke the silence. Gently he asked, 'Is this your first visit to Ireland, Mr Denman?'

Another problem was agriculture. How were we going to adapt to the Common Agricultural Policy, generally held in Whitehall to be the work of Satan? A few days after the trip to Dublin I got an urgent summons to see the Permanent Secretary. Sir Antony Part was in a mood of righteous indignation. 'Why had we been stupid enough to tell the Six that we "accepted" the Common Agricultural Policy? Everyone knows it's a mad policy. We shouldn't be accepting it, we should be tearing it up.'

I replied that if we had not walked out of the preparations for the Treaty of Rome in 1955 and had instead taken part in drafting the Community's rules, we could have made our case. As it was, if we took that line, we could save ourselves the cost of any further air fares to Brussels. The way to deal with the French, as I had found in Geneva, was not by staging a confrontation over principle but arguing over detail. Moreover we had just received confidential information from Brussels about the reaction of one French Commissioner. He had ruefully remarked that in accepting 'in principle' the CAP, the British had been more intelligent than usual. He had hoped that we would reject it and thus straightaway provoke a veto.

Part was cross. He had summoned this recently promoted devotee of things European to take him down a peg, only to find that the upstart did not humbly accept Part's wisdom. Moreover he could see that in this particular case he was not going to win. So when we parted his mood was far from genial. 'I hope you're not going to get too attached to all this Common Market stuff. It's not exactly popular in Whitehall,' he said in a voice with some of the flavour of the icebergs crashing and grinding round the *Titanic*.

In between these diversions the team began the task of writing position papers which would have to be approved by Whitehall and then Ministers before negotiations actually started. In the middle of all this an election took place. The opinion polls foretold almost without

122

exception a Labour victory. Gathered in Cabinet Office, the negotiating team drew up a brief for the incoming Labour Government, larded, as is the Whitehall custom, with laudatory references to the wisdom and foresight of previous Labour Ministers. 'There's no point in wasting much time on a brief for the other lot,' said one of our group, to general agreement. Two days later, when the results started coming in, we hastened back to Cabinet Office to rewrite the brief.

I was elated by Wilson's defeat. This was not because of any antipathy to Labour; Civil Servants are mostly disillusioned Liberals, who greet with resignation the prospect of working for either party. Nor was it a dislike of Wilson; I had worked for him and liked him. And George Thomson, the Labour Minister who would have been in charge of the negotiating team, was a thoroughly decent, shrewd and sensible Scot. But for two reasons I could not see a negotiation led by Wilson working.

A few weeks before in a corridor of the House of Commons I had encountered Fred Peart, the Minister of Agriculture. He waved me with a conspiratorial wink to a corner. 'Harold's gone off the Common Market,' he said in a hoarse whisper. He raised a finger in the air, giving a creditable imitation of an old countryman testing the direction of the wind. And then with a cunning smile he was gone.

Knowing Wilson, I could see what he meant. Had Labour been returned the negotiations would have started briskly. But when the crunch came the following year the Party would have been badly split. Callaghan would have moved against, as he did in 1971. And Wilson, anxious as always to keep the Party together and to prevent himself being supplanted, would have broken off the negotiations. To the minority of pro-marketeers he would have said that he had done his best but had been unable to move the stubborn French. To the antis he would have declaimed to great applause that he had not been willing to sacrifice the country's vital interests and those of the

Commonwealth. Britain, with a Churchillian gesture of defiance, would stand alone.

But I doubted whether it would even have come to that. Pompidou, De Gaulle's successor, had visited London in 1966 when he was Prime Minister. He and Wilson had not got on. Wilson had cancelled a meeting at short notice and had cut a dinner party which Pompidou had given. My French friends told me that Pompidou had returned to Paris convinced that Wilson would always place the interests of the Commonwealth and the United States before those of his Continental partners. Wilson would have been shown the door in short order. But of the Conservative leader Edward Heath's commitment to the European cause there could be no doubt.

Heath, now in Downing Street, quickly appointed his Cabinet. The new Ministerial head of our negotiating team was Anthony Barber, small and nervous, with the air of an accountant brought in to supervise a merger, uneasily aware of unexplained depths. With him we flew in an ancient Andover on 29 June 1970 to the opening session of the negotiations in Luxembourg. A mass of journalists also attended and had cornered all the available hotel accommodation so quickly that the British Delegation found itself in a hotel in Mondorf, miles away. Cars had been efficiently laid on for us, the only difficulty being that whatever instructions we gave the drivers they invariably headed for the residence of the British Ambassador.

The next day Pierre Harmel, the Belgian Foreign Minister, as the outgoing Chairman of the Council of Ministers of the Six, made the opening statement. It defined the basis of the negotiations. Unlike the first negotiations in 1961–3, when Britain had negotiated with six countries (aided by the Commission), the Six would now negotiate as one; they would speak only through the President of the Council, advised by the Commission, although the Six would all be present at negotiating sessions, silently observing and ready to caucus if a new line were needed. The applicant countries, the UK, Denmark, Ireland and Norway, would have to accept the '*acquis communautaire*' – that is all Community decisions so far taken and the decisions which would be taken up to the date of their entry. Any difficulties which applicant countries might encounter in accepting these rules would have to be met not by altering them but by transitional measures. Barber's statement in reply was a far cry from the comprehensive list of demands which Heath had put forward in 1961 at the start of the first negotiations for entry. We had learnt in the meantime to be more realistic. In the main the British Government accepted the Community approach. It would be necessary to find solutions 'which are Community solutions' in a limited number of cases, including New Zealand, the budgetary problem and certain Commonwealth questions. He hoped the negotiations would be kept short and limited to essentials. This was well received. So were the Danish and Irish statements which took a similar line. The Norwegian indicated that the Treaty of Rome was not a bad basis to work on. At this a subdued growling noise, like lions at feeding time, issued from the Commission benches.

The Luxembourg meeting was followed on 21 July in Brussels by the first Ministerial negotiating meeting. This and subsequent meetings were held at two levels – Ministerial and what was called Deputies. The first would include the Foreign Ministers of the Six and the Member of the Commission, Jean Francois Deniau (a Frenchman) who dealt with the negotiations, each with their senior advisers – and on the British side the Lord Privy Seal, as the Minister in charge of the negotiations, the members of the negotiating team and the British Ambassador to the Community in Brussels. At Deputies level the Six would be represented by their Permanent Representatives in Brussels, i.e. their Ambassadors to the Community, and the Director General in the Commission dealing with the negotiations, Edmund

Wellenstein, a Dutchman. On our side Con O'Neill and the negotiating team plus our Ambassador would attend. At one stage a sub-
group was set up including representatives of all the applicants and the
Six, in effect Deputies of Deputies. The Norwegian Ambassador
achieved temporary fame when his Nordic gloom yielded to an unexpected sense of humour. 'Dep Deps,' he said.

Ministerial meetings would be held once a month; meetings of
Deputies twice a month. Similar meetings, though less frequent, would
be held between the Six and the other applicants. After each of our
meetings we would brief in turn in Brussels our colleagues from the
Commonwealth, the European Free Trade Association and separately
the Irish. The other applicant countries for their part kept us in touch
with their progress.

A bizarre pattern was set which was to become familiar. The British
would make a proposal; we then withdrew while the Six considered
their reply. At the start Barber proposed that fact-finding groups be
set up to get to work on our various problems. (Raymond Bell had
shrewdly warned that without adequate preparation on our part the
Six would baulk. He was right. They were suspicious. What were the
British up to?) When Walter Scheel, the German Foreign Minister,
proposed an adjournment, Barber said in all innocence, 'This will allow
me to have a cup of tea.' The Germans told me later that after he had
left, Scheel had said to his colleagues, 'Mr Barber is clearly not well
acquainted with our customs. He will have time not only for one cup
but several.'

The adjournment lasted for hours. Someone in the press room
pinned up a notice: 'If anyone finds a fact it should be returned immediately to the British Delegation.' Finally the Six agreed. It became
clear that this would be a long negotiation.

So the fortnightly trip to Brussels became a routine. We arrived in
the early evening, had a late snack and then a Delegation meeting

where we jointly went over whatever statements were being made the next day. On one occasion Freddy Kearns turned up late. He had clearly dined well and was smoking an extra large cigar. 'What are you going to say about pigmeat, Freddy?' asked the Arch.

Fred expansively waved his cigar. 'Tell them the tale, Con, tell them the tale.' The brow of the Arch furrowed.

'What sort of tale?' he asked.

London was also active. Visitors came from the four corners of the earth. John Marshall appeared from New Zealand to make what he called as a lawyer 'My statement of claim'. There was about it a charming simplicity which only those of guile can affect. 'New Zealand,' he said, 'is an island, thousands of miles from anywhere, and covered in grass. On the grass graze many sheep and cows. That is our problem.' The New Zealanders had the good grace not to refer to their effective power of veto. They took the line irresistible to Englishmen, that they were on a sticky wicket and could we possibly, as decent chaps, give them a helping hand?

The Canadians played their hand intelligently. Admittedly they were not always impressive. Our team had dinner one night with a Canadian Minister and his entourage, rambling on until midnight about the GATT and world trade. One senior Canadian official distinguished himself by making only three interventions, all identical: 'I think the Minister has a good point.'

'Surely,' I said afterwards to Raymond Bell, 'that man will not go far.'

'Don't bank on it,' said Raymond, 'that kind of fellow does go far.'

A few weeks later he was appointed Canadian Ambassador in Brussels. But there was an excellent Chargé d'Affaires, Randy Gherson. We explained to him that we were in negotiation to help ourselves, not Canada. But where we could amend to our mutual convenience a tariff definition on – say – plywood, a major item in Anglo Canadian trade, we would gladly do so.

Randy knew nothing about plywood, but he knew people who did. On the last plane one night into Brussels I collected a Canadian plywood manufacturer. 'I'm from the rhubarb belt,' he said cheerfully. 'Thought this bag of plywood samples might help. Solid one side.' We shipped them off next morning to the experts of the Six. The result was tariff-free access to the whole of the Community market for a large part of Canadian plywood exports.

The Australians employed different tactics. Their Trade Minister, 'Black Jack' McEwen, descended on London like a raging bull – in so far as one can imagine a raging bull speaking Strine. His language nearly set fire to the wallpaper. The tactic was ill judged. It availed him little.

A Jamaican Delegation turned up and Michael Noble, the President of the Board of Trade, gave them dinner at Lancaster House. He made a graceful speech of welcome. But his financial circumstances were clearly in a different league from ours. A stunned gathering of impoverished bureaucrats heard him say expansively, 'All of us with houses in Jamaica . . .'.

Our dealings with the other applicants did not present major problems. Denmark had had two major markets for its agriculture. Of them, Germany had long been behind the Community wall; if Britain entered Denmark could not afford to stay out. And the Danes saw that under the Common Agricultural Policy Danish farmers would prosper. Their only main difficulty was a constitutional one: the Folketing, their Parliament, with an impertinence often found in the elected representatives of the people, wanted an uncomfortably dominant role in the control of Danish affairs in the Community.

With the Irish we still had to settle the details, which we had first discussed in Dublin, of merging our free trade agreement with a wider customs union. I suggested drafting an exchange of letters. 'Brilliant,' remarked my Irish opposite number. 'Let's get our teams together over dinner.' They asked us to a restaurant off the Grand Place. Seamus began by telling a few stories. There is something extraordinarily beguiling about the lilt of an Irish accent and their story-telling capacity. We laughed uproariously, and the more we laughed the better the stories became. Some time after midnight we parted in high good humour, only dimmed the next morning by our recalling that we had not touched on any serious matter from start to finish.

I rang up Seamus. 'Thank you for a splendid evening,' I said, 'but you know we didn't really deal with anything serious.'

'There's nothing wrong with having a few laughs now and again,' remarked Seamus. 'But I absolutely agree with you. Next time we must really get down to it.' We and our teams met again the following week. The entrée was quickly demolished, our glasses were charged, our pens and paper were at the ready. Then Seamus intervened. 'I know we're in for a brutishly serious evening', he said, 'but let me lighten the gloom for just one minute. Have you fellows ever heard the story of the clergyman and the goat in County Kilkenny?' Slowly, inevitably and delightfully, the evening went the way of the one the previous week.

After that, as the Americans would say, the question 'kinda fell into desuetude'. Other crises intervened. And it slowly became apparent that there was after all no real need for a ponderous exchange of letters. Trade would be freed and things would sort themselves out, as in due course they did. I suspect the Irish knew this all along. But rather than waste time and energy on a theological wrangle with the stiff-necked Brits, they preferred an indirect approach.

Some months later a meeting in London discussed how the different members of the Community would tackle the Presidency – that is the six months in turn when each assumes the chairmanship of Community business. A rather pompous official doubted whether this could be done by those without the magnificent machine of Whitehall. How, he asked scornfully, could a small country like Ireland possibly manage? I replied with some asperity that from what I had seen they would manage a damned sight better than some of the big ones.

The Norwegians lived in a different world – one of Nordic twilight and a palpable distrust of Southern, Catholic fat cats. Their tactics were to play it long and get at the end of the day some special concessions on agriculture and fish. This could have been difficult for us. In fact no major difficulty arose, mainly because the Community thought throughout that Britain was the main problem and were reluctant to fork out for minnows more than they were prepared to give to a medium sized whale. But Norwegian doubts about membership were never far from the surface. In late 1971 I had dinner in Brussels with some of the Norwegian team whom I had got to know in Geneva.

At the end of dinner, feeling playful, I said, 'Now boys, once we're in we'll need to concentrate on taxation. We're all paying far too much tax to keep bums and layabouts in a state to which they should not be accustomed. Let's combine to get personal taxation down to not more than 20 per cent.'

The Norwegians went red in the face with indignation. 'You must reckon,' they said in that sing-song Nordic accent, 'with our Norwegian social democratic conscience.'

I went to the Arch the next morning. 'Con,' I remarked, 'those fellows aren't going in.'

Ian MacLeod, the Chancellor of the Exchequer, died soon after the negotiations started and Anthony Barber went to replace him. Geoffrey Rippon arrived as the leader of our team. There was a rasp in his voice and an air of conviction; he could put details in their proper place and showed no distaste for travel. He had something of the earthy self-confidence of the Radio Doctor; on occasions this was too much for the House of Commons. 'When we enter,' he once said. 'If, if,' chorused the doubters. Gilbert and Sullivan would have made of 'When, when' and 'If, if' a fine duet. But as Christmas came and went

130

the two major problems, New Zealand and money, were still far from solution. The French argued that agreement on our part to pay a substantial contribution to Community coffers from the beginning was a touchstone of our European commitment. And with the Community awash with milk and butter they saw no need to help a faraway place like New Zealand. 'Why', Couve de Murville had once asked in a meeting of the Six during the first negotiations, 'should we help New Zealand? Their farmers are richer than ours.' 'Because,' said Paul Henri Spaak of Belgium, 'twice in a generation they came to Europe to die for freedom.'

The decision was taken that the Prime Minister, Edward Heath, would see the French President Pompidou. The meeting took place in Paris on 12 May 1971. The negotiating team travelled to Paris to be on hand if advice were wanted. In fact we were hardly needed. The meeting was essentially between Heath and Pompidou, with only interpreters present. Pompidou was not concerned with the detail. He wanted – as a former banker – to know whether he could do business with Heath. Did Heath want a Europe with its own identity – a European Union? Pompidou liked what he heard. He and Heath had not a word of a common language. But they were on the same wavelength. One small example was an agreement on language. Pompidou was nervous at the prospect of French being submerged by a torrent of English. He asked for an assurance that the British would only send to Brussels officials who could deal in French. He got his assurance.

Pompidou decided that day that Britain could be admitted. At a joint press conference afterwards he was asked about the future of the negotiations. He smiled. He had no doubt, he said, that the negotiators would talk far into the night. They liked that sort of thing. But his conclusion was that 'it would be unreasonable to believe that agreement is impossible at the Conference [the next Ministerial meeting] in June.'

131

Thus the scene of battle shifted back to Luxembourg (where Ministerial Councils are held in April, June and October). It was not an easy fight. In the French ranks the split between Pompidou's men and the hardliners in the Quai d'Orsay was clearly visible. On the New Zealand side it was obvious that there was a struggle between Marshall and the hardliners in Wellington. This did not exactly help our fight on the budgetary contribution, which the French insisted on linking with the New Zealand question. Discussion with the Six started late on 21 June. It was not and could not be a tidy affair. The most important discussions were held in our Delegation office between Geoffrey Rippon and Jean François Deniau of the Commission (who in turn had to leave us from time to time to consult the Foreign Ministers of the Six). But the whole building was buzzing with contacts and news. Someone would whisper in a corridor, 'The Six are near deciding on X.' A brisk dialogue would follow in the bar; some thoughts of ours would be fed into the meeting. Shortly after three the next morning we received an offer from the Six on New Zealand. We decided to bid for more. But it was clear that no further progress could be made that night so we adjourned.

The next day's discussions went on until dawn on the 23rd. After much battling we got an increase in the New Zealand offer which Marshall, smuggled into the Delegation office late at night, said he would recommend to Wellington. A hard fought compromise was reached on the budgetary issue – a starting position just about acceptable and a formula which should prevent too sharp an increase towards the end of the transitional period. Two other questions were also settled. We had proposed a short period for moving to the Community's industrial tariff and a longer one for moving to Community agricultural prices. We agreed to make the periods approximately the same. The last question to be settled was Commonwealth sugar, which had contractual access to the British market and a favourable price to the extent of 1.4 million tons. We settled on a formula which fell short of our demand for bankable assurances, but which was acceptable to the Commonwealth sugar producers and to the British sugar kings.

Finally at dawn we reached agreement. Our Delegation filed in to the Council Chamber. The long windows were blood red with the dawn. Everyone began to clap. The proceedings were formal and short. Then a press conference. Champagne was handed round. A French journalist asked Maurice Schumann, the French Foreign Minister, how, as an old Gaullist, he saw the agreement. There was a hush. Schumann hesitated for just a moment. It would not have been too fanciful in the eerie half light of dawn to have glimpsed a menacing Kepi. In fact with a wave of the hand Schumann imagined the General before him. He would, he pronounced, have had far less difficulty defending this event than many others.

At six o'clock we streamed back to the hotel, tired but triumphant. Freddy Kearns wondered whether the bar was open. Fortunately for us it was not. We got a few hours sleep and then went out to the Delegation plane. There was an atmosphere of elation. Telegrams of congratulation began to arrive. The buzz of excitement increased. History had changed. We were going in. At Brussels we saw the headlines in the London papers: 'CHAMPAGNE AT DAWN'. The Foreign Secretary was coming out to Heathrow to greet us but the plane delayed too long in Brussels. We reached home tired but happy.

The press coverage the next day was favourable. From the start we – that is Raymond, Fred and I – had made it a habit to lunch every fortnight with David Spanier of *The Times*, Reggie Dale of the *Financial Times* and Andrew Knight of the *Economist*. We did this because the regular briefing by the official spokesman cannot, since the spokesman is a generalist, go much into detail. We thought the serious press deserved more. So at these lunches we were frank, explaining not only what we were doing but why we were doing it. Our friends never let us down. We had a good press. When they criticised us – and anyone who deals with the press and expects a diet of unalloyed praise should emigrate to a dictatorship – it was fair criticism based on knowledge. And we learned from them. In a negotiation where all depends at the end on public acceptance it is no bad thing to have a regular exchange with critical but fair minded observers. A certain camaraderie developed. At one point Reggie Dale urged us to beware a certain move we were considering. 'If you do that,' he said, 'then' – for once he was at a loss to express the enormity of the consequences – 'Wooffo.' This expression passed into the vocabulary of the negotiating team and their friends. People would say: '*Il y aura beaucoup de Wooffo ce soir*' or '*In diesem Fall wird es sehr viel Wooffo geben*'.

At the Paris Summit on 12 May our friends from the press had noticed that Raymond, Fred and I had not been invited to the various banquets which were being given for the Prime Minister and the Whitehall team, though some junior members of the Embassy staff were. This exclusion had struck us at the time as rather churlish, for, in general, it is not a good thing to signal to the other side that most of your negotiating team are below the salt. But I suppose that Christopher Soames, our Ambassador and no great friend of the Whitehall bureaucracy, thought that too much had been made of the bureaucrats on the negotiating team, and that he for one would cut them down to size.

Some weeks later (26 June 1971) Reggie Dale wrote a sympathetic piece for the *Financial Times*. Under the heading 'The team that got the terms', it read: 'Britain's successful Common Market negotiating team combines a judicious mixture of the austere and the irreverent. The austerity is largely provided by its leader Sir Con O'Neill . . . enormous contribution . . . dry sense of humour and extraordinary clarity of his logic . . .'. Friendly comments followed on the rest of the

team: 'Roy Denman and Freddy Kearns with the slightest encourage-
ment will put on a knockabout comedy act for journalists in which
Denman provides the wisecracks and Kearns the picturesque
language.' But worse was to follow. The piece continued: 'When not
on duty Denman has the remarkable gift of being able to order the
best vintage wines in most top Brussels restaurants without even asking
for the wine list.' (This was well meant but not entirely true. In the
restaurant near the hotel where we entertained I found that there was
an excellent but moderately priced Sancerre and similarly a Julienas; it
was quicker to order these than to pore over the wine list.) But the
grinding of teeth among Permanent Secretaries – particularly in the
Treasury – could almost be heard in the Channel Ports.

Con O'Neill was not entirely happy with these freebooting private
contacts. One day he approached me at the airport. 'I'm a bit worried',
he said in those canonical tones, 'about the contacts you and Freddy
are having with the press.'

'Someone's got to talk to the press, Con,' I replied, 'and X, with great
respect, knows as much about agricultural prices and tariff quotas as
the Dalai Lama.' I then introduced him to a nearby journalist, Squire
Barraclough. They fell into deep conversation.

At Heathrow I approached the Arch with an expression of funereal
concern. 'God knows what will be in the press tomorrow, Con,' I said,
'I just meant you to shake hands. That fellow is from the *Daily Express*.
Do you think it wise to have spent so much time with him?' A wintry
smile crossed the face of the Arch. He made no further comment. Our
contacts with the press continued.

Despite the triumphs of Paris and Luxembourg, not everything was
settled. Experience in negotiation often shows that after everyone has
finished celebrating a breakthrough, details remain which can turn out
to be so difficult as to endanger the whole settlement. In this case we
needed to settle a number of details on the trading side – among them

the handling of imports of cotton textiles, some mechanics of our transition to the Common Agricultural Policy, and finally fish. Fish at first seemed a minor problem; it turned out to be one of the most difficult. The timetable was tight if we were to clear up these issues by the end of 1971, because it would take the whole of 1972 to get the detailed enabling legislation through the House of Commons against the bitter line-by-line opposition of the Labour Party. If we were unable to meet our planned date for entry of 1 January 1973 doubts would be cast on our sincerity; it was not inconceivable that the whole enterprise could still run into the sand.

We drafted a White Paper with little internal argument. It concluded with a paragraph which may seem tame now but was rousing at the time: 'Every historic choice involves challenge as well as opportunity. Her Majesty's Government are convinced that the right decision for us is to accept the challenge, seize the opportunity, and join the European Community.'

The critical vote on the terms of entry set out in the White Paper was set for 28 October 1971. I was in Brussels most of that week but took the afternoon plane back. The Prime Minister was kind enough to decree that those members of the negotiating team in London could have a place in the official box. The debate was patchy. The Labour leadership was uninspiringly derisive. Enoch Powell spoke on sovereignty in terms which could have made a Rip van Winkle believe that Hitler's armoured divisions had landed at Dover and were advancing on London. The Prime Minister made a first-class speech. It had no rolling Churchillian phrases, but Heath was a man of action, not words. He set out simply and convincingly how he saw Britain's position in the world and how entering the EEC was the only valid choice before us. The House began to fill up with all the atmosphere of crowding and drama which attend these occasions. Then the Division. The House emptied. The tension rose. With MPs off to the

Division lobbies an attendant approached us in the box. 'What do you think the majority will be?' he asked. Privately I thought the pro-Europeans would be lucky to have more than thirty. But modestly we said that we hadn't the faintest idea. 'I reckon it'll be more than a hundred,' he said sagely. 'Seen some very interesting faces going into the Ayes lobby.' He continued, 'See the Ambassadors' Gallery over there? Haven't seen it as full since the days when we used to matter in the world.'

The Division ended and the tellers appeared. I began to feel slightly sick.

'For the Ayes,' someone cried, 'three hundred and fifty six!'

Then, 'For the Noes, two hundred and forty four!'

A majority of one hundred and twelve. Hardly credible. Magnificent. A tremendous cheer burst out from the massed Conservative benches.

On the Labour benches there was pandemonium. All the jeering xenophobia of the Labour party of 1971 bubbled to the surface. Some of those who had voted for were almost physically assaulted. 'Fascist bastard!' someone shouted at Roy Jenkins. It was a very nasty scene.

The House began to empty. Wilson slumped by, grey and defeated. Peter Shore stalked out with Judith Hart, smacking his hands together like the villain in some Victorian melodrama, and crying vehemently, 'We counted wrong.' We – the officials – laughing and jubilant, moved off to Admiralty House where Geoffrey Rippon was dispensing drinks.

I rang Moya, who collected me from the House of Commons and we drove across. The party when we joined it was going strong. We talked to John Davies, then Secretary of State for Trade and Industry. Heath came across and I introduced Moya. He was very genial. Referring to the Kennedy Round, where our paths had crossed before in 1964, he said, 'We've both been through quite a lot in the way of negotiation.' Moya asked about sailing off the Kentish coast and said that she thought sailing would be a good thing for me. This was about the only time I had ever seen Heath moved to violent and genuine mirth. We talked to many others, then looking at our watches suddenly realised that it was half past one. Happily we drove home.

With that hurdle behind us our efforts in Brussels to settle the remaining issues were intensified; there were only seven working weeks to the end of the year. Fish began to assume a menacing importance. Feelings aroused by fishing were deep and passionate. Like the Home Guard in 1940, every British fisherman pictured the combined fleets of the Six sailing up to his particular coast and sweeping all the fish away. Lord Boothby and Jo Grimond, two of the most prominent British supporters of our entry, were passionate on the fishermen's behalf. And many of the ill disposed, who cared nothing for fisheries but were out to scupper the negotiation, leapt on the bandwagon.

It became clear towards the end of 1971 that another major effort would have to be made with the French. The Prime Minister concluded that he had, as the Americans would say, already cashed most of his chips with Pompidou. It must be the French Foreign Minister and the French Minister of Agriculture who were to be approached. At the beginning of December the negotiating team gathered gloomily in the Foreign Office room of the Arch. We were deep in discussion when the door flew open and the British Ambassador in Paris, Christopher Soames, stamped in. He had a face like Dorian Gray's portrait, a voice like the gurgling of a beer barrel, and a manner towards those he considered not his social equals reminiscent of a Russian Duke towards his serfs. But in discussion he was forceful and quick. Freddy Kearns – whose agricultural domain included fish – explained our difficulties. The Arch gave Soames a large map of our fishery limits, that is the line round our coasts within which fishing would be reserved for our fishermen.

The sequel came a couple of days later in Brussels. Peacefully asleep in my hotel room, I was wakened in the early hours by a tapping on my door, like the raven in Edgar Allen Poe. I knew who it was. When I opened the door there entered a cloud of whisky fumes with, improbably at its centre, a glowing cigar. This was shortly followed by Fred, who was nevertheless perfectly coherent and indeed in excellent form. 'I have', he said, 'a stirring tale to tell.'

The previous afternoon he had been telephoned by an exquisite young man in the Paris Embassy.

'How did you know', I asked, 'that he was an exquisite young man?'

'He sounded like one,' said Fred. 'You know the sort.'

His Excellency, said the exquisite young man, had just settled with the French the main lines of an absolutely splendid deal on fish. Could Fred hop on a plane and come out and settle the details? It should be explained that to anyone in the negotiating trade this situation is what is known as a bummer. Fred would have been perfectly capable of negotiating in the utmost detail a deal on fish. But to do so within a framework suggested by someone not an expert would be like asking a chef to put the finishing touches to a dish prepared by another and then present it to a circle of rather blasé and critical diners. So Fred had reacted briskly.

'Fuck off', he said. There followed apparently a pause. I could picture the scene. On international lines in those days a silence was usually accompanied by some faint ethereal humming.

'The line's frightfully bad,' said the young man. 'I couldn't quite get what you said.'

Fred repeated rather more loudly his advice. A longer pause followed. The humming continued. Finally the young man spoke. 'I can't quite understand what you mean.'

'In that case,' said Fred, 'you must have had a very sheltered upbringing.'

After further alarms and excursions over the next few weeks we

139

reached the Ministerial meeting on 11 December. At about six the next morning we got a cast-iron guarantee for 95 per cent of our fishing take with a completely open-ended review by the end of 1982. Clustered together in the UK Delegation room we decided that this was acceptable. Elation. We filed in. Rippon accepted. We got to bed by seven.

Back in London later in the day, Fred and I exchanged various telephone calls with the *Financial Times* and *The Times*. We had the feeling that the press reaction to the deal on fish would be positive. I got home at the same time as Moya arrived with James – aged three – from a children's party.

'Where have you been?' asked James.

'In Brussels.'

'What were you doing in Brussels?'

'Working very hard on something called Europe. It will be very important one day for you and Julia. Would you like me to tell you about Europe?'

'No.' And with the air of someone brushing aside trivia to get to the essentials, he added, 'At Marcus's party I got a red balloon.'

One thing which mattered far less than the negotiations but began to be talked about towards the end of the year was Honours. Twice a year the Honours List is issued. Civil servants, ambassadors, the deserving of the land are made Knights, Companions of the Bath, or appointed to lesser Orders. At the end of the last negotiations knighthoods had been awarded to the members of the team. This time it became known in the whispering gallery of Whitehall that Geoffrey Rippon had proposed the same but that William Armstrong, the Head of the Civil Service, had vetoed it. I cannot say that any of us on the team were touched by this generosity. Fred was furious. He went about quoting the reward offered the Pied Piper: 'A thousand guilders? Come, take fifty.'

While any outside observer might regard all this as a piece of trivia of interest only to the egos of bureaucrats, something deeper lay behind. There was in the upper reaches of the mandarins throughout Whitehall a cold hostility to the whole idea of joining the Community. I asked someone in Cabinet Office about this. 'Simple,' he said. 'The last negotiations failed. If these had failed you would all have been welcomed as returning heroes. But these negotiations succeeded. This will in time mean the biggest revolution in the government of Britain since Cromwell. If Whitehall is about anything it is about resisting change. So you and your friends are dangerous revolutionaries. Watch it!'

Encouraged by this warm support at home we continued to tie up in Brussels the remaining loose ends. On 23 December we closed down for a few days. On 4 January we resumed. In the meantime the New Year's Honours List came out. There were grand rewards for the Whitehall generals; for the troops in the field the cupboard was bare. But the Arch did get a GCMG (Knight Grand Cross of the Order of St Michael and St George). The pleasure with which he received my congratulations must however have been tarnished by an incident a couple of evenings later.

Fred and I were having a drink in the bar when a couple of Belgian acquaintances approached us. 'Tell us something,' they said. 'We do not understand your honours system. This award to Sir Con. He was Sir Con. But now he has a Grand Cross is he Grand Sir Con?' That, Fred and I said with enthusiasm, was exactly it. It would be a grave *faux pas* to address him now as Sir Con; it was Grand Sir Con. We were sure he would be touched if the Belgians were to go across and greet him correctly. Smiling politely, the Belgians moved in the direction of the Arch. Fred and I moved quickly out of the bar. Delayed for a moment by a German tariff expert, I saw the Belgians and the Arch in conversation. As we disappeared from the room a baleful glance from the Arch turned in our direction.

The end was near. The Canadians were kind enough to give us a farewell lunch. I thanked Randy Gherson for his cooperation and asked that our thanks be conveyed across the frozen tundra and the rhubarb belt to our cheerful friend with the bag of plywood samples 'solid one side'. The New Zealanders gave Fred and me dinner at the Comme Chez Soi, just about the grandest restaurant in Brussels. I recalled the words of the New Zealand Prime Minister on 3 September 1939, which I had read as a schoolboy: 'Where Britain stands we stand. Where Britain goes we go.' It had given me a lump in the throat then; it did now. We talked of the war which we had fought together, of the impeccably loyal support we had always had from the Kiwis and the debt of honour we had owed them. Fred and I told them not exactly of a British marching song but of a diversion used from time to time on a long march when the troops were getting weary. Someone at the head of the column would sing out

> *Today's my daughter's wedding day.*
> *Twenty thousand pounds I'll give away.*

The chorus would follow from all: 'Hooray, Hooray'. Then

> *On second thoughts I think it best*
> *To keep the money in an old oak chest.*

Chorus: *You stingy old bastard*
         You miserable old sod

This produced so much in the way of laughter and applause that we narrowly escaped being thrown out of the restaurant.

Then on 17 January came what we hoped would be the last meeting of the Deputies. At about 2.30 on the morning of 18 January we reached agreement. After the drama of Luxembourg in June 1971 it was something of an anti-climax. The Arch and we filed in; the remaining items were formally run through. Clapping broke out. But although shorn of all panoply and drama it was still a considerable milestone on Britain's journey into Europe.

The signing of the Treaty of Accession was fixed for 22 January. The Prime Minister and Geoffrey Rippon flew to Brussels with the Shadow Foreign Secretary, George Brown, Harold Macmillan, and the wives of those of us on the negotiating team. (Harold Wilson had been invited; he declined and spent the afternoon at a football match.) The signing in the afternoon was delayed because someone threw a bottle of ink at Heath and he had to find another suit. Then he signed, square-jawed and impassive but with something of a sparkle in the eye. I thought back to when I had been a grubby schoolboy in 1940 and fog in the Channel. The fog seemed to be lifting.

Rippon very generously distributed to the team golden medallions he had had struck himself. Michael Palliser, who had taken over the previous autumn as Ambassador to the Community from James Marjoribanks, gave a reception. The Arch presented the team in turn to George Brown. When it came to me, George Brown, remembering Douglas Jay's hostility as President of the Board of Trade to the Community, gave a strangled cry. 'The bloody Board of Trade!' he cried.

'Mr Denman', said the Arch gallantly, 'has been a tower of strength in the negotiations.' George Brown looked at me in disbelief.

'So he bloody well should have been.'

Then he turned to a passing waiter. 'Put some gin in this bleeding tonic,' he cried. The following day a lunch was given for us by Jean François Deniau, the French Commissioner responsible for the negotiations. Geoffrey Rippon, Harold Macmillan and George Brown were all invited. I kept the menu duly signed and five years later, when I moved to Brussels and could afford it, I had it framed. It hung in my office for twelve years. I regarded it as my card of entry to the Community.

As we moved off after lunch I fell into conversation with the Arch. I said that I was sorry that this would be the last time we would be working together. I had much enjoyed serving under him. This was not the small change of valedictory politeness. Con was a great man. I shall always be proud to have been associated with him in a considerable venture and to have become a friend. He never changed. The last time I saw him was fifteen years later, the year before he died. I had then been four years in Washington as the EC Ambassador (then the Head of the Commission Delegation) and I ran into him at a Christmas party in the European Commission office in London. He looked just the same as when I had first called on him in 1970. We greeted each other warmly. 'Hi, Con!' I cried, 'Great to see ya. How ya doin?' A suspicion of a smile crossed Con's face. And in those grave tones I remembered so well he said, 'I must say, Roy, you seem to have adapted uncommonly well to the United States.'

Returning to Whitehall was rather like a cold shower on a winter morning. On the team we had averaged in Brussels over the last fortnight of negotiation about three hours sleep a night. The Monday morning meeting in the Department on my return was devoted for the first twenty minutes to the heroic deeds of some of those dealing with electricity supply, who had been hauled in for a few hours on the previous Saturday and Sunday. They were given a general benediction and three days' leave. I asked modestly for a few days off and got a distinctly sour reply.

The year 1972 saw a long drawn out, closely fought battle in the House of Commons to get the necessary Community legislation through. From the first it was a near run thing. Five days after the signature of the Treaty of Accession, the European Communities Bill was presented to Parliament. The omens were not good for the second reading on 17 February. The domestic scene was stormy; the miners' strike had produced record unemployment and general gloom. Heath made it clear that if the vote went against the Government he would call a General Election. The Labour Party saw a real, quite unexpected chance of bundling the Tories out. With the Tory anti-marketeers determined to vote against and the Labour pro-Europeans under-standably unable to cast a vote in support of the Government, it was a tacit understanding between a few sympathetic Labour members and the Conservative Whips and the tiny Liberal Party that saved the day. Heath on one occasion got a slender majority of seven. The clause-by-clause battles later were equally narrow. But Heath was grimly deter-mined. Without him the venture would not have succeeded, either in 1971 or in 1972.

In this I was not much involved. My job was to deal with the Department of Trade and Industry's interests in the run up to 1 January 1973, when we would actually become a part of the Community. Partly this meant escorting across to Brussels colleagues who dealt with subjects such as company law and regional policy. Partly it meant writing papers for Whitehall on the industrial, regional and commercial policies which we should pursue in the Community – not an easy task when it had to be made clear that there was no crock of gold for the UK, whatever Whitehall mandarins and Foreign Office plenipotentiaries might think. Partly there were the occasional meetings where the members of the negotiating team were consulted by others in Whitehall on the workings of that mysterious body, the European Commission.

One afternoon a high official of the Civil Service Department descended on us. He explained with, I thought, more than usual pomposity, that his Department was concerned not only with keeping standards of administration high in Whitehall, but with bringing up to scratch this new lot we had to deal with in Brussels. For good or ill (he implied mostly for ill) we would be dealing more and more with the Commission. And they would need to shape up. He continued for some time in this vein.

Raymond Bell, who never wasted words, removed a cigarette from his mouth. 'Do you know what they'll say, if you tell them that?' he enquired.

'No.'

'They'll tell you to bugger off.'

Our visitor withdrew in high dudgeon. Reports reached us later that certain high panjandrums had been displeased. Raymond was not in the least perturbed.

The rest of the year was marked by two excitements. One was a battle royal with the Scandinavians. The second was a huge conference in Paris chaired by President Pompidou.

The row with the Scandinavians was about paper. The Six had agreed to move in stages to free trade with our EFTA partners. But the Scandinavians were such formidably competitive producers of paper that a slower timetable was fixed for this commodity. This in turn meant that if our industry were not to be squeezed, the UK would have to go back on its EFTA commitments and reimpose – for a time – tariffs on paper imports from the Scandinavians. This was about as popular with them as the lions in the Colosseum were with the Christians. 'I shall watch your activities carefully,' the Prime Minister told me with a grim smile.

Feeling like a Christian among the lions I set out. Our main suppliers were the Finns and the Swedes. I went to Helsinki. Our Ambassador was kind enough to ask me to stay. I got there at twilight. I asked the Ambassador what the local sentiment was. The essence of his reply was that I would be lucky to get to the airport alive when I planned to depart, two days later. Digestion of these gloomy tidings was helped by the appearance of a statuesque Nordic beauty in a housemaid's uniform wordlessly bearing a silver tray on which was perched a large whisky and soda. After some ten minutes further chat I went up to unpack. A minute or so later there was a knock on the door. The Nordic beauty was there again, expressionless and wordless but with a silver tray and a whisky and soda. Even with this cheering episode the next couple of days largely bore out the Ambassador's forecast. Back in London the pressure from our EFTA partners grew. The Foreign Office became concerned. I was summoned to Cabinet Office to explain myself.

I explained that I was only carrying out the Prime Minister's instructions and that the uproar from EFTA would be a mouse-like squeak compared with the uproar from the British paper industry if we did not succeed. But if we stuck to our guns it would work out. Negotiation, I said, was essentially about who had whom by the balls. In this case we were in the favourable position because it would not be in the interests of the Scandinavians to smite us hip and thigh. But we needed to agree a timetable; this would take a few wearisome months of Kabuki theatre, not least because whatever we agreed had to be concerted with the Six.

So it turned out. I went to Paris and Bonn; the former was clear and unhelpful, the latter helpful but unclear. We negotiated in Brussels; we negotiated in London. At one point the Finns took me aside. 'When we are in Brussels,' they said, 'you tell us that the final decision will be in London. But when we are in London you shrug your shoulders and say that the final decision will be taken in Brussels.' I congratulated them on having been the first to have seen through our negotiating ploy, and said that to mark my appreciation I would send them privately a bottle of champagne. From that moment the atmosphere began to improve. In the early summer we settled. It had been a tough skirmish. But the Finns shook hands; indeed their negotiator, Paavo Karlehto, later Ambassador to the Community in Brussels, and later still Permanent Secretary of the Finnish Foreign Office, became a lifelong friend. The Swedes on the other hand let it discreetly be known that I would not be welcome in Stockholm for a good year or so.

There was not much time for anything except work and travel. But that autumn we bought a house in Wiltshire. It was more than a cottage, far less than a country mansion. A stream ran through the garden and on the nearby river swans could be seen. For two small children and the two of us it provided at the weekend a haven of peace and country air.

Suitably encouraged, I embarked on the other main venture of 1972 – a conference, summoned by President Pompidou, for 19–20 October of the Heads of Government of the Six and the acceding members – now Britain, Denmark and Ireland, since the Norwegians had that autumn lost a referendum on entry. There was a frenzy of briefing. This moved into overdrive when a message arrived from Pompidou, as Chairman, proposing that the conference should endorse the aim of a European Union by 1980. I happened to be with the Private Secretaries at No. 10 when the telegram arrived. Heath had just finished reading it when the Foreign Secretary, Alec Douglas-Home, appeared. He read it.

'Don't think the House will like that,' he said.

'But that,' said Heath, 'is what it's all about.'

This was the first of the many Eurosummits that British ministers would attend, so it lacked the panoply of officials which would adorn later versions. Indeed, on the plane to Paris it began to dawn on me, viewing the fleet of Foreign Office personnel, that representation of other Whitehall departments was sparse. John Hunt, the Permanent Secretary dealing with European questions in Cabinet Office, would be our team manager. Alan Neale, now his opposite number in the Treasury, dealing with overseas finance, would answer on sterling. The rest of the waterfront – regional policy, company law, the new GATT Round, and raw materials – would have to be dealt with by the only other Whitehall hand: me. The inescapable conclusion was that I would be stretched. I was.

While part of the meeting was devoted to sessions in which the Heads of Government boomed at each other, the rest was a pretty fair madhouse of *ad hoc* meetings of officials.

At one meeting raw materials were being discussed. Fighting off a formulation which would have given Whitehall a collective heart attack, I rushed to another where the Concorde was being discussed. Wandering out from that I went, impelled by curiosity, into an adjoining room. Here I found a full-dress debate on trade policy, where our proposal to set a date for the next round of GATT trade negotiations was being fiercely opposed by the French. With the help of Emile Noel, the legendary Secretary General of the Commission, we got some conclusions we could live with.

Other similar nerve-wracking excitements followed.

The final meeting of Heads of Government considered the draft communiqué. Under Pompidou's chairmanship, brackets round alternative drafts disappeared like snow in the sunshine. A dinner was postponed. At nine in the evening we were through. The Heads of Government of the Six and of the three acceding States had agreed on the aim of European Union by 1980. To say that this would need much defining would be an understatement. But it was a step onwards in the unification of Europe. Champagne was served. I slipped away. 'Where', asked a colleague from our Delegation, 'are you going?'

'I'm going to check the translation,' I said.

'Translation?' he said incredulously. 'That's a job for the technicians'.

'Not in the Community,' I replied.

One phrase in particular had caught my eye. The French text of the communiqué spoke of agreement on the '*participation des travailleurs dans la marche des entreprises*' – that is, worker participation in the running of firms. Feeling that this would be anathema when read out in London, I went up to the translators' room ready for a clash. I got one. The English translation, I argued, should be 'the involvement of workers in the progress

149

of firms'. Uproar followed. Finally, with a threat of waking up the Prime Minister, I got my way. The following day in London the translation provoked not a murmur. I was content, but my contentment was short-lived. A fortnight later I got a call in Brussels from Copenhagen.

'Vee have been looking at the communiqué from Paris,' a puzzled Danish voice said. 'Vee do not think the English version on worker participation is correct.'

I persuaded him to desist. What was past, I said, was past. We needed to concentrate on the future.

On social policy the future was to hold many a rift between Britain and Europe.

European Union by 1980 had been agreed, but the road ahead was going to be as stony as it had always promised to be. In 1973 came the first oil shock. The following year the Conservatives were voted out of office.But these horrors were still in the future. On 1 January 1973 we were in Wiltshire. At midnight Moya and I raised our glasses to a new year and a new world. Britain was now part of the European Community; history had changed; the future for our children would be different.

In the meantime there was much to do. The biggest immediate change on our joining the Community was in external relations. In foreign affairs and the mysteries of international finance the Foreign Office and the Treasury would talk to their Community partners from time to time, but they were still captains of their own destiny. In matters of trade it was now the Commission which spoke and negotiated for the Community. For us this posed both a challenge and an opportunity. The UK's voice would only be one among nine Member States, and that only in internal debate. Yet to the extent that we could persuade our partners and the Commission of a line which would suit us, the clout of a Community of over 250 million people (as it was then) was huge.

So I began to attend a body known as the 113 Committee, named after the relevant article of the Treaty of Rome. This is a gathering of the Directors of Trade Policy from the Member States which meets once a month in Brussels. Its function under the Treaty is to advise the Commission on trade negotiations. The Commission works on the basis of a mandate agreed by the Member States, itself based on a draft proposed by the Commission. But while the Commission's powers of initiative and execution are formidable, it needs at every stage of the journey to get the Member States on its side. That is what the meetings of the 113 Committee were about.

The Commission followed the agreeable habit of inviting the Trade Policy Directors to lunch. We would debate all morning and then adjourn to the dining room on the thirteenth floor of the Berlaymont. Over a gin and tonic, viewpoints which had been vigorously opposed seemed in some mysterious fashion to soften. Over lunch – away from the interpreters and the large crowd at the plenary session – discussion would be to the point and frank. People would say such things as: 'This is off the record so I couldn't put it in these terms this morning. But the difficulty here is that my Minister is having a row with the Minister of X. I doubt whether he'll win. But there's no way at the moment I could sell Y to him. On the other hand, if someone else, say the Commission, could suggest something a bit different, perhaps on the lines of Z, and this were acceptable round the table, I think I could swing it.'

This procedure had two consequences.

The first was a radical change in the conduct of business between Community governments. In the days before our entry into the Community, if someone in the Department of Trade wanted to know what his opposite number in another European capital thought of a certain proposition an elaborate and time-consuming gavotte would be performed. A telegram would be drafted in the Department of Trade and sent across to the Foreign Office. They would send it to their Embassy in the capital concerned. Someone from the Embassy would then get in his car and call on a foreign official. Returning to the

151

Embassy, he would dictate a telegram. This would then find its way the following day to the Department of Trade via the automatic Whitehall circulation of telegrams. Now all began to change. The Department of Trade official would pick up his telephone and call his opposite number. 'Hans,' he would say (or François or Roberto), 'you remember we had a word about X at the 113 lunch the other week. My Minister's pressing me on this. What's the form?'

The second result was the gradual emergence of a family feeling. Nine (as it then was) intelligent people cannot meet each other, month in month out, for discussion of mutual problems without a certain feeling of commonality developing. I tried to explain this once to a Labour front-bencher and was vigorously rebuked. That, he said, was the whole trouble. Our representatives were being seduced by pleasant lunches and by the traditional Foreign Office all pals together act. Instead we should be fighting our corner. I tried to explain that we were doing precisely that. But it had to be done intelligently. No one could go along to the group and dictate to them his own line. There had to be a common approach, put forward to third countries by the Commission because that was laid down by the Treaty. The trick was to know enough about the disparate interests of the group to advocate a common approach which would get a majority but would also suit our interests. This is what happened at a meeting of Departments in London. Now we had to learn to do this on a European scale. For those of us who had spent some time in the new world this was not so difficult. For Whitehall as a whole it was a revolution.

'You mean,' an incredulous voice from one Ministry asked one afternoon, 'that we have to change what we've been doing for several hundred years because of some bloody foreigners in Brussels?'

'Yes,' I replied crisply.

'Look,' he said, 'there is a dividing line between lunacy and common sense.' 'Since 1973,' I said, 'you've been on the wrong side of it.'

The Commission began to draw up the mandate it would propose to the Council for the new world trade negotiations, the successor to the Kennedy Round, which had finished in 1967. The world watched with interest. Would the enlarged Community be mainly occupied in absorbing the new members, which were facing the gradual abolition of their tariffs against the Six? Or would it take the long view?

The Commission – under the leadership of Christopher Soames, now Vice President responsible for external relations – rose to the occasion. A general statement of our aims, known as a *conception d'ensemble* was drawn up. This struck the French as too liberal, and battle raged for months. We went so often through every line of the paper that I was reminded of someone I had known in the Gurkhas. Near his regimental depot there had been a hill. In manoeuvres his battalion in turn advanced on the hill, attacked the hill, withdrew from the hill and fortified the hill. He got so tired of the hill that he was almost ill when he clapped eyes on it every morning. This became the prevailing sentiment in the 113 Committee. Comic relief came when the Japanese suggested that the negotiation should be opened not in Geneva but in Tokyo – a mad idea because Tokyo instead of Geneva would be outrageously more expensive for the long-suffering taxpayers of the world; and anyone who thought that agreeing to this would commit the Japanese to liberal trade policies was wrong in the head. But as my cynical Italian opposite number remarked, 'If this goes to Ministers, I fear they will accept it.' They did.

So in September 1973 I led to Tokyo a small official delegation, with Peter Walker, then Secretary of State for Trade and Industry, in overall charge. Bob Goldsmith, now the Deputy to our Permanent Representative in Brussels, joined us to help in dealing with the other Member States. Over a hundred Ministers from all over the world attended. All would make speeches. But the speeches of the nine trade Ministers of the Community countries had to be broadly in line. And

153

this meant Community decisions on a number of points. The Ministers of the Community met, the first time that a Council of Ministers had met outside Europe.

Two Commissioners had come out to Tokyo: Christopher Soames, who had been a politician and Ambassador in Paris but who knew nothing about the GATT, and Finn Gundelach, a Dane who had not been a politician but knew everything about the GATT. Soames was late; it was reported that he was on the telephone to the Americans. But reaching a common line ahead of the GATT meeting would be a lengthy business.

Gundelach, who had been the Number Two official in the GATT and who periodically ate people for breakfast when he found them insufficiently intelligent or well briefed, raised the first item. 'This', he said, 'is what the Commission proposes. Does anyone disagree?' He looked around with a wolfish smile. No one spoke. With a slight air of disappointment he passed to the next item. He posed the same question and then licked his chops. The Ministers sat silent like rabbits before a snake. In no time at all the meeting was virtually over. Soames hurried back. With a sigh of relief at being freed from the tiresome detail of the GATT, Ministers plunged into an interminable political discussion. Peter Walker, used no doubt to the cut and thrust of more practical discussions in the City of London, showed signs of impatience.

The background to the meeting had been laboriously discussed not only in the Community but also with the whole world in Geneva. Only one major point was still in dispute. That concerned the link between tariff reductions and exchange rates. The French were reluctant to agree to a programme of tariff cutting without some guarantee that this could be suspended if exchange rates moved against them.

'Protectionism!', cried many. It was true that France was traditionally less open on trade matters than Britain or Germany. But the French reservation mirrored one of the many culture gaps that still divided Europe. French industry was run by engineers; British industry was run by accountants. Exchange rate fluctuations had few terrors for the British; they simply sought cover from a merchant bank. The links between French industrialists and the banks were less intimate; for a French engineer running a major company to see the exchange rate moving against him – and suspecting that this was the result of an Anglo-Saxon conspiracy – smacked of unfairness or worse. I pointed out that we could hardly embark on a major negotiation, lasting several years, if it were to be called off at any moment because of exchange rate fluctuations; it would be like embarking on a war but halting it at any moment if the weather turned bad.

The Germans were supportive, the French resistant. Finally Giscard d'Estaing, then French Minister of Finance, gave way.

To a packed assembly of all the Delegations the Director General of the GATT, now a Swiss, Olivier Long, read out the text of the conclusions. 'Is this now agreed?' he asked. There was a pause. Had it lasted for only one or two seconds there would have been a protest about steamrolling the conclusions through. Had it lasted ten seconds someone would have intervened. Olivier Long judged the moment to perfection. After five seconds his gavel came down. 'Agreed,' he said.

Thus the Tokyo Round of trade negotiations was launched. In a reporting telegram that evening from the British Embassy I wrote: 'The show is on the road.' I did not know how long the road would be or that at the end I would be one of the actors. Happy at concluding, we packed and departed.

On the way to the airport Goldsmith was in a reflective mood.

'Things,' he said,' are going to go badly.'

'Come, Bob,' I commented, 'this is not the moment for gloom. We've just started a major negotiation. There's every prospect that it will work, just as the others have.'

'I wasn't thinking of the negotiations,' he said. 'Just raise your eyes

155

a moment from GATT land, temporarily in Tokyo, and look around. These Japanese are working their arses off from morning till bloody night. What chance have we got of competing with them? Mark my words, mate, the great old UK is slowly moving to the knacker's yard.'

Events since have not shown him markedly wrong. But we were cheered when we boarded the British Airways plane and saw a copy of *The Times*. Freddy Kearns had joined the ranks of Permanent Secretaries and his K now would not be far away. We raised a glass to him; justice in Whitehall had temporarily broken out.

In Britain the struggle with the unions, the miners' strike and the prospect of a General Election cast their shadow. The election was announced for 28 February 1974. From the opinion polls a Labour victory did not seem likely. So I was not disturbed when at a party given by the New Zealanders someone broke the news to Fred and me of a Labour MP urging that the team which had negotiated our entry into the Community should be impeached. Indeed, there was general hilarity at the suggestion.

Election day came. Moya and I gave a dinner party and put several bottles of champagne in the fridge. After dinner the results started coming in; the champagne stayed in the fridge; it was clear that Labour was back. The last guest to leave, well after midnight, was an affable American engineer. He paused on the doorstep. 'Boy,' he said, 'you've sure got problems.'

BRITAIN ALMOST OUT OF EUROPE

The election results became definitive on the morning of 29 February 1974. For a couple of days the Heath Administration considered continuing with Liberal support and thus a tiny majority. But this came to naught. On 4 March a Labour Government took office. The next morning, as soon as I reached the Department, I was called in by Max Brown, the Permanent Secretary who looked after trade affairs.

'Sit down, Roy,' he said. 'I have some bad news for you. Peter Shore is our new Minister.'

'This is not the moment, Max,' I said, 'for ill timed jests.'

'It is not a jest,' said Max. 'He is upstairs. He wants to see us. Now.'

The shock was considerable. Peter Shore was the Arch Demon of the Anti-Marketeers. Being summoned to see him was like one of Trollope's canons being bidden to Lambeth Palace and finding Beelzebub installed there. Max explained on the way up that the Department of Trade and Industry was to be broken up forthwith into three parts. There had been no alternative since Harold Wilson – now Prime Minister – had promised the job to three different people. Peter Shore would be in charge of trade, Tony Benn of industry, and Shirley Williams of some rump devoted to prices and the consumer.

In Peter Shore's office the atmosphere was glacial. At least, I reflected, with Beelzebub the furnaces would have been roaring. The new Minister addressed us gravely. He knew that some officials had become devoted to the Common Market. But the people had spoken. Our membership would have to be reviewed. A silence followed. It seemed a long silence. Finally I spoke, as by implication the guiltier of the two. I said that we operated in a democratic system. A Government had been elected. It was the duty of officials to serve it. The Department had operated for many years on this basis and no serious complaint of political bias had ever been made by either of the main parties. I had no doubt that this was how we would continue to conduct our affairs. A faint hint of an Arctic spring appeared and our discussion drew to a close.

In fact dealing with Peter Shore turned out to be less arduous than dealing with Beelzebub. He was always courteous. I told him openly what the reaction would be from the Commission and the Council to whatever proposition he thought of advancing, and what was and what was not allowed under the Treaty. On some issues – the continuation of the Tokyo Round and a stand for liberal trading policies – we were at one. But I cannot claim it was a comfortable experience.

Two other factors were enough to drive me to cumulative despair. The first was encapsulated in Denis Healey's promise that he would squeeze the rich until the pips squeaked. The maximum rate of income tax was set at 83 per cent on earned incomes and 98 per cent on so-called unearned income. That was not taxation designed to ensure a fair burden between taxpayers: it was confiscation driven by class hatred. I did not think that class hatred needed to apply to me. I had started without any inherited money; what I had been able to save had come from taxed income and hard work. But the levelling attitude applied to any who were not among the ranks of the working classes. *The Times* was to calculate in 1976 that the pay of the top ranks in the Civil Service had fallen in real terms by 50 per cent over the previous two years. As a Government economist acquaintance remarked, that was not a social democratic rate of change but a revolutionary one. Our house in Chelsea had been bought but we were still paying off a mortgage on our house in Wiltshire. And we had two children to educate. Certainly we were better off than some. But the future looked bleak.

Even bleaker was the feeling that the country had slipped from a rational to a dark and irrational world. Conservatives on the whole live in the real world, though some may emphasise the seamier sides of it – the selfish, snobbish, grasping, uncaring sides. But a large part of the Labour Party was then living in Loonyland, where no worker, however incompetent or idle, could be sacked; where barbed wire would be erected at the ports against imports but it was expected that our exports would be welcomed by foreigners with glad cries, whatever their quality or price; where water ran uphill and pigs with wings flew by

158

every window. Tony Benn was one of the high priests who, I was not sorry to read, later fell so out of favour with the Party that he was observed by one correspondent roaming the Labour Party Conference of 1990, unheard and unattended, like Marley's ghost.

The new Labour Government decided on 'a renegotiation of the terms of entry'. To have announced that the UK was going to withdraw from the Community would have split the Cabinet: Roy Jenkins, Shirley Williams and some others would have walked out. So it was decided to improve on the terms which the Heath noodles had blithely accepted.

The beginnings were not auspicious. James Callaghan, then Foreign Secretary, summoned a meeting of British Ambassadors from the other capitals of the Community. Distrust hung in the air. He was reminded by one of them that he was now a member of the Council of Ministers. He replied that he did not feel like one.

At another point an assiduous aide whispered to him: 'But, Secretary of State, I don't think this will be acceptable to the MAFF [Ministry of Agriculture, Fisheries and Food].'

Callaghan, who had clearly forgotten this Whitehall term, was tetchily mystified. 'What's the Mafia got to do with it?' he asked.

Our man from Rome ventured unwisely into the fray. 'Ho, ho, Secretary of State!' he cried. 'The Mafia is in my domain' – and received, metaphorically speaking, a brisk kick in the breadbasket. So did several others. Readjusting to Europe was going to be a long and painful haul.

The next meeting of the EEC Council of Ministers was to be held on 1 April 1974. In preparation for it, the Cabinet agreed a defiant statement on our membership and what needed to be changed if we could condescend to remain members.

Depressed, I went off to Luxembourg as part of the supporting cast, and speculated with Freddy Kearns and some of our Permanent

Delegation over lunch how long it would be until we were expelled bag and baggage from the Europe which we had taken so long to join. A considerable quantity of white wine was consumed – on the basis that there might not be many other such occasions – and violent anti-Labour sentiments were expressed. Afterwards in discussion in the delegation with Callaghan it was fortunately agreed that a section of the Labour Manifesto, which the Cabinet had insisted on including in our opening statement, should simply be entered in the minutes of the Council. Had it been formally read out tempers among the Six might have exploded.

As it was the day was largely saved by the newly appointed German Foreign Minister, Hans Dietrich Genscher. For those six months it was Germany's turn to hold the Presidency of the Council of Ministers and so he was in the chair. Doubts had been expressed about him: he was formerly Internal Affairs Minister – how could a fellow like that deal with delicate external questions? He did so with weight and grace. 'Our British colleagues have a problem,' he said. 'There has been an election. We all understand that. Let us look together at their difficulties in a spirit of Community solidarity.' This carried the day.

But beneath the surface a major danger lurked. My French friends told me that President Pompidou was exasperated. It had not helped that during the election campaign Harold Wilson had been cheered by a West Country audience for a mocking reference to 'Pom Pee Doo'. Pompidou, I was told, was prepared to blow the whistle. He had negotiated an arrangement with his friend Monsieur 'Eath. If the new British Government was not prepared to accept this deal, then there was no place for Britain in the new Europe. He would not be prepared to make any further concessions. The British could pack their bags and go. A few days after the Council meeting he died. Had he lived, history would have been different.

There were other dissonances. It was no secret that Chancellor Schmidt of West Germany detested Wilson. And Wilson did not later endear himself to Pompidou's successor Giscard d'Estaing. Giscard, with his glacial politeness, asked Wilson whether the simultaneous translation at a conference in Paris had been satisfactory. 'Prefer the channel with music myself,' Wilson had replied. Gales of laughter in Huddersfield, no doubt, but hardly likely to appeal to a President of France.

Gradually, in the course of renegotiation, fig leaves began to be produced, and to aid their manufacture there was much journeying between London and Brussels. One Sunday morning I got on the same British Airways plane in London as Christopher Soames, then the senior British Commissioner. The press was full of the news that a Mrs Thatcher – not at the time the household name she later became – had displaced Edward Heath in a vote for the Conservative leadership. Interested to have the assessment of a politician as shrewd as Soames, I asked him what he thought of Mrs Thatcher. Emptying in one swig a generous glass of brandy and soda, Soames gave his view in stentorian tones. 'Margaret Thatcher,' he boomed, 'is Ted Heath with tits on.' A nervous tic seized the British Airways stewardess and she hastily drew the curtains behind the forward cabin. From time to time in later years, when we met, Soames would express a certain malevolent curiosity at how the story had travelled far and wide on both sides of the Atlantic. I would always reply that I had no idea, but the best stories always travelled far.

One of the most difficult features of this period was adjusting, under the hostile gaze of many in the Labour Cabinet, to the Common Agricultural Policy – then, as now, about as popular in British non-farming circles as a polecat. Here Freddy Kearns – now a Permanent Secretary – did a considerable job. The Minister of Agriculture was once again Fred Peart. He was no extremist; he was parked in Loonyland, not because he was one of those who owned the title deeds of the car park, but because there was nowhere else to go. He was a decent, jovial, dimwitted gladhander of the kind often encountered in politics and rotary clubs. Amid the fearsome intricacies of the Common Agricultural Policy he did not know his rear end from a hot rock. Here the other Fred came into his own, and Peart soon became entirely dependent on him. In the Council of Agricultural Ministers he would make some crisp and well phrased statement that 'I therefore suggest that what we need to do is . . .' – then over the microphone would come a hoarse whisper, 'What's this word, Fred? Can't read your bloody writing.' When Kearns slipped out to the men's room, Peart would become agitated.

All this did not go unnoticed by the Anti-Marketeers. At one more than usually bitter meeting someone said across the table to Peart, 'You know what they say about you? Enter the Minister of Agriculture, followed by Mr Peart.'

The relationship I had with my Minister, Peter Shore, was different. Shore was a clever man who knew something about the Community, but his heart was firmly against the enterprise. While always polite, he made no secret of his view that the sooner we left the Community the better. We both came from Liverpool. His father had been a ship's captain; my grandfather had been the captain of a windjammer. My grandfather's view of the world, formed about 1900, was simple. The best people were British Empire people – meaning in effect Canadians, Australians and New Zealanders. Very close came the Americans, with whom grandfather had had many dealings and of whom he approved. Then, going down the scale, came the Scandinavians, who did at least wash and speak English. Bottom of the heap were the French and the Italians, always drinking wine and chasing women, and the Germans, always waving huge swords and starting wars. I told Peter Shore of this one night in Luxembourg after we had dined late and well. From the gleam in his eye I think that he and my grandfather would have hit it off.

So we coexisted uneasily. We only had one sizeable clash. The time had come for Britain to make a further step to align its customs tariff with that of the Community. Shore opined that, with renegotiation not completed, with the Cabinet split and a referendum on the terms still to come, we should not be expected to increase our duties against the Commonwealth and, by so doing, raise the cost of living. I pointed out that this was simply not possible under the Treaty of Accession. It was possible to accelerate our movement to the Common Tariff; it had never occurred to us in drafting the Treaty that anyone would want to delay. Nor would it have been acceptable had we proposed it; this would have been regarded as an attempt to avoid our obligations as a Member State.

Peter Shore was unconvinced. So I alerted the Cabinet Office, and rang up Bob Goldsmith in Brussels. We needed to get Shore to Brussels. The President of the Commission, François Ortoli, Christopher Soames, as the senior British Commissioner, and Finn Gundelach, as the Commissioner responsible for Customs tariff adjustments, were the ones to provide the most authoritative advice possible on whether Shore's proposal was compatible with the Treaty.

A couple of days later Shore and I appeared in Brussels. A discreet limousine whisked us from the deserted military part of the airport to the house of Michael Palliser, the Permanent Representative. Ortoli was solemn. Given the importance of the occasion he would speak in French and Palliser could translate. He explained that he saw no way the British request could legally be met. Gundelach said that he had spent all morning looking for any possible loophole. He had found none. Soames spoke as a politician's politician. He understood the case Shore was making. Equally he understood that it was unwise for politicians to press beyond the limits of legal advice. Shore took the rebuff with dignity. But on the way back he observed with a sardonic glint in the eye that he knew what had been going on. I felt – not for the first time – a breath of the fiery furnace.

Christopher Soames played an impressive role on the international stage, and his personal staff was of high calibre. David Hannay, his Chef de Cabinet (private office) in Brussels, had been in the Permanent Delegation in the accession negotiations. If Soames was a sixteen-inch gun, Hannay was the gunlayer. It was a formidable combination. And Jane Morton of the Cabinet kept the show on the road with a cheerful ease and grace. Someone in the Commission remarked that the Soames Cabinet was arguably the most efficient on the thirteenth floor (where all the Commissioners had their offices) but in the relaxed style of a country house. Worse things have been said about the British.

But even with the best of supporting staff Soames did not find the Commission a natural habitat. He was one of nature's proconsuls: he later performed as one in Rhodesia with great distinction. Had history been different he could have been a Viceroy of India, Foreign Secretary, perhaps in a less technocratic age Prime Minister. But Commissioners are expected to deal with a degree of detail strange to a politician brought up in the House of Commons. A wit said in London when Heath was considering appointing our first Commissioners that they needed to be either a politician who should have been a Permanent Secretary, or a Permanent Secretary who should have been a politician. Soames was of a different stamp. On the big issues he was a man of force and fire. On the foothills his step was less sure. But he remains one of the major figures in the tale of the unification of Europe.

In 1975 the renegotiation of our terms of entry was concluded. A White Paper was cobbled together under the skilful chairmanship of Brian Cubbon of the Cabinet Office, and the date was set for a referendum. Some wit in the Cabinet Office circulated privately a draft of the question to be put: 'Are you really prepared to submit to the foreign, Catholic, capitalist conspiracy into which you have been lured by the reactionary Government of Heath?'

A vigorous, at times passionate campaign began, and the element of farce which had marked the outset of the negotiations persisted to the end. For the process had achieved the minimum of result with the maximum of Continental ill will. Some ingenious drafting of a vaguely reassuring kind had been done. Virtually nothing of substance had been changed. Only the blind or the credulous can have been deceived. People voted on their basic feelings, with a sharp look at who was championing which cause.

The day of the referendum came. Moya and I voted and then drove down with the children to the Isle of Wight for a couple of days. Afternoon came. I went for a long walk on the beach. If it went wrong and we had to withdraw from the Community then I thought that however difficult it would be I would chance my arm somewhere else than Whitehall. Civil servants are used to changes in policy. If they resigned every time they thought a political decision wrong there would be no administration with any continuity. But leaving the Community would be such a betrayal of the national interest that I could have had no heart in conniving in it.

Coming back with these gloomy thoughts I found the results beginning to come in. With tremendous relief I learnt that we had romped home with a two thirds majority. We dined happily, our pleasure increased by the gnashing of teeth there must have been in the Benn/Shore camp.

Later that summer I had a call from John Hunt's secretary in the Cabinet Office. John was now Cabinet Secretary, having been promoted from his previous job, Second Permanent Secretary dealing with the European Community two years before. Could I come along that afternoon and see Sir John? I anticipated that this was doubtless about a coming European Community Summit. But the trade part of the agenda was devoted to Third World questions which, happily, were not in my bailiwick. There was a hint of amusement in her voice. Sir

John wanted to see me on a personal matter. Should we say 3 p.m.? After lunch with some Australians I approached the Cabinet Office with some curiosity – which John soon satisfied. Pat Nairne, who had taken over from him on the European front, was going off to run the Department of Social Security. Would I like to take his job, on promotion to Second Permanent Secretary?

I could hardly believe my luck. I hoped that at some stage I might be promoted – but being concerned with European questions was hardly a recommendation. One comment had been reported to me. 'Why should we promote Denman?' someone had asked. 'All he does is to go to Brussels once a week, talk French and drink wine with his foreign friends.'

A few days later Christopher Soames asked me to call on him at Claridges. He explained that the Director General of External Relations, Edmund Wellenstein, was retiring early on health grounds. Would I like to succeed him? It was of course exceptional for a Commissioner to have a Director General of the same nationality. But he would be there only for another eighteen months; in the meantime he thought he could swing it. I thanked him warmly, but explained that I had just agreed to go to the Cabinet Office. Becoming Permanent Secretary was rather like making Admiral in the Navy. It was a lifetime's aim. Soames understood. I only later found out that he had then blocked a British appointment at the same level elsewhere and made an interim appointment to succeed Wellenstein. This was to pave the way for me to succeed to the job two years later.

On my last day in the Department of Trade I lunched with Philip Brown. We happened to go down in the lift with an attractive young woman who had spent a year with me in General Division and was now engaged in some research project. I asked her how she was getting on with it. 'Oh,' she said, 'I'm leaving General Division. I'm going to work for Mr X. Do you think I'll like it?'

Brown and I exchanged glances. It was rumoured about Mr X that no woman under the age of eighty could spend more than two minutes alone with him without her feeling an exploring hand. I was caught in a typical bout of Whitehall indecision. On the one hand, the rumour might not be true, and thus it would be unfair as well as slanderous to repeat it. On the other hand, if it were true then it would be unfair not to give some warning. Brown rose to the occasion. 'I think,' he said gravely, 'that you will find Mr X has a firm grasp of the essentials.'

Working in the Cabinet Office was the most agreeable experience of my Whitehall life. It was small: everybody knew each other and got on with each other. John Hunt ran the office on the basis of urbane good humour, a shirtsleeves informality but relentless efficiency. Part of the job was to take the minutes of that part of the weekly Cabinet discussion which related to Europe. This, I discovered, had complications. Writing the record of a discussion was one of the longstanding skills of Whitehall. But it was not always easy to catch at the end of the table something said in a quick aside at the other end of the room. And while some Ministers were bored by the Cabinet minutes some – including the Foreign Secretary, James Callaghan – would go through them meticulously the following morning and set telephones jangling if they found anything they thought inaccurate. There is a myth – found in the memoirs of some Labour politicians – that the Cabinet Office systematically cooks the records of ministerial discussions. The record is in fact painstakingly, and to some of the participants disappointingly, accurate. What is sometimes resented is that it can be terse. Aneurin Bevan, it is said, was once enraged by the record of a Cabinet in which he had launched a long tirade, glowing with Welsh eloquence, against proposals for cuts in Health Service expenditure. He concluded with the words, 'and all for a paltry few million pounds.' Hearing Bevan pronounce the word 'paltry' at the climax of some oratorical flight was apparently like hearing Beerbohm Tree play

Hamlet. The only record in the minutes was one sentence as point (j) under 'the following points were made in discussion'. It is a long-standing tradition that records of Cabinet discussions should not encourage Ministers to declaim eloquently simply for the record.

Another episode, remembered with even greater affection, centred on the summing up of a Cabinet's conclusions. In the days before Thatcher and Blair, when there used to be Cabinet discussion, the Cabinet Office would prepare a brief for the Prime Minister on every item: this would set out the subject for decision, identify the views of those Cabinet members known to have them (mostly by summarising the papers they had circulated) and then venture on a feat of imagination. 'Subject to discussion,' we would write, 'the Prime Minister might wish to conclude . . . .'

The purpose would not be, as left- or right-wing theorists might imagine, to twist ministerial decisions to suit bureaucratic wishes. Neither Wilson nor Callaghan would have tolerated this for a moment. But a hard pressed Prime Minister might find his thoughts straying momentarily to matters of greater immediate importance. And while the Cabinet Secretary by his side would always be ready with some deftly drafted conclusions, it would be of help if there were a first estimate before him, of what his staff, from what they knew of him, thought he would want and could persuade his colleagues to accept.

Sometimes this worked; sometimes discussion would spiral far beyond the expected. As a Cabinet Secretary once observed, discussion among Ministers reflected diverse social backgrounds. Labour Ministers were often intellectuals who would talk at the drop of a hat about anything in the universe. In the Conservative ranks, at least in those days, senior boys spoke and junior boys remained silent. In one Labour Cabinet, discussion of an item not of the first importance had lasted well past one o'clock and had left any conclusions imagined in advance as far behind as the Stone Age. Wilson was getting bored.

More importantly, he was expected for lunch at the *Daily Mirror* and the brandy served there in abundance must have seemed to him as attractive a prospect as a clear stream to a thirsty hart. So he rose to his feet, announced that he had a very important engagement and asked the Deputy Prime Minister, Edward Short, to take over. Short was a Bear of Little Brain and would have been as capable of under-standing, let alone summarising, the previous discussion as he would have been at delivering a lecture on quantum mechanics. He presided wordlessly over the discussion for a further five minutes, then spoke. 'I find we have agreed as follows' – and read out the draft conclusions penned before the discussion had begun. The astonishment of the intellectuals present could not have been greater if he had burst into 'God rest you merry gentlemen'. Their mouths were agape. In this momentary interval Edward Short snapped his folder shut and made for the door. Cabinet was over. Not without a modest satisfaction, the Secretariat recorded the conclusions read out by the Deputy Prime Minister.

Another of my tasks was to service the Ministerial Committee on European Affairs, chaired by the Foreign Secretary; parallel with this was the duty of chairing a Committee of senior officials on the same subject. Also involved was responsibility for advising the Prime Minister direct. The significance of this was that if the Foreign Office wanted to put a point to the Prime Minister they had to go through the Foreign Secretary. He might not agree; or if he did, might not think it worth while intervening with the Prime Minister. But I could and did, when I thought it necessary, minute the Prime Minister direct, with naturally a copy to the Foreign Secretary. I hope it helped to inject now and again a view of what was going on in Europe, rather than what some thought should be going on.

For my two years in the Cabinet Office I served under two Prime Ministers and three Foreign Secretaries. When I joined in the late summer of 1975 Harold Wilson was Prime Minister and James Callaghan Foreign Secretary. In 1976 Wilson resigned. Callaghan took his place and Tony Crosland became Foreign Secretary – to be succeeded after his sad and untimely death in January 1977 by David Owen.

Wilson and Callaghan never cared much for the Community, and internationalism was not exactly widespread in either of the two main parties. Christopher Soames once told me of entering his London club, White's, after a couple of years in Brussels. An elderly member greeted him with mild surprise. 'Haven't seen you for some time, Christopher,' he said. 'You been in Kenya?'

In the Labour Party xenophobia had a different tinge: it was a deep-rooted fear that in a united Europe socialism in one country would no longer be possible. And there was also a question of generation. Callaghan was over sixty and Wilson nearly that age when they began to grapple with the problems of Britain in the Community. Their world was that of the late 1940s, of a victorious Britain as a great world power, the centre of a great Commonwealth, with a special gold-plated key to the White House ('Attlee flies to tell Truman no atom bomb on Korea'), and a patronising smile for the defeated, rubble-clearing, foreign language-chattering lot across the Channel. For Wilson and Callaghan the emerging unification of Europe was as unreal and as improbable as the Constitutional Convention in Philadelphia must have seemed to George III and Lord North.

Wilson I found easier to get on with than Callaghan. I had worked for him before; Prime Ministerial office had not changed his attitudes; the complications of Labour Party politics and the international stage afforded ample scope for his constantly flickering private computer. He had none of the uneasy resentment of some Labour politicians towards grandees. If people were richer than Wilson, then they could buy him a brandy. He remained as friendly, quick of wit and approachable as he had always been, but showed from time to time that he was becoming very tired.

170

Callaghan gave the appearance of an avuncular village policeman, though the manner was not always avuncular. He had a mind both sharp and well stocked, but he seemed uneasily conscious that he had not been to a university. And he did not like those who were grand and rich. When he thought that anyone was condescending to him, either intellectually or socially, his temper could ignite with the speed of a striking match.

The generational gap between Wilson and Callaghan and the rest of Europe soon found expression. In the autumn of 1975 a huge conference – CIEC (Conference on International Economic Cooperation) – was called in Paris, a meeting between the Haves and the Have-nots. It was meant to bridge the gap between the rich and the poor. Needless to say it did not. But such conferences, involving much travel, entertainment and writing of memoranda, are always extremely popular with the practitioners of power. It was a major event. Yet now in the dealings which the European Community had with third countries Britain had no independent Ministerial voice. As always in the Community there was an internal discussion and then the Commission, or in this case the country holding the Presidency of the Council of Ministers and the Commission, would go off and deal the hand. Britain was no longer, in Churchill's phrase, at the top table.

To Wilson and Callaghan this seemed extraordinary. So in October 1975 Callaghan proposed that Britain should have a separate seat – apart from the Community – at this jamboree. I asked him why. National prestige, he replied, and let it be known among his Ministerial colleagues as well as officials that if his advisers stopped wringing their hands and instead manfully pressed our case his demand would be met.

My heart sank at this. There were points which we wanted featured in the Community approach. Inside the Community we were free to argue for these as resolutely as we wanted. But in 1975 to leave the

171

Community ranks and make a separate case from the back of the room, would be as about as acceptable to our Community colleagues as a proposition to the United States that Alaska should, in an international gathering, raise the state flag and make a separate case.

I reflected. As Roosevelt once said, he did not hire lawyers to tell him what he could not do. There was a precedent which might help. Before I had left the Department of Trade a few weeks earlier we had had much argument in a Geneva working group about how the Community should operate in a new Steering Committee which was to be set up to oversee the GATT. The French had suggested that the Commission should not, as the Treaty of Rome provided, be the single spokesman. They had, as usual, a clever point. In the course of discussions in Geneva, issues could arise not simply of commercial policy but of monetary or social questions where the Commission did not have an exclusive right to speak for the Member States. Using this as a precedent, we could argue that Britain had a right – together with other Member States – to speak on questions which went wider than commercial policy.

At the same time we were preparing for a forthcoming Community Summit in Rome, where the question of representation at the CIEC would come up for decision. I went across to No. 10 and put this point to the Prime Minister. Wilson looked gloomy. Barbara Castle (then Secretary of State for Social Services) was engaged in a furious row with the doctors. On the separate seat affair, while blustering noises had been made round the Cabinet table, Wilson had become uneasily aware that we were dangerously exposed. (He was not alone. A few days before, as Callaghan was finishing his weekly report to the Cabinet on foreign affairs and the Cabinet was about to move to the next item, Roy Jenkins had intervened. In the silkiest possible manner he asked, 'How are you getting on with that separate seat business, Jim?') So the Prime Minister's unease was understandable. 'Got to get Barbara off the hook,' he said, 'and Jim off the hook on this one.'

MASTER

I explained my thoughts. His gloom seemed momentarily to diminish.

In Rome a couple of days later for the European Council, Callaghan seemed friendly. My suggestion did not fully meet his point but it was a step in the right direction. After the first morning of the Council, I was summoned from our Delegation's back room to see the Prime Minister. 'Do me a note on that separate seat thing and the French argument', he said. 'Bit of the GATT, bit of the Treaty of Rome. You know the form. Want it by 2.15.' Abandoning an excellent lunch provided by the Italians for visiting officials, I went away and dictated a note. I hope it helped.

But the result later that afternoon was not a victory. We did not of course get a separate seat. We did get a formula which would allow Member States to speak separately on matters not of Community competence, after certain consultations, and we got somewhere on our other demands, so it was not a total defeat. But the press thought it was. And the jeering uproar on the Opposition benches when the Prime Minister reported on his return was not exactly a welcome for a conquering hero.

The *Economist* wrote in a kindly vein:

> Mr Callaghan is one of Britain's best post-war Foreign Secretaries and this reverse, borne of trying to hit too far off his own bat, will make him a better one. With Mr Roy Denman, a formidable bureaucrat now in charge of the Whitehall EEC unit in Downing Street, it is to be hoped also that in future the Prime Ministerial hand will know better what the Foreign Office one is doing.

The next time I appeared before Callaghan was a few days later, for a meeting of the Ministerial Committee on European Affairs. Looking at me as if I were the dog's dinner brought in by mistake for the cat, he said, 'So you're the formidable fellow who's going to keep me in order, are you?' I thought silence the better part of discretion.

I began to realise that British Ministers' view of the world was not simply that coloured by memories of the past for elders of the tribe. There was something in the atmosphere of No. 10 Downing Street which acted on them as a distorting mirror. It was the mahogany and the silver candle-sticks on the Cabinet table and the echoing sense of history in the house. Here had been brought the news of the victory at Waterloo. Here Viceroys had been despatched to India. Here Chamberlain had returned from Munich with – he claimed – peace and honour.

So it was difficult to sit at the Cabinet table and mingle with the ghosts of the past without feeling that despite all the fashionable pessimism Britain was still a great power. Pathetically enough, a Minister would occasionally retail to his colleagues some polite banality uttered by a foreigner: 'I was talking to Signor Tutti Frutti the other day, and he said that Britain was still frightfully important.' This would be followed by a rumble of approval and a thumping on the Cabinet table.

Reading about Britain in the European press after such forays, the gap between the perceived world of Ministers and the view outside seemed to me not only thousands of miles wide but widening by the month. So I suggested that we should compile once a fortnight, for circulation to the Cabinet, extracts on Britain from nine or ten world newspapers which Ministers would not normally see, ranging from the *New York Times* to the *Asahi Shimbun*. Our compilation would have no element of interpretation, leading to possible accusations that officials were pandering to the prejudices of foreigners. It would be a straight reproduction or translation of a substantive article on Britain – with any accompanying cartoon. If over a fortnight there happened to be no substantive comment that in itself would be a message. I was rather pleased with this idea. That will sharpen the noodles up, I thought.

My colleagues thought the same, coming unfortunately to a different conclusion. Heads were shaken. It would be controversial, I was told.

'Controversial' in Whitehallspeak has the same sort of connotation as 'junk bonds' and 'defaulting' in a respectable banking house. 'How so, controversial?' I asked. The British press often printed views critical of foreigners, usually representing what a lot of British people thought; if foreigners wanted to deal with us, it would be wise on their part to take these points on board. No, I was told. I had not quite understood. Ministers would not like it. I began to say that this was not the idea. But I realised regretfully that there was nothing doing. Shattering the glass panels of a dream world would be bad enough. Organised by the domestic staff it would be intolerable.

Life in the Cabinet Office went on. I had been given – as my predecessor had – a palatial room, meant originally, I assumed, for a Minister who had been promoted or sacked. As a Permanent Secretary I had a car to take me to the office and back. I borrowed from the Ministry of Works some rather attractive oil paintings to hang on the office walls. And I now went to the weekly meeting on Wednesday morning of Permanent Secretaries. The attitude of the older Conservative Ministers to this gathering, in so far as they would have bothered to have heard about it, would have been that they had nothing against the servants' hall getting together, providing of course there was no unseemly or riotous behaviour – a possibility, which looking round the grey faces of my colleagues, seemed about as likely as an outbreak of carnival spirit in Glasgow on a rainy Sunday morning. Labour Ministers, on the other hand, suspected that the purpose of the meeting was to plot against the Government. (Had they ever heard a tape of the meeting they would have been agreeably surprised.)

I also went for the first time to the annual meeting of Permanent Secretaries, held in some hideous Victorian mansion in an area that was fighting a losing battle with suburbia. I was the youngest Permanent Secretary and it would have been wise to have kept my trap shut. But someone started the meeting by complaining about the falling standards of those joining the Administrative Class. I tried to point out that we were apportioning national talent in 1975 in a manner appropriate to 1875; now more of our brighter young should go into industry; this is what had happened in Germany and their economic success had been far greater than ours. These points cut little ice. The first questioned the existence of the talent. The second was an indecent reference to that thing called Europe. The Treasury seemed the most resolutely anti-European of Departments. Later, in the bar before lunch, one of the Treasury mandarins was heard saying ' ... so I said that was a lot of Eurocrap.' This was greeted by a sympathetic titter. It was going to be a long road to Rome.

Some relief from Whitehall meetings was afforded not only by European Summits but the monthly meeting in Brussels and Luxembourg of the General Affairs Council, in effect a meeting of Foreign Ministers which dealt with general business. I had agreed with John Hunt, who had had some fear that I would want to take over negotiation in Brussels from Michael Palliser, that I would make a monthly sally for these. This gave me the chance of seeing foreign colleagues and getting the feel of the situation in a way that telegrams can never give you. Here Bob Goldsmith, Palliser's Deputy, was an invaluable asset. In advance of a Ministerial meeting on the Monday I would arrive the day before with a stack of briefs. I would explain our line. Bob would explain in turn that discussion in Brussels over the last few days had made this line quite unsaleable. I would reply that what he was suggesting was quite unsaleable to Ministers. After much discussion, and reasonable refreshment – always generously dispensed in the Goldsmith house – we would reach a compromise. We would then have to explain this to Ministers when they arrived the following day. At least our final advice to Ministers was up-to-date and realistic.

It was on one of these occasions that I caught a last glimpse of Freddy Kearns in action. His speciality was the Council of Agricultural Ministers. Here he would work round the Delegations, sounding views and sewing up deals in a manner worthy of a floor manager at an American Party Convention. Exceptionally, a joint meeting had been called of Foreign and Agricultural Ministers. It was June, so we gathered in Luxembourg. The Foreign Secretary was not due to arrive until the next day. Our Ambassador asked the Minister of Agriculture and Freddy Kearns to dinner, and was kind enough to invite me as well. I arrived at the appointed time and chatted to my host. After a while Antony Acland looked at his watch. 'I hope they're not going to be late,' he said. I was about to reply that if the two Freds had found a convenient pub on the way they might be very late, when we heard on this drowsy summer's evening, through the half opened windows, a noise. Some way along the street two people were singing. They were not in tune and it was apparent that, as they say in Dublin, they had had a few jars. As they neared it became clear that they were British. They were in fact the two Freds. And to the doubtless astonished passers-by they were belting out

> *Old Macdonald had a farm*
> *Ee I Ee I O*
> *And on this farm he had a dog*
> *Ee I Ee I O . . .*

A momentary expression of alarm crossed Antony's face – only momentary because he did not have to acquire diplomatic skills, he was born with them. As the two Freds neared the residence the noise increased. There was a momentary pause while they knocked on the door. At least it would be a laughable understatement to say that they knocked on the door. It sounded as though a platoon of US Marines was demolishing it. A terrified domestic flung the door open. And up the stairs, in splendid full-throated chorus, came the guests of honour.

> *With a bow-wow here*
> *And a bow-wow there*
> *Here a bow, there a bow*
> *Everywhere a bow-wow*

Antony turned to our small group. '*Courage, mes braves,*' he said.

It was not long after this that both Freds fell from grace. Peart was moved; a lawyer – John Silkin – was appointed in his place. Silkin had heard of the Svengali-like role of Freddy Kearns, and arrived determined to make a change. In the British Civil Service senior officials are not sacked at a Minister's whim for the good reason that this would lead to a bureaucracy staffed at the top by political creeps. But Silkin made it clear that he disliked Fred and was not prepared to listen to him. It was equally clear that this attitude extended to foreigners in general and the Community in particular.

A climax was not long in coming. At a meeting in Brussels there was the usual council of war in the Delegation office. An exasperated Fred, his advice once more ignored, asked for a bowl of water. Thinking that this eminent man had been taken ill, a young sprig rushed out and returned with one. With an air of drama which would have done credit to the London stage, Fred, now the centre of attention, plunged his hands in the bowl and slowly washed them. 'That's what I think of you, Minister,' he said. 'I wash my hands of you.'

It must have been a splendid scene, one that will be talked of in hushed voices in Whitehall for years to come. It should have been commemorated in one of those engravings found in London clubs, with a key identifying those present (No. 26 Captain Fitzwallah, No. 27 Ensign Bumble). In any event, it finished Fred. He was forbidden further trips to Brussels. Some months later he was eased out on early retirement. A few years later he was dead.

Taking part in a major and difficult negotiation is rather like serving in a war. There are moments of triumph and despair; living through these together creates a bond. But I do not think I am moved simply by a friendship formed in difficult times if I judge Fred to have been a remarkable man. He rendered great services to the state and had a distinguished career. But he should never have become a civil servant. There was about him something of a *condottiere*. He had an unerring eye for a deal, a ruthlessness, a quickness and a willingness to take risks. In a more mobile society like the United States he would have become a celebrated figure on Wall Street. With Fred the predator on the prowl, any chief executive with one quarter's bad results and doubts about the next would have been advised to take tranquillisers or flee to a monastery. And he was also a very complex person. For all his colourful language he was a devout Christian, a lay preacher, a lover of English poetry. When he went, I am sure the trumpets sounded for him on the other side.

The Whitehall scene was enlivened, after Callaghan took over from Wilson as Prime Minister, by the arrival as Foreign Secretary of Tony Crosland. Roy Jenkins, who made a pitch for the job, would undoubtedly have been a considerable Foreign Secretary. But there was no love lost between him and Callaghan, and it began to be thought that Roy Jenkins might move to Brussels as President of the European Commission.

I found the arrival of Crosland a breath of fresh air. Some Foreign Secretaries are seduced by the pomp and circumstance of foreign affairs, but Crosland regarded it all with a certain quizzical amusement. I think that as an economist at heart he suspected diplomats of spending large parts of their lives waltzing in white ties under

179

glittering chandeliers and of having little regard for economic reality. To the consternation of the Foreign Office, he greeted me as a long lost friend from the Department of Trade who had spent his life not on frivolities but on serious economic matters.

I remember a briefing meeting in Luxembourg one evening when Crosland arrived late. He had already read his briefs and he wanted to relax. So, waving aside the Foreign Office contingent, he started to chat about Permanent Secretaries we had both known. He opined that one of them would not have recognised a Phillips Curve (a formula linking inflation with unemployment) if it had walked up to him in the street and shaken hands. Going out of the room, the Foreign Office men were indignant. One was heard to say, 'Who the hell was Phillips, and where was he Ambassador?'

Towards the end of 1976 I fell ill. I became increasingly short of breath and white faced. Coming back from a European Council in the Hague I could barely complete the usual mile long hike from where the plane came in to the baggage counter. I went to see our doctor the next day. 'You have no blood,' he said after a short examination. 'I hope it's nothing nasty.' I was shipped into hospital the next morning. Crosland sent me a friendly message. Some impression thus got about in the hospital that I was associated with 'Them' – the Labour Government, hated by the medical fraternity. In the course of innumerable X-rays someone thrust a probe relentlessly up my rear.

'Gather you're part of the Government,' he said conversationally.

'No,' I cried desperately, 'I'm just a civil servant. I advise.'

The treatment grew kinder.

Later the specialist came to see me. They were not sure quite what had been wrong but after a blood transfusion and some pills I would be released. Fate seemed to want to celebrate. A letter arrived from No. 10 asking in traditional fashion whether I would accept a Knighthood in the New Year Honours. So after all the year ended well.

FIVE

A Greater Guild

EUROPE IN THE WORLD

A few days into the 1977 New Year our Ambassador in Brussels, Donald Maitland, appeared in my office. My room was large, Maitland small. Now and again he would leap up and rush round the room like a clockwork mouse.

'There are some senior appointments to be filled in the Commission,' he said. Lulled by Christmas, relieved to be out of hospital, I listened with benevolent impartiality. Maitland fixed me with a look rather like that of the Ancient Mariner. 'One of them is the Director General for External Relations. It is one of the key jobs in the Commission. If we field the right candidate we could get it.' This was the job which Christopher Soames had offered me eighteen months before.

I began to see what was up.

'Do you mean me?' I asked.

'Yes,' he replied.

I thought hard. With a new US Administration coming into office the Tokyo Round of world trade negotiations – the biggest yet – was due to be relaunched. The Commission would have a decisive role; indeed the role of the UK, as only one of nine member States, would be a minor one. I was already an Admiral, but on the staff. The new job would mean hoisting my own flag with my own battle squadron. But breaking with Whitehall after nearly thirty years would be a wrench. And the intrigues and backstabbing in Brussels were on a scale unknown in London. I took counsel with friends. If I decided to stay in Whitehall I would be more than satisfactorily looked after. But the more I thought about it, the more the change seemed a great adventure. The Prime Minister agreed to the move. So, after a week or so, did the Commission.

There was one difficulty of timing. In January 1977 Britain assumed for the first time the Presidency of the Council of Ministers of the Community. The country which has this responsibility for six months finds itself not just a member of the team but its captain. Ministers – not just the Prime Minister or the Foreign Secretary, but departmental Ministers, whose main preoccupation may have been the drafting of standards for dogmeat – find themselves, to their surprise and sometimes their dismay, chairing meetings in Brussels of their European counter-parts. And something more is required: uplifting statements need to be made about the visionary goals which the Community is pursuing, and tribute paid frequently to the glorious progress being made to this end. To expect this from the Labour Government of 1977 was rather like moving, in the full glare of television, a confirmed alcoholic into the chairmanship of the Band of Hope.

Perceiving that the task of Assistant Ringmaster, even at official level, of this variegated circus would be more than usually difficult, and that it would be unfair to pitch in a newcomer, those concerned in Whitehall agreed, with the assent of the Commission, that I should remain in the Cabinet Office until the end of June. In the meantime I would go to Brussels one day a week to read myself in.

Thus started a period of bluebottle-like activity. Watching over events in Brussels, briefing from time to time the Prime Minister and the Foreign Secretary, servicing and chairing endless discussions between Departments in Whitehall became ever more frantic, the backcloth ever less encouraging. The Foreign Office found it difficult to realise that other Departments needed to deal with Europe; other Departments found it difficult to realise that Europe was there at all. The Labour Party had heard of Europe but wished quite simply that it would just go away. I began to wish fervently that the Labour Party would go away, but without any great hope, now that Mrs Thatcher had displaced Edward Heath, that the alternative would be better.

The end of our Presidency began to approach. In May a Summit of the Industrialised Countries (the G7) was held in London. I was not more than marginally concerned, but I observed with interest that the recently appointed President of the Commission, Roy Jenkins, attended, although Giscard d'Estaing, the President of France, had done his best to stop him. ('The Commission', Giscard said, 'is not a sovereign state.') Roy Jenkins had the support of the Italians and the smaller Community members but none from Callaghan, who made him as welcome as a polecat. (By a process of osmosis Whitehall takes its tone from the top, where the position was that, while by what must have been some oversight in the drafting of the Treaty of Rome the Commission had been given responsibility for trade policy, for the rest they were overweening bureaucrats who should be cut down to size.)

Of more direct concern to me was the European Summit (a meeting of the Heads of Government of Community countries) held in London in June, the climax of our Presidency. I had to chair a meeting of officials which lasted until three the next morning and produced a statement which even by the standards of Summits was of ponderous banality. The Council adopted it later that day without enthusiasm – and I am glad to say that it had no discernible effect on events.

This being the last day of June, deliverance was at hand. So I cleared out my desk in the Cabinet Office, gave a drinks party there that evening, and the next morning, with two suitcases, got on a plane to Brussels. It was a Friday. There was no real need for me to be there until the Monday. But I had said several times that I would be in my new job on 1 July; it seemed best to keep the appointment.

For the month of July (August being the traditional holiday month for the Commission) I rented a small service flat near the office. The amount of work to be done was awesome. The people and the work were mostly familiar, but a lot of decisions had simply been deferred. And contrary to popular myth, staff were very thin on the ground – I reckoned that in DG 1 (as the Directorate General for External Relations was known) the senior staff amounted to about a third of what would have been provided in Whitehall. So I found myself getting into the office about 8.30 and leaving in the early hours of the next morning. Finding somewhere more permanent to live posed a problem: it is usually inadvisable to seek to view a prospective house at 3.30 in the morning.

Moya came out for a few days and we registered our two children in the European School. It was a good school: every Community language had a separate stream, and from an early age all pupils had to have part of their instruction in another Community language. We put Julia, who had started at the Lycée Français in London, down for the French stream. This caused raised eyebrows. Do you realise, I was asked, that she will increasingly be brought up as a French citizen? I said laughingly that I could imagine worse fates. We also found a house to rent, a comfortable, rambling one in a pleasant area of Brussels. The work may have been hard but financially things had improved a great deal. My take-home pay trebled, though in New York it would have been regarded as modest. But we no longer had to worry about money.

Back in London for August I went to get a reservation for our car on the cross-Channel ferry. This done, the girl looked up expectantly. 'And the return journey?' she asked. 'There is no return,' I said and paying for the ticket walked out light of heart.

When we got across the Channel we stopped for a picnic on the Belgian coast, and I felt an enormous relief. It is difficult to remember now the trade union-dominated anarchy, the sheer hopelessness of 1977, the joy of escaping.

That joy was partly the exhilaration of a new job with a very large freedom of action. In Whitehall, it seemed to me, a Permanent Secretary was smothered by layers and layers of Ministers. In the Department of Industry there was at the top of the pyramid the Secretary of State. Under him there toiled two Ministers of State, under them two Parliamentary Under Secretaries. Then there came the Parliamentary Private Secretaries. I had asked John Davies once, when he was Secretary of State for Trade and Industry, for a formal meeting of DTI Ministers. At the appointed hour they entered in columns of three. In France and Germany, where the economic performance since the war has been substantially better than in Britain, there would have been two. In the Commission a Director General operated much more on Continental lines, with far less direct supervision than in Whitehall. There was political control, exercised by the weekly conclave of the gimlet-eyed Ambassadors of the Member States (the COREPER), where the representative of the Commission appeared, often feeling like a prisoner in the dock. And the Council of Ministers would take the final decisions. But in the Commission the only political figure set directly above a Director General was one Commissioner, who might or might not be active. So many questions which in London would laboriously go to Ministers at various levels would be decided by the Director General. And he also had to deal with the press. At the end of my first week I was told that something we had just decided would be coming up at the Commission's midday press conference. I nodded without much interest. My staff saw I was missing the point.

'Is it not time,' they said, 'that you went?'

'But officials don't take press conferences,' I expostulated.

They do here, I was told. I went.

Of course an exposure far greater than in Whitehall had its dangers. But it was tremendous fun, and it was also fun dealing with my colleagues. A variant of Murphy's Law decrees that in every organisation some are Lulus. But the overwhelming majority in DG1 were people of high calibre – able to expound the most complicated brief in at least one language other than their own – and more than a few of them were world-class negotiators.

Different nationalities and different backgrounds were bound together by a common cause: we all believed that the only hope of a war-torn continent was in a union. The Member States regarded the Commission with a mixture of caution and suspicion. But they were sailing ships – often as magnificent in their rigging as the Spanish galleons of old. We were the steamship. We were the future.

Dealing with the Commissioners was a more variable pleasure. At the time of writing there are twenty – an absurdly high number for the real jobs available. When I joined the staff there were twelve. They were in effect our Ministers, though by no means all had been politicians. Commissioners were nominated by their Member States every four years (now five), and often a Commissioner stays on for two or more terms.

If politics is a lottery, the selection of Commissioners has resembled a kind of blind man's bluff played in dense fog on ground riddled by deep holes. The President of the Commission had little say in the selection of Commissioners. Who are occasionally appointed because they are able men well qualified for the job. Sometimes they are appointed because they have the right friends. Sometimes they are appointed because someone wants to get rid of them. So the quality is variable. At the top end of the scale, there have been Commissioners who would have done credit to any national Government. At the bottom end of the scale, there have been people who were quite simply awful.

If anyone is disposed to think this an unduly dyspeptic judgement they should remember the Commissioner who threw a bottle through a mirror in the bar of a Strasbourg hotel, the Commissioner whose expenses reached a level so Homeric that there was an outcry in the press followed by a formal enquiry, and the Commissioner who was told by a President of the Commission at one of its meetings that he was not capable of running a Greek taverna. In cases such as these it would have been far better if the Commission could simply have gone to Central Casting. It is not difficult therefore to understand the wish long expressed by the European Parliament, and now on the way to being accepted, that it should have a decisive voice in the selection of Commissioners.

NEGOTIATING ON TRADE

So the Tapestry of Everyday was much more brightly coloured than in Whitehall. It did not take long to unfold. In the first week of July 1977 the Multi Fibre Arrangement – an agreement restricting the imports of textiles into developed countries from the less developed – ran out. Would it be renewed? The question was due to be discussed at a meeting of the GATT (the forerunner of the WTO) in Geneva at the beginning of the week, and as usual the Commission would speak for the European Community. It might seem that the liberal answer would be to let the agreement lapse. But this would not have helped the developing countries. The MFA did guarantee them a steadily rising share of the markets of the developed countries; if the agreement were to lapse, the way would be open for emergency restrictive action by importing countries. This is what the French wanted, and their anxieties were not difficult to understand. Because of a chapter of accidents, imports of textiles into the Community were running not at the overall rate of increase of 6 per cent specified in the agreement but at over 20 per cent. The Community was becoming the world's dumping ground for surplus textiles.

For a decision on whether the MFA should lapse, a meeting of the COREPER needed to be held, and one had to be called over the weekend. I made the mistake of arranging it with the country holding the Presidency and not the Commission's Secretariat General. So there were no interpreters. A Dutchman courteously said that as a gesture to the newly arrived Director General they would be content for the proceedings to be held in English. At this the French nearly had a fit. Their representative said icily that since the beginnings of the Community the French had in its meetings only spoken French. He had no intention of changing this custom. It was agreed that French, German or English could be used. Temporarily mollified, the French put their case. Others were not persuaded.

Not to renew the agreement in Geneva would be a major move backwards for world trade. A Community decision to allow this could be made only at Ministerial level. So at the end of the discussion I said that the Commission would in a famous Community phrase 'take its responsibilities'. That meant that if the Commission thought a certain course of action was within its mandate, it could go ahead even if some Member States dissented. If they wanted nevertheless to press their objections, they could have an open row in the Council of Ministers. So it was a risky proceeding. But I felt as if a bugle had sounded. There had been no bugles in Whitehall.

That was not the end of the textile pageant. But an even bigger pageant, the current world trade negotiation, the Tokyo Round, came to occupy the stage. Trade negotiations under the auspices of the GATT are hung around with technicalities boring enough to stun an ox. Consequently they are never mentioned in any Ministerial memoirs. Yet the stakes were high. Successive negotiations since 1947 to reduce barriers to world trade had ushered in the greatest period of prosperity in the recorded history of the West. Yet if one negotiation, this time the Tokyo Round, already long under way, were to fail, then the rule of law in world trade, laboriously built up over thirty years, would begin to crumble. New trade barriers would spring up; others would follow in retaliation. Jobs across the world would drain away. The economic wasteland of the 1930s would suddenly seem as near as a neighbouring valley, seen on turning a corner on a mountain, in the clear still air.

Whether the negotiation would succeed depended on two factors.

The first was how far the European Community would back it. Here there were doubts. It was not only the French who by tradition dragged their feet when it came to freeing trade. The British, long keen on free trade but now with an economy enfeebled by strikes and low productivity, were apprehensive. It had been put to me before I left London that in the current condition of the British economy boldly reducing barriers to imports would be like someone with incipient pneumonia taking a Christmas swim in the Channel. The Commission's ability to bring the Member States along would be crucial.

The second was how far the United States would back the negotiation. The GATT had never been popular with Congress. Americans had a long-standing disposition to believe that in every international trade negotiation Uncle Sam was taken for a sucker by cunning foreigners. Much would depend on the personality of the chief American negotiator and how far he would be able to persuade, convince and cajole Congress.

189

Here we had the enormous good fortune that Robert Strauss was appointed. He was one of the great Washington wheeler-dealers, Chairman in 1976 of the Democratic Party (and manager of Jimmy Carter's successful Presidential campaign in that year), later President George Bush senior's Ambassador in Moscow.

The first news I had had of him had been a few months back in London. A telegram from our Washington Embassy had reported that 'a well known attorney, Robert Strauss has been nominated for the post of Trade Representative. CV follows.'

But CV never tells you very much about what a person is like. My American contacts were not in those days numerous. On the telephone I tracked down a friend in New York. He asked me whether I had heard of Strauss's first press conference. I said I had not. Strauss had made, it seemed, a good deal of money in Texas and appreciated his creature comforts. But President Carter had decreed that in the interest of economy, austerity and God knows what else, even Cabinet members should travel coach. Strauss was having none of that. So at his first press conference the first question was, 'Mr Ambassador, are you still flying first class?' A hush came over the room. Strauss would now have to eat humble pie. He did nothing of the sort. Picking up the microphone genially he said, 'Yeah, until they think of something better.' As they used to say in Edwardian times, Strauss was a card.

A month or so later Strauss had made a tour of the European capitals. He appeared in London looking like a cross between a dancing bear and a travelling salesman and speaking softly and clearly in the unmistakable accents of Texas. He had deep-set blue eyes which looked straight into you and could uncover any secret, a fund of stories which could reduce even the most straight-laced to helpless laughter, and a Texan's originality in phrase and speech. In short, he was the most remarkable American I have ever met.

In London he was given a warm reception by Ministers and the top brass. It was hands across the sea and a glorious progression together to the sunlit uplands.

Strauss seemed pleased by these sentiments. After the meeting I took him aside and said that what he had been listening to was hypocritical baloney. The British had become closet protectionists. This would not help. But in the negotiations he would be dealing with the European Commission. I had dealt with them for many years and I could tell him that they were the meanest-minded bastards in the business. Representing a clutch of Member States, some of whom were roaring protectionists, they had little choice. Communication between the Americans and the Commission had not always been good. I would at least be prepared to tell him, when I got to the Commission, at any time of day or night what our position was and why. I later gathered that on his return to Washington he said that his impressions in Europe were generally favourable; the only negative note had been struck by a guy called Denman, who would unfortunately have something to do with the negotiations.

In September he appeared again in Brussels with his Deputy, Al McDonald, who had been the senior partner of McKinsey's, the management consultants. One day he had received a call from Strauss.

'I want you to be my Deputy.'

'See here, Mr Strauss,' said Al, 'I'm not a friend of yours. Why are you offering me this job?'

'I wouldn't be offering this job to a friend of mine,' replied Strauss.

Al had lived in Paris and London, and had a quick understanding of how Europeans thought and how to put to them an American view. And he had an ingenious management consultant approach.

I was fortunate in the formidable and friendly team from our side which performed the real work of the negotiation. They had between them not just talent and ability to work longer and harder than anyone else, but together a breadth of experience equalled by none, either from

191

the Member States or our negotiating partners. To name only a few –
Paul Luyten, Roderick Abbott, Peter Klein and Raymond Phan Van
Phi, all old friends from Geneva – they made a negotiating team with
which it would have been difficult to go wrong.

After a long pause in the Tokyo Round for the American elections
it was necessary to do business. The first question to address was how
deeply the negotiating countries should cut tariffs. The Europeans,
with trading conditions bad, wanted shallow cuts. The Americans said
they could only sell to Congress something ambitious. Al McDonald
and I worked out a scheme which would have something for everyone.
We would aim at tariff cuts in stages averaging 35 per cent; the result
in practice would be less, say 20 per cent, because of the inevitable
exceptions. Then after three years or so, if the world economy was
going well, we could move to a total of 50 per cent (again less with
exceptions, an average of say a third). That way both sides in the
dispute – the modest and the ambitious – could claim they had won.

The solution was accepted at a large meeting with the Americans
in the Commission, presided over by Roy Jenkins, and after some rapid
clearing of our lines with the Member States, Al and I went to Geneva
and managed to sell it to the other participants.

The next problem was agriculture. This had made a late entrance on
the GATT scene. In the immediate post-war period and in the 1950s
the Americans had not wanted to deal with agriculture: Congress was
not going to stand for some bureaucrats in Geneva telling them what
they could and could not do with agricultural assistance programmes.
And in the 1960s the Americans had not attacked the formulation of
the Community's Common Agricultural Policy: the Administration
had thought (and this was a statesmanlike decision) that it was politically more important to encourage the unification of Europe. But in
the 1970s, with the United States becoming a major exporter of food-
stuffs and with production under the CAP rapidly increasing,

Americans began to have second thoughts. In 1977 they had a choice. Either they could stage a frontal attack on the Common Agricultural Policy – much as the Americans were to do in the next negotiation, the Uruguay Round at the end of the 1980s – or they could press for increased access for specific products. Strauss was an extremely tough negotiator, but he was also a shrewd one. He could see that, no matter how anyone outside the Community walls huffed and puffed, there was no practicable chance of abolishing the CAP. The policy had to change.

But this would not be a rapid process. Nor would this be welcome to the Americans if it were; Congress would not welcome any resulting pressure to cut American aid to dairy and sugar producers. So Strauss said to us 'You've got sacred cows. We've got sacred cows. I'm not in the business of slaughtering sacred cows. But here's a list of products where I've got to have increased access to the Community market.' It was a tough list but we agreed to tackle it seriously. There was no option.

So by the summer of 1978 a good deal of progress was being made. Then there drew near the annual summit of the industrialised countries, the same cast of characters that had met in London in May 1977. Al McDonald and I were agreed that at this meeting – in Bonn in July 1978 – the great ones of the world needed to focus on the Tokyo Round. It was not for them alone to decide the fate of this negotiation. Nor could they hope to settle the very complicated points still under dispute. But an outline deal was beginning to emerge between the EEC and the Americans. If the Bonn Summit could give a final political impetus then we would be quite some way to a successful conclusion. So we thought it sensible to take stock and present the Summit with a progress report on what had been achieved and what still needed to be done. Al and I called a meeting in Geneva of the developed countries, which by agreement was held in the Commission Delegation.

We began shortly after dinner and finished at breakfast time the next morning, and it was at times a tense discussion. At one moment a delegate said 'I got that from the horse's mouth.'

'I hope' shot back a Canadian, 'that it comes from that end of the animal and not the other.'

But we ended with an agreed text.

Later that morning a tripartite meeting – USA, EEC, Japan – and the Director General of the GATT, Olivier Long, reviewed the preparations for the Bonn Summit. Our report was noted approvingly. 'What steps', asked Long, 'were being taken to inform the other contracting parties of this important communication?' This was a sensible question. The developing countries, always touchy, would be quick to regard as a slight not being consulted on a summary of the state of the negotiations. The answer was simply that there had not been time to widen the circle. Including the developing countries would have taken weeks. But Long had asked the question in an English so polished that it probably grated on the ears of a Texan. And as Strauss saw it, Long had not featured prominently in the previous discussions. There was a moment's pause. Then Strauss said, 'Everyone knows Ah drink too much. After midnight Ah just tell everyone everything Ah know.' There was a shout of laughter and the meeting broke up. Bob Strauss had the Churchillian gift of using a phrase or a joke not just to divert the assembly but to move it the way he wanted.

There was not just a question of the developing countries. A number of the Member States were cross. Events had moved on since 1960 in Geneva. The Commission now negotiated alone with third parties, without Member States in the room; we simply reported to them at intervals. The more recently joined Members in particular resented having had to kick their heels all night, with only occasional visits from the Commission representatives, while the real action was taking place elsewhere. This was not helped by increasingly violent telephone instructions during the evening to the British team from one senior official in London who saw all this as a chance, as he happily put it, to 'get Denman'. The French for their part found that the President of the Republic was displeased at what seemed to him an assault on his lofty prerogatives as a member of the Summit. My French colleague was confronted on the telephone with a panic-stricken Minister. Back in Brussels later that day and feeling somewhat weary, I was summoned to a meeting of COREPER.

The mood was questioning. The reports from capitals had been hostile: what had I been up to? I was in that mood of exaltation and defiance which fatigue and a conviction that one's cause is just can bring. And I also by circumstances knew more about the document we had spent all night agreeing than the Ambassadors. So I gave doubts short shrift. The Frenchman, finally reduced to silence, said sulkily that he would report what I had said to Paris. The British showed me later their reporting telegram. It said: 'Sir R. Denman gave a robust defence of his actions.'

With this as background, off we went to the Summit in Bonn. More precisely, Roy Jenkins attended as President of the Commission and a small number of officials went along to advise. I found that I was quartered – together with the Commission's Deputy Secretary General – in the gloomy remains of a castle on the Rhine. Joining the bustling throng the next morning I encountered my French opposite number – a man of considerable intelligence and charm, who later became a banker. He was, he explained, having a difficult time with his Minister. Could he come along and see me for a private word? I assented readily and gave him the number of the room assigned to me in a headquarters block which looked rather like council flats. I went up and unpacked my papers. Then in breezed Bob Strauss in his shirt sleeves, twanging a couple of bright red braces. He gave me in salty terms his assessment of the situation and to illustrate this told a couple of Texan stories. I was laughing heartily at these when the door opened and my French colleague walked in. He entered with a courteous smile and his hand outstretched in greeting. But seeing Strauss and myself, sitting in our shirt sleeves, clearly on friendly terms, filled him with roughly the same horror as an ancient Greek on glimpsing Medusa, 'whom no man shall behold and draw again the breath of life'.

Here was the so-called Community representative unmasked – *'Perfide Albion'* – closeted with his Yankee friend, selling the European store. Later in the day I saw my French colleague at the side of his Minister and President Giscard. The Minister saw me and whispered in Giscard's ear. The two of them gazed at me with an air which in Stalin's Russia would have meant a life expectancy of several minutes.

The rules for attendance at Summits were strict. A Head of State or Government can only be accompanied by two of his Ministers, almost invariably the Foreign Minister and the Finance Minister. In the back seat he can have a note taker. When the time came for the Summit to discuss the Tokyo Round I sat behind Roy Jenkins. Bob Strauss sat in a front seat, temporarily displacing the US Treasury Secretary. This has never happened since; I can only say that trying to exclude Strauss from such a discussion would have been like trying to contain a nuclear explosion.

Roy Jenkins was asked by Chancellor Helmut Schmidt to introduce the subject. He explained that the document which had been drawn up in Geneva was not an attempt to short-circuit the negotiation. It represented a photo of the state of play; it showed that a good deal had been achieved but some important progress remained to be accomplished. He suggested that the meeting put its weight behind a speedy conclusion; a success could be a major boost for world trade.

President Giscard was mollified by the reference to a photo. That was how he saw the document. He agreed generally, as did the others, with the need for the negotiation to succeed. Strauss added his comments. These were upbeat. 'Mr President,' he said, 'this is a first class package.'

Giscard was critical. 'Was it in good taste to speak so well of one's own accomplishments?' he asked.

Strauss at this point threw into the discussion a linguistic bombshell. 'As Dizzy Dean used to say, it ain't braggin' if ya done it.' This provoked a hum of surprised conversation round the room.

'Dizee Dean. C'est un homme de politique quoi?'

'Wer war denn dieser Bursche?'

Across the room I could see the British Prime Minister asking his Foreign Secretary, David Owen, a question. Owen seemed nonplussed. The British told me later that Callaghan had asked who Dizzy Dean was. Getting no reply he said, with only a faint smile of satisfaction, 'He was a pitcher for the St Louis Cardinals in the 1930s. Thought as Foreign Secretary you might have known that.'

Fortified by this Summit endorsement, the negotiation moved on. Finn Gundelach, the Agricultural Commissioner, did wonders with the American list requesting access for specific agricultural products. Finally in January 1979 we came to settling the tariff chapter – the full range of duties on industrial goods on which we could swap concessions. After last-minute consultations with Stevy Davignon, the Commissioner for Industrial Affairs, I took a plane to New York to meet Al McDonald.

It was not encouraging to have before I left a warning call from Christopher Soames, formerly Ambassador in Paris, to the effect that the French were trying to get together with the Americans to settle the negotiation bilaterally, bypassing the Commission and the rest of the Community. In New York the Americans told me what had happened. A message had been received by the President from President Giscard, who was tired of having affairs important to France bungled by those fellows in the Commission. So he had proposed that

J. F. Deniau, the French Foreign Trade Minister, should take a Concorde to Washington and settle the remaining questions in the Tokyo Round with the Americans. The American reply had been that they would be glad to discuss these questions with the French Government, or indeed any other. A member of the White House staff would be in Paris the following week and would gladly call on M. Deniau, thus saving him the inconvenience of a transatlantic trip. But the Administration of the United States was in negotiation (a word gently underlined) with the Commission of the European Communities.

Al McDonald and I and our small teams argued about a possible package of industrial tariff cuts. We argued all morning, all afternoon and all night. On Sunday morning about breakfast time we decided to call it a day. Al rang 'Lord Robert' (Bob Strauss) in Texas. I rang Davignon in Brussels. Comparing notes afterwards, we concluded that while it might be colouring the tale a bit to say that we had both received a considerable rocket, the reception in both cases had been far from enthusiastic. We had both been given briskly to understand that we had not secured points which were vital and had compromised unwisely on several others. I pointed out to Al that if we had both got the same message we had done rather well. He was not convinced. When I got on the evening Sabena flight to Brussels, I did wonder whether I had not got dangerously out on a limb. Fortunately exhaustion took its toll and I fell asleep before dinner was served.

Back in Brussels I had hardly got my nose in the door at home when the telephone rang. It was the French Ambassador. What, he enquired suspiciously, had I been up to in New York? What vital interests of the Community had I negotiated away? I suddenly had a thought. With an airy nonchalance I was far from feeling, I said that we had only been discussing possible bargains. One could be compared with a Citroen Deux Chevaux, limited but cheap. Alternatives were a Peugeot – more in the way of gadgets but more expensive – or at the extreme a Rolls Royce – everything we could want but fiendishly expensive. We would of course discuss these possibilities carefully with the Member States before we came to a choice. He rang off only partly mollified, declaring grimly that he was looking forward to hearing of the discussions.

This was not in fact an approach easy to defend in detailed argument, since the price for a Rolls Royce was so horrendous that we had not dared put it on the table. But time was short. The American legal authority for trade deals ran out in only a few months. Getting approval from the Member States in the time was not easy. But after many skirmishes on the telephone with Washington and in Geneva, a deal on tariffs was put together.

In this last phase we had to fight on two fronts. There were the remaining details to be tied up not only with the Americans but also with the other participants, particularly the developing countries. And we needed to get the endorsement of the Member States, first at official level and then at the level of the Council of Ministers.

It was the job of the Commission to prepare the detailed documentation, explaining and defending to the Member States the outline deal emerging. This involved much drafting, arguing about the presentation, filling in the slots with new results from the negotiating front as they came in. We set ourselves the deadline of the Council of Ministers' meeting in April. We began to work round the clock, seven days a week. Among the Commissioners, Davignon for industry and Gundelach for agriculture gave invaluable help.

At the meeting of the Commission when this was discussed, another Commissioner, whose heart was not exactly in the details, perked up when it was announced that we would have to operate over the weekend. In that case, he said jovially, refreshments would have to be provided. Simply ham and cheese sandwiches would be a bit austere. After all, we were working very hard. Roast beef sandwiches would be helpful; indeed a side of roast beef, suitably garnished, should be provided. Elaborate fish dishes would be difficult, but a little dressed crab together with some salmon would be very acceptable. Some thought that this lengthy and thoughtful intervention verged on the incongruous. But we were grateful for his consideration.

From the American side Bob Strauss's two deputies, Al McDonald and Alan Woolf, were a considerable help. They did not set out, as Americans sometimes do, to show the folks back home how they could sock it to the foreigner. They negotiated toughly but – conscious always of the danger of some sudden storm in Congress – they wanted a solution.

I remember from this time a discussion with Bob Strauss. I said that things seemed to be going well. We would doubtless have to have a ritual row; but the result seemed in the bag. Strauss disagreed. Senator X was dying. I commented that with great respect I did not see what difference the death of a Senator would make to the Tokyo Round. 'You fool,' said Strauss. 'I always told you you'd never know a goddamned thing about American politics. [Being insulted by Strauss was a mark of respect and friendship.] Once a Senator dies there'll be a funeral. All the other Senators will turn up. Then they'll sit around and compare notes on what I'd told them. That way there'll be death and disaster.'

With the developing countries we held numerous meetings. The reaction was normally a mewing cry that the whole operation was being rushed along by the European Community and the Americans. My reply was to say briskly that the negotiations had been in train for six years; where the developing countries had problems we would tackle them – against counter-concessions in the case of the richer of them. But if the Community and the Americans had not taken the ball and run with it the Tokyo Round would have died of old age.

With the Member States we worked either in *ad hoc* bilateral

meetings or in the 113 Committee, which met often on the spot in
Geneva. Americans would ask me years later how we could possibly
agree on a position with nine separate countries, to which I used to
reply that the 113 Committee had learnt to operate as a family. We
knew each other; we could discount high bidding and low bidding; we
knew our strength was in hanging together. From the accounts we had
had of the arguments in the American Delegation – several times
larger than ours – between the representatives of the various
Washington Agencies, differences inside the Community ranks
seemed friendly and minor.

The Council of Ministers of April eventually arrived. Everything
was in place. If we could get the agreement of the Council we would
be home and dry. Being April the meeting was in Luxembourg. But
France for this six months had the Presidency of the Council. A
French Minister would take the chair. Never enthusiastic about open
markets and foreign trade, they were going to be difficult. The French
Foreign Minister, François Poncet, would pass the ball to the French
Foreign Trade Minister, Jean François Deniau. He had formerly been
a Director General in the Commission and later a Commissioner: he
was brilliant, conceited and abrasive. He was also sardonic and destructive. We tightened our seat belts for a rough ride. Then happened one
of those minor accidents of history. Shortly before the Council was to
start after dinner there was a sudden flurry of activity. The concurrent
negotiations for the entry of Greece into the EC were at a critical
stage. François Poncet reflected. 'There will have to be two Councils,'
he said. 'I will chair the one about Greece. Deniau will chair the
Council dealing with the Tokyo Round.'

This changed the situation at a stroke. Deniau, as a consummate
technocrat, now had another objective. Instead of using his considerable talents to demonstrate how difficult France could be, the intellectual challenge was now to bring a difficult Council meeting to an

201

agreed conclusion. He succeeded. It took some six hours. The French were not the only ones to be difficult. But Count Lambsdorff – the German Trade Minister – was in good form and a steadfast defender of free trade. John Smith, the British Trade Minister (these were the last days in 1979 of the Callaghan Government), was dogged, reasonable and commonsensical. Davignon and Gundelach had the right answer to every question. And Deniau sparkled. 'Exercising ruthlessly my prerogatives as Chairman,' he would say, 'I find we have now discussed this matter enough. The Council's conclusions on this point are . . . .'

Some time after four the next morning it was over. Elated, we started the two hour drive back to Brussels.

On arrival I just had time for a shower, a shave and a clean shirt before the office and starting to draft speaking notes for our Commissioners at the midday press conference. A Dutch journalist asked rather acidly why it was that Jean Rey (at that time the Commissioner for External Relations) had presented the results of the Kennedy Round on his own, but a report on the Tokyo Round needed four Commissioners. The reason was that the Tokyo Round had been more complex and had involved more Commissioners. But on the whole the reception was friendly. Success has many friends.

After a few weeks of getting some of the technicalities straight, the day for signing the agreements was fixed. On a sunny April afternoon I took a plane to Geneva. Bob Strauss had other engagements and was understandably reluctant to travel for this all the way from Washington. So next morning Al McDonald and various Ambassadors appeared. The French telephoned from Paris to ask that as a gesture – presumably of malevolence – I should ask for the signing to be delayed to the afternoon. I replied that I had no such intention. So at eleven we signed in the Palais des Nations. On a page headed 'The European Communities' I wrote my name. I wondered what

Edgar Cohen would have thought if he had been given this vision of the future when I had joined his staff as a neophyte nineteen years before. That spring day in 1979 was one of the prouder moments of my life.

For the United States, the signing of an agreement with foreign powers is not the end but the beginning. The Congress still has to give its assent. Here Bob Strauss entered into his own. He spent hours with the Chairman of the Senate Finance Committee, hours with individual Congressmen, equal time with groups of Congressmen. He flattered, wheedled, persuaded and cajoled. I had to go and see him once on something we thought important to get in the legislation. It was July and Washington was like a steam bath. People were tired and tempers were getting frayed. But Bob was his sardonic cheerful self.

'Doing deals in smoke filled rooms?' I asked.

Bob grinned. 'I'll tell ya something. People aren't smoking as much as they used to. Guess we might have to import some smoke.'

A few weeks later the legislation was through with a record majority. Strauss operated with Congress like Menuhin playing the violin

What was the deal? Was it worth the six years it had taken to piece it together? It had taken six years not only because the number of participants was just short of a hundred and the subjects covered much wider than any previous negotiation, but because getting the necessary authority on both sides of the Atlantic took time. And when this was obtained the outcome of the US Presidential election of 1976 had to be awaited. Thus it was not until the spring of 1977, when the new Administration had shaken down, that the negotiations could get fully under way.

The final results were worth the long haul. Industrial tariffs were cut by about a third. A whole range of non-tariff barriers, ranging from subsidies to anti-dumping, Government procurement, dispute settlement and customs procedures, were brought into the multilateral rule book. On agriculture, the Community conceded increased access for an important list of US products. And there emerged an agreement – which for a time worked – on restricting agricultural export subsidies so that no contracting party could use them markedly to increase its share of world trade. So the deal was the biggest yet in the liberalisation of world trade.

But it represented something more. It prevented a lurch into trade wars and protectionism which would have made the West a poorer and more dangerous place. Instead the success of the Tokyo Round laid the foundation for a massive increase in world trade and world prosperity throughout the 1980s. It was my conviction then – and remains so now – that without Bob Strauss this would not have been possible.

And the success of the negotiations gave a boost to the Commission, negotiating for the Community, just as the success of the Kennedy Round in the 1960s had reinforced the position of a Commission then still young.

I have already mentioned the Commission team which made this possible. On my personal staff a particularly valuable contribution came in early 1978 from a new recruit. On starting in Brussels I had inherited an assistant. But he was occupied full time with the administrative chores involved in a Directorate General of several hundred people with its burgeoning Foreign Service, so I would get back to the office after two hours of meetings and find a dozen files stacked on the desk, and would have to ask my secretary which were the most urgent. 'They are all urgent,' she would reply. So I would buckle down to reading them. Immersed in the second file down I would get a telephone call. I was to go at once to see Commissioner X.

'What', I would be asked, 'did I think of the Doodledank affair?'

'What the hell', I would counter, 'is the Doodledank affair?'

It would be pointed out to me that the file had just been sent to my office. I badly needed a troubleshooting additional assistant who would be able to say to me when I got back from a lengthy meeting, 'There are two files here which are urgent. Commissioner Y will be on to you any moment about one of them. And on the other you need to give a call to Director General Z before ten tomorrow. Two files should not have been sent to you. The rest you can take home and deal with after dinner, but you haven't got to deal with them all tonight.'

Such a role required talent; at the right age and grade it was difficult to find anyone on the ground in DG1. But visiting our Mission in New York I was impressed by the First Secretary (Information). I found that she had served on the staff of the European Parliament, in the Cabinet of an Italian Commissioner and also in Washington. She was German, spoke impeccable English, French and Italian. So I offered Barbara Jacob the job. She was highly intelligent, hard-working, and had a very shrewd judgement of affairs and people. She soldiered with me in many battles, was an immense help, and became a friend of the family. Four years later I was to take her to Washington where she was as much a tower of strength as she had been in Brussels.

HOW WE OPERATED

If I have recounted the tale of the Tokyo Round consecutively, this is partly for the reader's convenience, and partly because it was the major external challenge for the Commission when I joined. But progress on that front was intertwined with many other alarms, excursions and crises, ranging from Japanese restrictions on Danish canned meat to an all night session with COMECON in a Moscow skyscraper.

From time to time – usually when the weather in the United States became uncomfortably hot – earnest American political scientists would appear and interrogate me on how organisationally the Commission dealt with these problems. How did we on the external

205

relations side consult with those dealing with industry and agriculture? Grasping their pencils with anticipation, they would ask about the Committee structure. I explained that there was no Committee structure. In a multinational organisation where there was no unified common background, such coordination as there was had to be mostly at the top. In the case of industry my opposite number Fernand Braun, a Director General and the equivalent in British terms of the Permanent Secretary of the Department of Industry, was an old friend; he and I would drop in on each other once a week for a drink and a chat.

Occasionally we would have a specific point to discuss; more often than not we would simply tell each other what we were doing. Communication in the Commission being far from perfect, we would often both learn something to our surprise, sometimes to our astonishment. But at least we kept in regular and friendly touch.

'You mean to say,' said one astonished American, 'that the optimal way of regularising these multidimensional discrepancies is not by a structured Committee approach but' – his voice faltered in disbelief – 'by having drinks?'

'Yes', I said, 'it works.'

He was only marginally mollified when I explained that consultation with our agricultural colleague was a shade more formal. Claude Villain, a recent arrival, was a brilliant French administrator who came from the Elysée. He was a magisterial Director General who ran a tight ship. I was with him once when a Head of Division was summoned to explain why something could not be done. *'Mais c'est impossible, Monsieur Villain,'* he explained, *'C'est contre la doctrine.'*

Claude pounded his chest like an orang-utan. *'La doctrine,'* he shouted, *'c'est moi.'*

Claude was too outspoken to last, and after a few years he was forced out. But while he was there we had a meeting once a fortnight – alternately in his room and mine. An agenda of half a dozen items was drawn up; attendance was limited to not more than three a side. Occasionally he would leap to his feet in rage and run round the room. Discussion thus had moments of excitement. But we always managed to agree.

COMMISSIONERS

Where, our American friends would ask, did our Commissioners come in? I was less frank then than I would be now. But five had the most impact.

First, Roy Jenkins – the President of the Commission when I joined. In his company it was possible to feel that the melancholy decline of British political life had been momentarily reversed, that Asquith and Balfour were in the next room, that the world had suddenly again become one of civilised conversation, remembered history and good food and wine. Roy Jenkins has said himself that much in Brussels – the multilingual and multicultural elements of the Community – were strange to him when he arrived. But I think history will judge that he made three major contributions to the unification of Europe.

He was the first, in his speech in Florence in 1978, to launch what later became the European Monetary System, now the single European currency, the euro. It is worth remembering that his initiative was opposed by virtually all his fellow Commissioners. They remembered an earlier ill-fated attempt at coordination of exchange rates – the 'snake' – and wanted gradualism. But Roy Jenkins, as a statesman, saw more clearly the path ahead. He lit the lamp; he showed the way.

Second, he gave the Presidency of the Commission, particularly in

the Industrialised Summits, a substantially increased authority. Jacques
Delors has since increased its role much further. But all ventures have
their early days; what has been achieved since would hardly have been
possible without the unrelenting efforts made by Roy Jenkins to roll a
heavy boulder uphill in the 1970s to the jeers of several of his partners.

Third, he attached major importance to the Community's partnership with the United States. He knew America extremely well and had
a sense of its history. He has written a short biography of Truman
which catches, as few books from English writers do, the way
Americans talk and do business. He watched carefully over the Tokyo
Round; he was concerned not to interfere with the detail but to see
that it went right. He knew that the Atlantic link was the most
important external relationship which the Community had. It is fair
to say that after his departure and that of Davignon the cultivation by
Commissioners of the link with the United States did not for some
time prosper.

Roy Jenkins was also a kindly and agreeable host. In my first week
he asked me to lunch with his Chef de Cabinet, Crispin Tickell. The
ostensible purpose was to discuss a draft reply to the Australian Prime
Minister, Malcolm Fraser. In fact he wanted to range over the external
scene and he asked a number of questions. He listened closely to what
I offered as comments and from time to time would say reflectively
'Myes'. This is a useful and widely used Whitehall and Oxbridge term
of art. It means: 'I have understood what you have said. I am inclined
to agree but I would like to reflect further before I give a definitive
reply.' This was a sensible reaction to the off-the-cuff views of an
official adviser on a wide range of subjects. His only difficulty – though
not of course with Crispin and me – was that both the expression and
its intonation, when it is pronounced, reflectively as it should be, were
strange to our Continental colleagues.

A year or so later a French colleague in the Commission came up to me in Belgrade and said, '*Cette expression anglaise – MYA – qu'est ce que ca veut dire exactement?*'

'You have got it wrong,' I replied. 'It is not MYA, it is MMMYEAAAH, and you need to have spent three years at least at Oxford or Cambridge before you can pronouce it.'

He went away with an odd look on his face – much like the French years before in Saigon, when I had tried to explain why the British did things in a certain way.

In day-to-day dealings, the star among the Commissioners was Viscount Etienne Davignon, generally known as Stevy. His grandfather had been Belgian Foreign Minister; his father Ambassador in Berlin in the 1930s; Stevy himself had become Permanent Head of the Belgian Foreign Office. I first came across him when I used to go from the Cabinet Office to the monthly meeting of the Council of Ministers. Each Delegation had three seats at the Council table, one occupied by the Minister, one by the Permanent Representative, and one by the principal adviser from the capital. I found myself sitting next to Stevy. He would simultaneously be reading what seemed to be the entire cable traffic of the Belgian Foreign Office, writing various letters, following the discussion, giving from time to time trenchant advice to his Minister on how and when to intervene, and making the occasional comment on the proceedings which made it difficult not to burst into unseemly laughter. As a Commissioner his intelligence and flair were such that although his nominal responsibility was limited to industry, his writ ran far and wide. In my five years in Brussels I was summoned to see him three or four times a week. I could – and did – telephone him when really necessary at ungodly hours from the other side of the globe. It was always worth while. I never finished any conversation without his having raised some new angle. And the discussion never took long because he was so enormously quick. Some said he was vain. I never found this. Many Ministers, when told a course of action which they favour is not possible, bridle. Stevy, when told of an objection, would – if he found it valid – accept it without demur. 'What do we do then?' he would ask. Then one had the classic, but in this case rapid-fire dialogue between a Minister and an official. The captain on the bridge knows where he wants to go, but a sensible captain will know what the boiler room can and cannot deliver. In forty years of public service, Stevy was one of the very best Ministers I had to work with.

And it was also fun, for Stevy had an agreeable sense of the ridiculous. I remember a lunchtime meeting of the Commission in April 1982, when I was summoned to report on the discussions within the Community on the Falklands crisis. The question was the extent to which Member States were prepared to align themselves with the British in an embargo on exports to Argentina not only of arms but of goods which could be used for military purposes. I reported that reasonable progress was being made and then relaxed and listened to the rest of. the discussion. One item concerned preparations for the annual Summit of the Industrialised Countries, this time to be held in Versailles. Gaston Thorn, the President of the Commission, reported that a grave situation had arisen. The membership of the Summit included – as well as the United States, Canada and Japan – four Community countries (France, Germany, Italy and the UK) and the President of the Commission. So the French had prepared eight handsome suites at Versailles for these great figures. But what had been overlooked was that the Head of Government of the Community country holding the Presidency attended. Usually this had presented no problem because it had turned out to be held by one of the countries already represented. But this time Belgium held the chair. So the Belgian Prime Minister Wilfried Martens would also attend. There would be nine VIPs and eight suites – a case of no room at the inn. As Thorn explained the full horror of the situation his voice dropped several octaves. There was a hushed silence. It was broken by Stevy. 'I don't see your difficulty, Gaston,' he said. 'You have a suite. It has a bed and a bath. Martens can sleep in the bed and you in the bath.' There was a shout of laughter round the table. Thorn, who in the presence of Stevy always showed the unease of a rabbit in front of a mongoose, gave only a little laugh.

The leading French Commissioner and a previous President of the Commission was François Ortoli. An Inspecteur de Finances, at one time a Director General in the Commission, then coordinator in Paris of French policy towards the Community (the equivalent of the job I had had in London), Minister of Finance under De Gaulle and the previous President of the Commission, he was in the tradition of the great public servants of France. His formal role in the Commission was to oversee economic and monetary affairs. But, like Stevy, he had a much wider role. He played an extremely important part as a link between the Commission and the French Government – then more central to Community affairs than any other. He lodged in Brussels but would go off to his Paris apartment every weekend. There he would get a feeling for what the mood was in Paris; he would also explain there with authority and precision (he would grill me once every few weeks on the Tokyo Round) why the Commission was taking the line it did. It was a considerable tribute to him that when the French Government changed in 1981 he remained – though at the other end of the political spectrum – their main interlocutor in Brussels.

Underneath a rather formal manner he was a warm and generous man. When the Falklands affair erupted he called me to see him. The Falklands, he said, was an affair in which we would not find everyone in the Community helpful. Old resentments would surface. But he had served under De Gaulle; he understood the force of national feeling. If ever he could help he would be glad to do so. He was – as always – a man of his word.

Ortoli also had a nice self-deprecating sense of humour. His father had been a high official in Indo-China; had there not been the war and independence, Ortoli might well have become Governor General. Finding that I had served there too we would occasionally lunch in a nearby Indo-Chinese restaurant. Once I asked him about the Inspecteurs de Finance, that formidable body in which he had started his career. What was it like to join, I asked? What had been his first job? 'I got a telegram,' said Ortoli, 'from the Ministry of Finance, saying that I had been accepted and asking me to report. I did so. They congratulated me and said they had a first job for me. I was to go to the Post Office at Clermont Ferrand and inspect the accounts.' Someone had given him a few tips and off he set. When he got there he found that the management – solidly in its fifties – regarded the intrusion in their affairs of a young whippersnapper from Paris with feelings ranging from rancour to contempt. So the atmosphere was tense.

He was equipped with a form with, from left to right, three columns. The first was for an observation by him; the second was for a comment by the Post Office staff; the third was for a final comment from the inspector. Searching desperately for something to say, Ortoli finally wrote in the first column, 'It seems that Regulation No. — has not been fully observed.'

In the second column the Head of the Post Office staff wrote silently: 'Regulation No. — was abolished three years ago.'

'What', I asked 'did you say to that?'

'There was not,' said Ortoli, 'much option. With what dignity I could muster I wrote in the final column "*Vu*".'

The fourth was Arthur Cockfield who came to Brussels in 1985 as a British Commissioner. First impressions of him were mixed. When he arrived he was heard to ask, 'Can one drink the water here?' He was nearly seventy, considerably older than his colleagues. His manner on first acquaintance had a certain grave formality and did not show any enthusiasm for Brussels and its works. He was a friend of Mrs Thatcher and had served in her Cabinet, and it was rumoured that she had sent him to Brussels to sort those Eurocrats out.

It did not work out like that. Cockfield soon became a convert to the European cause. Within a year he had clashed with Mrs Thatcher. When he was visiting her in London she had voiced an objection to the harmonisation of indirect taxes. This was not in the Treaty of Rome, she said. Cockfield disagreed. The following dialogue took place.

Mrs Thatcher: 'It was not.'

Cockfield: 'It was.'

Mrs Thatcher: 'It was not.'

Cockfield: 'It was.'

Cockfield then asked the Private Secretary on duty to fetch a copy of the Treaty of Rome and read out Article 99. He did so. 'The Commission shall present proposals for the harmonisation of indirect taxes . . . .' Mrs Thatcher was silent. But at the end of Cockfield's four-year term she did not renew his appointment. He had contradicted and found wrong the Great She-Elephant.

If Cockfield had not spared Mrs Thatcher, neither did he spare British Ministers when he appeared before the Council of Ministers. He had been one of the stars of the Inland Revenue, a barrister and a successful businessman; his knowledge was encyclopaedic, his logic ruthless. 'I am surprised,' he would say, slowly and deliberately, 'that the Minister has made that point. Surely even a cursory glance at the Income Tax Act of 1948 – which I played some part in drafting – para 235, sub para j, would have shown him . . . .' The dimmer-witted British Ministers approached these confrontations with quaking knees.

But Arthur Cockfield's main contribution to the European cause was in making possible the creation of the single market. It had

213

become apparent some years before his arrival that eliminating tariffs within the Community did not completely free trade. Regulations would provide that lorries in one Member State would have to have a certain type of windscreen, in another a certain type of brakes. Imports of certain foods would be prohibited ostensibly on health grounds. Attempts to negotiate the removal of these barriers had foundered on the argument that Member State A would only move if Member State B moved on another product, and Member State B, in turn, would only move if Member State C were to take similar action elsewhere.

Cockfield adopted a radically different approach. He drew up a list of nearly three hundred measures which would be needed to establish throughout the Community a single market. For each item there was a description of the problem, of the precise measures needed and a timetable. The whole operation was scheduled to be completed by the end of 1992. It worked. In December of that year a European Council meeting in Edinburgh declared the Single Market 'complete in all essential respects'. It was a milestone in the construction of Europe, and it would not have been achieved without the imagination, knowledge and tenacity of Arthur Cockfield.

Fifth in the list, and most formidable of all, was Jacques Delors. His appointment was agreed at a European Council in early 1984. The then President of the Commission was a Luxemburger, Gaston Thorn. His predecessor had been an Englishman, Roy Jenkins. There was informal agreement that this time it would be a Frenchman, and Claude Cheysson, a Foreign Minister of France and former European Commissioner, was in the running. But Mrs Thatcher did not take to Claude Cheysson. He was not the quiet and respectful bureaucrat she preferred. Instead she took to Jacques Delors, who had just resigned as French Finance Minister. He did not seem a man of extravagant views, was quiet and well behaved and had a reputation, despite being a Socialist, for financial prudence. She thought he would give her little trouble. This must have been the greatest misjudgement since Washington despaired, on Roosevelt's death, at the accession to the Presidency of Harry Truman.

I first met Delors in December 1984. I was then the European Community Ambassador in Washington. Wondering what the new man would be like, I asked through our Delegation in Paris whether I could call on him during some routine transatlantic trip, to *'présenter mes devoirs'*, as the French Army used to say. He made on me a considerable impression. His cause was the Union, and he pursued it with a zeal both religious and austere. His church apart, he would have ridden out with Cromwell at Naseby and struck down in the name of the Lord those of little faith. He was clearly one of those who change the world, and did not take long to show it. At a Summit of the Industrialised Countries in Toronto early in his term he arrived, ignored by the press who were mobbing Heads of Government. Then President Reagan made a proposal on trade. Delors opposed it. He got his way. The world's press sat up. The *Financial Times* ran a headline reading 'EC EARNS ITS CRUST AT THE TOP TABLE'. The Commission had arrived.

It was again Delors who saw that further integration, and in particular the Cockfield plan for the single market, would hardly be possible if a single country could block progress. So he piloted through the Council of Ministers the Single European Act that introduced majority voting for a whole range of decisions.

The legislation had other provisions. For the first time, certain aims were set out in treaty form – economic and monetary union, a social policy and greater convergence in foreign policy. Delors played the lead role in planning and bringing about the single European currency.

Administration of the Commission was not his leading achievement. Delors held himself aloof from his Commissioner colleagues, occasionally addressing them in terms which inspired a Spanish Commissioner to remark that even Franco did not treat his Ministers like that. There was a degree of bickering between Commissioners which had not been known before. Their personal staffs were allowed ever more authority; arrogant neophytes elbowed aside the Directors General, the Permanent Secretaries of Brussels. And when Member States allotted the Commission considerable sums of money to aid the economies of Eastern Europe, Delors did not insist on them also providing the necessary backup in the form of additional staff able to check adequately how the money was spent. Thus was laid the foundation of the troubles which later forced the resignation of one of Delors' successors, Jacques Santer.

But history will judge these errors to have been minor in scale compared with Delors' massive achievements. He gave a struggling customs union a massive and irreversible shift towards its ultimate goal of a European federation. And, as no single figure since Jean Monnet, he became in the press and on television Mr Europe.

JAPAN

The Tokyo Round over, relations with Japan took the limelight. The issue – which has still not been solved – was essentially that our balance of trade with Japan was worsening steadily. This in itself was no problem; any country or trading bloc has a variety of surpluses and deficits with its trading partners. The problem arose because our industrialists claimed that they were shut out of the Japanese market – while the Japanese were free to make hay in the European market.

This bone of contention was insoluble for three reasons.

The first was that even if we did have equal access to Japan, the Japanese could still take us to the cleaners, simply because they worked harder and consumed less than their competitors in the West. Asking factory workers – or managers – in Britain, France or even Germany

216

to work at the pace of the Japanese and with their restricted standard of living would have produced a revolution.

The second was that Japan did not fit into the post-war international trading order. This had been founded at the end of the Second World War by the United States and Britain and was geared to Western-style free enterprise economies. Reduce the barriers to trade, above all customs tariffs, then free competition would give full play to the theory of comparative advantage: everyone would produce more and more what they could best manufacture ever more cheaply and everyone would get richer. But Japan was another civilisation. Its customs tariffs were low. Protection came in other forms – for example, testing requirements of an esoteric kind: if we were considering the export of Western skis to Japan, we were told, 'Very difficult – Japanese snow different.'

Above all, the aims of society were different. Free competition, with devil-take-the-hindmost and an opulent life style for those who succeeded, was not for the Japanese. Their world worshipped consensus, harmony, the promotion of the interest of the firm or the country. They would buy from a Japanese, only in the last resort from the *gaijin* (foreigners).

The third reason was that European Ministers would always be reluctant to back their appeals for increased access to the Japanese market by the threat of action, for instance of restrictions on imports from Japan if there were no level playing field in the Japanese market. European Ministers would be profuse in their public determination to 'negotiate toughly'. 'We must not let the Japanese get away with this any longer,' they would cry. 'Officials have got to get tough.' But at the slightest sign of displeasure from the Japanese, European Ministers would panic like a herd of cattle encountering a tiger. (I give an example later.)

Events developed accordingly. In the early months of 1978 news came in from Tokyo that the formidable Bob Strauss had appeared and was pressing the Japanese for trade concessions. Strauss had told a gathering of eminent Japanese in the American Embassy, 'You're gonna have a trade treaty with the United States. Either Congress is going to write it or I am. Boys, what d'ya want?' The Japanese had never been talked to like that before, and Strauss made a considerable impression. Reaching Brussels, this news caused an even more considerable impression in the COREPER. Always suspicious of what the Americans were up to, the Ambassadors summoned me and asked what the Commission was doing. The clear implication of their questions was that, as always, the Commission had been caught napping. The cunning Americans were about to remove the plums from the cake. We would be lucky to get a few crumbs. Off we should go to Tokyo and repair this omission. It was about time we stopped uttering our polite platitudes and got tough. I asked what ammunition we were being given – what counter action on our part could we outline if the Japanese made no concessions? I was told briskly that we should rely on what was referred to as 'the diplomatic approach'.

So in March 1978 off we went. In Tokyo masses of journalists met us. Were we trying to get some trade concessions from the Japanese? Yes. What would we do if none were forthcoming? Taking a deep breath I embroidered on the theme often used in the House of Commons by Ministers at a loss for some instant cure to the British disease. It was from *King Lear*: 'I will do such things – / What they are yet I know not; but they shall be / The terrors of the earth.'

The Japanese were bland and hospitable. They were also unyielding. Tests? But, *Denman-san*, Japanese must be protected from unsatisfactory foreign goods. But why do Japanese insist on buying Japanese rather than foreign goods? Patriotic habit dating back from war, *Denman-san*.

'The war', I said, 'was a long time ago. Japanese people slow to change.' Like English people, someone added with a perfectly straight face.

In desperation I asked about one of the few products where Europe – Italy in particular – was competitive. Why the outrageously restrictive Japanese import quotas on leather goods? 'It is religious question,' explained the Japanese.

'What the hell has religion got to do with leather?' I asked. It appeared that one religious group, the Dowa sect, was regarded as low caste and could only deal with leather goods. So Japanese production was not competitive and had to be protected.

I said that in one important branch of industry Britain had a precisely similar problem. The Japanese seemed surprised. 'Yes,' I said, 'we had a large group called British Leyland sect. Their religion compelled them to spend most of the day on their backsides, drinking tea and smoking cigarettes, when not actually asleep.' By a piece of singular good fortune this did not get out to the press.

We did have one card which could be played. At that stage of their post-war development – with nationalism much less evident than it is now – the Japanese disliked intensely an open clash with a major trading partner. If we had been able to walk away openly proclaiming disagreement, the Japanese would have been disturbed; their senior officials would have lost face.

It nearly came to that. Miyasaki, the Vice Minister for Economic Affairs in the Gaimusho (Foreign Office), an old sparring partner from Geneva (known by us in those days as Ferret Face) would come along to my hotel for a chat on succeeding evenings looking increasingly worried. Finally, to consider what concessions to us could be agreed among the Ministries concerned – the concessions so far offered were meaningless – he called a meeting for 3 a.m. of Vice Ministers from all Departments. Tokyo was beginning to hum like a disturbed beehive. We had a real chance of a breakthrough. But I got instructions to back down. Grinding my teeth, I did my best to defend our decision to the press. But the Japanese Minister Ushiba gave the game away. Asked by the press what concessions Japan had made, his reply was short and clear: 'None.'

Back in Brussels, neither the press nor the Member States expressed enthusiasm for our efforts. So a pow-wow took place in the Commission. Sundry Commissioners and various officials congregated for a discussion on Japan over a working lunch. I turned up with Michael Hardy, my mainstay on Japan, an extremely clear-minded former United Nations lawyer with a refreshing sense of humour. One Commissioner led off by reading a statement from his brief. He spoke – as John Jay Chapman said of President Charles. W. Eliot of Harvard – 'with all the passion of a woodchuck chewing a carrot.' Outgunned by the intellectual firepower of his colleagues, he then relapsed into a sulky silence and devoted his attention to the food before him, to which he did ample justice. Ortoli spoke in measured and statesmanlike terms. Davignon, as usual, was rapid and brilliant; Gundelach, an old GATT hand, incisive and sardonic. But, as they spoke, I was put in mind of a guide for new entrants to the British Foreign Office written in 1945. While much of the advice would now be considered laughably old-fashioned, it was in fact worldly and shrewd. It advised a mythical new entrant, Third Secretary John Bull, to pay close attention to the opinions of barbers and taxi drivers, and to turn round quickly after taking his leave from a foreign host to see the expression on his face. It also stated that 'Foreigners are an excitable lot. They like to talk. Occasionally they will all talk at the same time.' Such was the case on this occasion. The result resembled a Mad Hatter's Concerto. The boom of the bassoon blended with the rapid hammer strokes of the piano and the astringent solitary notes of the flute, all against the drumbeat provided by the champing jaws of Commissioner Woodchuck. I did not dare to look at Michael Hardy. There was no conclusion.

Back in my office, Michael and Barbara Jacob and I discussed what could be done next. A paper for our Commissioners analysing the problem and recommending a course of action might help to focus their minds. The course of action was not difficult to frame – that if, after full discussion, we did not get access to the Japanese market then we should take the matter to the GATT and try to secure authority for counter measures against imports from Japan. But to liven up the paper and offer some inducement to weary Commissioners to give it their attention, I tried to make as graphic as possible one of the key points – the propensity of the Japanese to work and the miserable little apartments and low living standards with which they seemed content. So I wrote that we were dealing with 'a nation of workaholics living in rabbit hutches.'

The paper was duly circulated. Forty-eight hours later the *Financial Times* published lengthy extracts. To my chagrin I learnt that any document circulated to Commissioners or their personal staffs could be considered as handed forthwith to the press. A considerable uproar followed in the Community. One Ambassador, who had been the most thunderous in demanding decisive action against the Japanese, shook his head sorrowfully. 'Offence has been taken by the Japanese,' he sighed. Close scrutiny would, I am sure, have shown a glistening tear. The Danish Minister pressed for disciplinary action to be taken against me. But Roy Jenkins and Henri Simonet, the Belgian Foreign Minister, were stout in my defence. It was, they pointed out, after all an internal memorandum; and it was not only relevant but, in contrast with most official documents, it was also readable.

Not long afterwards we returned to Tokyo once more. At our first press conference a number of sinister gentlemen appeared – one with a particularly long television camera, which seemed to me to be capable of harbouring a projectile. Leslie Fielding, the Head of our Mission in Tokyo, was in the chair. I whispered to Michael Hardy, next to me, that if things got really menacing I would spring to my feet, and crying to Leslie, 'Sir Roy, I really think that this time you have gone too far!', make rapidly for the door. But the questioning, though edgy, was – compared with an American press conference in similar circumstances – like a mill pond instead of a tempest.

I was then told that the Japanese staff of the EC Mission wanted in a body to see me. They all filed solemnly in. Then their elected Chairman, a charming young man in his mid thirties, congratulated me on my paper. He explained that he was a bachelor and lived with his parents. If he got married, his wife would have to move into his single room. Japanese people worked hard, he said, just as hard as Europeans or Americans (he was of course being polite; what he meant was that they worked a good deal harder). Why, therefore, could Japanese not have separate houses, like Europeans and Americans – with, he added, and this provoked a loud murmur of approval – separate rooms for sleeping?

That evening, when I went to have a quiet chat with Ferret Face, I told him of this encounter. He nodded. There had been cartoons in the Japanese press about rabbit hutches. And at a recent May Day parade, trade unionists had appeared wearing replicas of rabbits' ears. 'One day', he said, 'they will put up statue in Tokyo to Lord Rabbit Hutch' – unfortunately spoiling this rather dubious compliment with a loud cackling laugh.

The statue has not materialised. But years later I received a copy of the bi-monthly magazine of MITI (The Ministry for International Trade and Industry), on the cover of which, with no title or attribution, was a sectional picture of a small modern Japanese apartment. Crammed in by the prefabricated bathroom and a mass of electronic equipment only a tiny area remained. It was occupied by a huge pink rabbit, with even bigger ears, contentedly drinking a cup of green tea. I had it framed. It hangs on my study wall in London and faces me as I write this. I prefer it to a statue.

As the gavotte between Tokyo and Brussels continued, Ferret Face would appear from time to time in Brussels with his troops. I was always glad to see him. I pointed out on his first visit that years before in Geneva he had explained 'special problems of Japan'. The world had now turned round and I had to explain 'special problems of Europe'. He spoke a fluent, rather abbreviated, slightly American-accented English. He was particularly fond of the phrase 'at this juncture' which he rolled round his tongue with the appreciation of a connoisseur. We were in a sense opponents but we remained good friends. He was tough but he was fair, and there was something about his sharpness and sardonic sense of humour which appealed to me. Once in Geneva during the Kennedy Round in a small gathering Mike Blumenthal – who had dealt with commodity policy in the State Department – had been holding forth on sugar. He proposed a certain course of action. Ferret Face shook his head. 'Okinawa,' he said. 'Much sugar.' Blumenthal was greatly disturbed. He had been caught out. No one had told him about the problem of sugar production in Okinawa. Aides were summoned. Telegrams were despatched. After some time Ferret Face spoke again. 'Okinawa,' he said. 'No sugar. Joke.' Only Goya could have done justice to the expressions on the faces of Blumenthal and his team.

It was rumoured that Ferret Face's final departure from Tokyo, on posting as Ambassador to the OECD, was because there had been a contretemps with his Prime Minister at the annual Summit of the Industrialised Countries in Tokyo. This particular Prime Minister was about as familiar with economic details as the Dalai Lama. He had expected the Summit meeting to consist of a series of incantations, followed by the laying before the Great of various sheets of parchment prepared by officials. Everyone would then bow to each other, cry 'Wah!' and adjourn for a cup of saké. It was therefore a severe shock when – without warning – President Carter opened a large briefing book and said in his twangy Georgian, 'Say, the figures in para 2 of our

223

draft conclusions aren't the same as the ones my guys have given me.' Miyasaki's successor was not someone whom Stevy Davignon or I found very appealing. And we were not, despite endless meetings, getting very far. Confronted once in Tokyo by the usual hordes of the press, I was asked what I thought of certain Japanese promises of better treatment for our exports. I replied that the proof of the pudding would be in the eating. This was an unwise reply since proverbs do not translate easily. How many puddings, I was asked, and how long should they be eaten for? Did Common Market have special pudding it was going to sell? So I fell back on ancient Chinese proverbs such as 'When tigers fight leaves fall from the tallest trees in the forest.' Bafflement but great respect greeted these, which was useful, if hardly surprising, since I had made them up on the spot. One Japanese journalist did actually bring himself to ask a question (questions from Japanese journalists are rare since with their love of consensus they hate to get out of step). Where had I found proverb about tigers? 'In the course of extensive reading,' I replied and moved relentlessly to the door.

Of course, something more serious than inventing proverbs was called for. We did manage to secure informal undertakings from the Japanese to restrain certain of their exports to the Community. But we needed above all to open up the Japanese market. Brooding on New Year's Day in 1982 on our problem, I remembered the article in the GATT which allows any contracting party to take another to court if trade concessions paid for by the first are 'nullified or impaired' by the second. To my knowledge it had never been used. But if we could convince the other members of the GATT that our exports to Japan were being unfairly treated the Japanese would be faced with a clear choice. Either they would open up their market or we would be authorised to take action against Japanese exports. I elaborated this in a paper.

It was remarkably unpopular. 'You mean to say that we could take action against the Japanese?' I was asked incredulously. But the

Japanese would be indignant. Member States would never agree. I replied somewhat tartly that it was bad enough being expected to fight a battle with blank ammunition. If in addition our generals took to their heels the moment the enemy fired a rifle shot, then we had better give up this negotiation and stage a comic opera, to which our talents would be well suited. After much argument – and with the help of Davignon – we got the proposal adopted. The Americans said that they would not come in – they wanted no part of 'ganging up against Japan'. But our hope – not unjustified from various contacts – was that enough countries from South East Asia would judge it in their own interests to support the case and thus Japan would be impelled to open up its market to some extent.

The enterprise, once started, developed well. Raymond Phan Van Phi got to work with the help of a young German, Jörn Keck, hauled across from our Mission in Tokyo. Keck had studied economics at Kiel and had gone to Japan to see how an economic miracle worked. He had learnt impeccable Japanese and his knowledge of the Japanese scene was impressive. The two of them assembled a formidable case and deployed it to some effect in Geneva. The Japanese were considerably disturbed. But then in the summer of 1982 I went to head our Mission in Washington. Getting any bureaucracy to take a firm line on anything is difficult; getting a firm line which will be unpopular with other countries demands efforts which border on the super-human. After I left the flower slowly withered on the vine.

CHINA

With China, our other main negotiating partner in the Far East, our dealings, while not spectacular, were more fruitful.

After the reign of the Gang of Four had ended in 1976, Christopher

Soames, then Commissioner for External Affairs had, in a successful visit to Beijing, blazed the trail for a subsequent trade agreement between the Community and China. The cultural revolution of the 1960s had made China incommunicado. But a market, however undeveloped, of over a thousand million people was important: when possible, the Community needed access to it. In December 1977 Bob Kawan, an extremely enterprising Belgian who seemed to have an inexhaustible store of knowledge about China and the Eastern bloc, put his head round my door. He grinned. '*Sie kommen,*' he said. And early in 1978 a Chinese team did indeed arrive in Brussels to negotiate a trade agreement with the Community. Such an agreement with a state trading country is difficult: how can one get reciprocal advantages for one's exports when free competition plays no role? What we set out to do was to offer to remove restrictions on a range of Chinese exports, providing we could get from the People's Republic an undertaking that they would consider seriously any offer which a Community firm might make. We were not, we explained, asking for preference for Community goods. That was against the principle of non-discrimination which, except for customs unions and free trade areas, was one of the cornerstones of the post-war trading system. But we did want offers from our firms looked at seriously, and not just thrown aside in favour of deals with our main rivals, the Americans and the Japanese.

The negotiation was not easy. It took several days and one session which lasted all night. Finally we got a text acceptable to our Member States – they had been on hand throughout the night – if we could get one further concession. We, that is our small Commission team, adjourned for lunch at the Chinese Embassy. Mao Tai was produced – the nearest thing to original firewater which I have ever encountered. The Chinese Ambassador told stories about the war against the Kuomintang. He was a fascinating man who had worked his passage from Shanghai to London as a deckhand and had then studied at the

London School of Economics. He spoke about the sudden collapse of the KMT in 1949 and the drama of the headlong Communist advance into Shanghai. He told his stories well and whether it was this or the Mao Tai, Bob Kawan and I laughed immoderately. I then explained that we needed one more move on their side. If this were not forthcoming not only would there be no agreement but Kawan and I would be taken into custody and shipped off to the EC equivalent of Siberia. This made an immediate impression on the Chinese, who had no difficulty understanding this point.

A vigorous discussion then burst out between them. Afterwards David Ting, our Chinese speaker, explained that the general line had been that Denman and Kawan, although running dogs of capitalism, were not bad fellows. If they were sent off to a Gulag, the replacements might be worse. The Ambassador added weightily that they had appreciated his stories about Chinese history – and they could drink Mao Tai. So the concession was gracefully offered and warmly accepted. Lunch lasted some time. But an agreement was reached.

The clause about looking seriously at Community bids came in for some criticism in Brussels: was this not a piece of window dressing? When we reviewed with the Chinese a year later the operation of the agreement, we found that they had meticulously met their obligations. They had circulated the trade agreement to all their agencies. The checks we could make with Community industry seemed to confirm this. Our exports to China began to rise substantially. The advice we gave to European firms was that it was not a gold rush. Dealing with the Chinese was a very long-term affair. It was difficult not to be conscious that it was a civilisation 4,000 years old. The Museum of History in Beijing showed the great inventions – printing, the compass, gunpowder – which the Chinese had discovered centuries before the West. There was about them a calm, a continuity, a sense of history strange to the West. A week seemed a long time to Harold Wilson. For the Chinese, short term was a hundred years.

We told European firms that if they could afford it – and clearly only the major firms came in question – then it was worth considering investing in China. They would need to keep someone there for a long time. With leaders like Deng about there would from time to time be blood on the floor. But in the end a firm which had maintained a presence in China for many years would get its reward.

When in February 1979 Roy Jenkins paid an official visit to China, I went along. The Chinese were pleased that the President of the Commission had come. They attached importance to the Community, not least because the Soviets detested us (this was the age of Brezhnev) and they detested the Soviets. So we were lodged extremely comfortably in Number One Guest House, where Nixon had stayed only a few years before.

On our first evening some of us put the finishing touches to a speech which Jenkins would be making at a banquet in the Great Hall of the People. While it was being typed we asked for Scotch and water. After some clearly difficult confabulations a waiter appeared with a bottle of Mao Tai. At this point Emile Noel, the Secretary General of the Commission, appeared. I recommended the drink strongly to him. But I said that it had to be taken in one gulp so as not to miss the flavour. Emile, with his invariable courtesy, took me at my word. He downed in one a fair sized glass of Mao Tai. For a moment he seemed gratified. Then frightful internal convulsions began to grip him. He turned white and then green and was unable to speak. It took him minutes to recover. His manner towards me for the rest of the evening was distinctly cool.

The next day we saw Deng. He was short, had a face strangely reminiscent of pictures of Napoleon, and bristled with nervous energy. He was deaf and spoke in a stentorian voice in what I was told was a strong Szechuan accent. He was well briefed. His questions came at us like hailstones. How many nationalities were there in our team? How did we manage to get on together? What was our relationship to the European Parliament? When were we going to achieve a European Union? Deng spoke about the war then being waged between China and Vietnam. His views were clear and forceful, and he had a habit of emphasising them with a cutting motion of his right hand. Chinese generals, he said, had got fat and lazy. Only way to learn about war was to make war.

I remembered a story I had been told about him when he had been in the Central Committee in Beijing before the depredations of the Gang of Four. A strike had broken out in a silk factory in Soochow and Deng had been sent down to deal with it. He called the strikers together. They talked for an hour, but no progress was made. Deng brought the meeting to a close and suggested that they continue at eight the next morning. The meeting, he said, was open to anyone with any interest in the dispute. The next morning a fair sized crowd turned up. They were taken out in groups and shot. The strike ended.

It was decided that we should give a reception. It appeared that there was one problem. Whisky, gin and of course Mao Tai were available without difficulty. But tonic to go with the gin seemed hard to come by. That evening, going up to my room in the Guest House, I passed a gaggle of somewhat downcast Chinese being harangued by a sinister figure, a cross between a retired boxer and a prison warder. Endymion Wilkinson, from the EC Mission in Tokyo, who spoke Chinese as well as Japanese, was doubled in laughter. I asked him what he was laughing at. When he could speak he gave me a rough translation of what Chief Bully Boy had been saying. It ran like this. 'O miserable sons of village jackals, listen carefully to me, otherwise it will be the worse for you. Foreign devils are giving party tomorrow. We can give them their Western drinks. But we cannot find drink called TOHNIK. It is important that Leadership of People's Republic should not lose face.

So we must have TOHNIK. Now get out and scour Beijing and find this infernal drink. Otherwise I shall myself bury your evil features in a pail of dung.'

The next day there was tonic. It was a good party.

OTHER PORTS OF CALL

Trips to other countries were less exotic than China or Japan, but they had their moments.

Yugoslavia, in the days of Tito before its break-up, took up a good deal of our time. The rationale was simple. The Cold War was on. Yugoslavia was defiantly at the edge of the Soviet Empire. If its economy collapsed there would be Soviet tanks at Trieste and a time of great danger for the West. Perceiving this, the Foreign Ministers of the Community had signed a stirring declaration promising aid to Yugoslavia, which it was the Commission's job to implement.

The difficulty was what in practice we could do. Their economic system – being Communist – was lousy. Goods of export quality which could be sold in the West were hard to find. But where they had an eminently marketable product, such as a high quality meat called baby beef, the farmers in France and Ireland found this inconveniently competitive and wanted to exclude it. And Yugoslav expectations tended to be high. On one of my first visits, their Foreign Minister conveyed with great emphasis that Yugoslavia was living beyond its means and that therefore the Community should do something about it.

Nevertheless, the Commission decided to negotiate a trade agreement with Yugoslavia. This would open up the Community market in return for some guarantees of access for our exports. My opposite number was a woman Permanent Secretary named Milica Zhiberna. She was straightforward, intelligent and formidable, and defended her cause with an ardour which was less Communist than simply patriotic. Her lode star was Tito. It was he who had freed them from the Germans, who had unified the country, who had defied the Soviets. In conversation occasionally, when we could relax, she would worry about what would happen when he went. Our final negotiating session in Brussels in February 1980 started after lunch on a Thursday, went on for most of Thursday night, continued all day and night on Friday and finished at breakfast time on Saturday morning. The agreement was modest but worthwhile, opening up a number of channels of trade. At the end the Yugoslavs rose and sang a song of the partisans.

One loose end remained, however. The post-war constitution of the Federal German Republic (the Basic Law) swept up and incorporated a whole mass of German subordinate legislation. Unnoticed apparently at the time, this included one order signed in 1943 decreeing that citizens of areas now in Yugoslavia who were of German background and sympathy were to be considered German citizens. This was not something which the Yugoslavs could accept. I had sought political guidance on this before the session and had been told that the question would present no difficulty. It soon turned out that it did. In Brussels the German Ambassador rang up and urged me to go to Belgrade to negotiate a solution. I said that I would do no such thing. I had negotiated a trade agreement. The remaining question was a constitutional one between the Federal Republic and Yugoslavia. But the next day I went with a German Chef de Cabinet to see the Commission's Chief Legal Adviser.

As he heard us out his eyes widened with surprise. 'And who signed this order in 1943?' he asked.

'Hermann Goering,' my colleague replied.

'Herr Froschmeier,' said the Legal Adviser, 'it is not legal advice which you need; it is divine intervention.'

231

But somehow a form of words was finally found which papered over the cracks.

Yugoslavia represented an odd paradox. The long and bitter feud between Serbs and Croats and the country's basically flawed economic system meant that sooner or later, once the legendary unifying influence of Tito had disappeared, Yugoslavia would self-destruct. In the meantime we could offer some help, but this was essentially like applying Elastoplast to a body wracked by a slow moving deep disease.

Yet it was not possible to feel for them indifference. They had courage and independence, a charm which was half Slav, half Mediterranean, and their hospitality came from the heart. In the evening they would sing haunting melancholy songs. They would talk of the time of the partisans, and of the day in 1948 when Tito broke with the Soviets, when the frontier was closed, when they had petrol for only forty-eight hours for their tanks, and when all stood ready to take to the hills with their rifles. They had a natural nobility.

Our journeys never seemed to stop. There was for instance a running series of disputes with Australia. Europeans and Australians do not always find each other easy. Australians are a rumbustious, irreverent lot quick to bridle when they think, often rightly, that the Poms are being condescending. Our Continental colleagues thought Australian straightforwardness was crass; Australians thought that European circumlocutions were pompous and insincere. And we had that jewel in our international crown, the Common Agricultural Policy. Malcolm Fraser, then Australian Prime Minister, had visited Brussels in the early summer of 1977, just before I got there. He and Roy Jenkins did not get on; one observer said that they nearly ended up throwing bread rolls at each other.

Australia had vast mineral resources. Europe had money and technology which could help with their development. Australia and the Community had much to offer each other. Could we not reach a broader agreement rather than perpetually seeming, as one Australian cartoon put it, like two farmers grunting incoherently and threatening each other with pitchforks over a couple of thousand tons of Australian beef?

The idea did not prosper. I asked a senior Australian Minister, Doug Anthony, why not. 'Would you rather,' I asked, 'have the cheers of several hundred Australian cattlemen, when you gave the Community a tongue lashing, or go down in history as the statesman who put Australian–EC relations on a new footing?'

Doug looked at me shrewdly. 'I'm in politics, mate,' he said.

I accompanied Gaston Thorn, then President of the Commission, on a visit to Canberra, where we were summoned to a meeting of the Australian Cabinet. In dispute was EC retaliation – fully justified under international trading rules – for some quite indefensible action they had taken against our exports.

In the Cabinet room there was uproar. Malcolm Fraser – about whom his friends would use the word aggressive, and those who were not his friends the word bully – tore into us. Our conduct, he claimed, had been scandalous. I asked if I could speak. Permission was granted. I pointed out that our action was perfectly legal. The Australians had in the past taken precisely similar action against us. Malcom Fraser then turned to agriculture and our villainies on this front. This was the only occasion in my life that I ever had the chance of a major public row in a good cause with a Prime Minister. I took it. I asked when he was going to apply his high-sounding principles of free trade to the Australian industrial tariff, which was the highest of all developed countries. The temperature rose. Harsh words began to be exchanged. We finished inconclusively. But we had not yielded.

Afterwards, Gaston Thorn was appalled. Not only had an official publicly taken the lead from a politician on an official visit; an official had no right to talk to a Prime Minister in those terms.

'You have ruined everything!', he cried ' They will cancel our dinner invitation this evening.'

'They won't,' I said, 'Australians aren't like that. In Australia people speak their mind. They think there's something wrong with you if you don't.'

We set off that evening in funereal silence for dinner at The Lodge, the Prime Minister's house. As we neared our destination Thorn, visibly apprehensive, burst out, *'Ils vont nous conspuer!'* (The most expressive translation, though not exact, is 'They will give us the bum's rush.')

We arrived. Malcolm Fraser and his Deputy, Doug Anthony, were standing by the door. I tried to break the ice. 'Real nice of you, Prime Minister,' I said, 'to have two disputatious bastards like us along.'

The two Australians roared with laughter. 'You were only being yourself, Roy,' said Doug Anthony. 'Come and have a large Scotch, mate.'

Thorn, to his surprise and delight, was treated like a long lost friend. The evening was a great success.

With the world at our door, to echo *Alice in Wonderland*, 'it takes all the running you can do to stay in the same place.' Bilateral forays, and discoveries, were in all directions.

In Brasilia I remember the bells ringing out in the church given by the King of Spain, the audacity of the architecture of the House of the Congress, the way in which the Foreign Ministry had preserved in their building something of the elegance of the Palacio Hidameraty in Rio.

'Where do you live?' I asked a journalist.

'No. 64,' he said.

'64 where?' I asked.

'It's clear you've just arrived,' he replied in an amused tone. 'Just No. 64.'

While in Brazil one might wonder whether it was a good thing for a country to be run by generals, but at least things worked. In Mexico no fewer than three gentlemen seemed under the impression that they were my opposite number. Having weeded out, as we thought, the wheat from the chaff and negotiated a communiqué which recorded our far from breathtaking conclusions, I was confronted late at night by a rival communiqué from another group. How we solved this particular conundrum now escapes me.

But I do remember a very pleasant dinner with the British Ambassador in Mexico. He had been brought up in Spain and was a Latin American specialist reputed to speak not only perfect Spanish but to know everyone of any importance in Mexico. After recounting many fascinating details of British dealings with Mexico, he looked at me quizzically. I could see that he was about to put some major question.

'Tell me,' he asked. 'You are here with this "Commission" Delegation. What is all this Community business?' (None of my European friends in Brussels would believe this story. No senior Brit could be as comically ill informed as this. History since has shown that many could.)

I came back from Latin America impressed, like any neophyte, with the enormous potentialities of the continent. It seemed to me to resemble the United States before the railroads. When I discussed this with a French friend who had served in Latin America, he smiled. 'Have you read,' he asked, 'the novel *Le pays ou on n'arrive jamais* [The country where one never arrives]? It is rather like that. One is always travelling to a great destination, but somehow one never gets there.'

A paper I wrote for the Commission, proposing nothing sensational but pulling together the threads of what we were doing in Latin America and suggesting some modest further steps, was quietly done down by the French. They did not want anything which might deflect money and attention from their former colonies, with which they still retained special and profitable links.

If our meetings in Latin America had been friendly, this was more than could be said for our meetings with the Soviet bloc. In pre-Gorbachev days this was cold, hostile and monolithic. The Community represented a uniting, strong, prosperous capitalist Europe – anathema to the Soviets. In the mid 1970s the Community had suggested to the Eastern bloc countries that diplomatic relations should be established; it seemed an anomaly that we had diplomatic relations with over a hundred countries across the world, but not with trading partners on our borders. The satellites consulted Moscow – linked as they were by their treaty of mutual economic assistance, COMECON. Mother Russia said that such relationships could only be established if the Community first concluded an agreement with COMECON. After discussion with the Member States of the Community it was agreed that a Commission team would go to Moscow. There was much interest in the German press. The enthusiasm of Germans for dealing with the East (as they called it) was prodigious: at any such prospect a strange light would come into their eyes. So the brief would have to be carefully written. I asked the resourceful Bob Kawan what line the Soviets would be likely to take. Bob had an extraordinary – if cynical and disenchanted – feel for Soviet reactions. He explained that they could take one of three possible lines. Our own basic position was clear: we were not going to pay the Soviets to recognise us; we were a fact and sooner or later they would have to come to terms with it; we did not want a series of meetings which the Soviets could use simply to attack us publicly. I suggested that Bob set out the three possible COMECON approaches (A, B and C) and – tailored to each one – a speaking note in reply (A, B and C). He produced the best brief I had ever seen. Armed with this we set off for Moscow.

The German Ambassador welcomed us warmly. It was slightly disconcerting that at his house people would say, 'Of course it depends on . . .' and then, with a warning gesture to the ceiling, write something hastily on a piece of paper and pass it around. Back at the hotel, I said loudly to the ceiling that the success of the discussions would be gravely impeded if Kawan and I did not have delivered a large jar of caviar each. Unfortunately the ceiling must have been turned off, and this was to prove fruitless. The next day we appeared at the COMECON headquarters, no long journey since we were lodged next door in the COMECON hotel. We were greeted by Fadaev, the Executive Secretary, an old-style Soviet party functionary, a shambling bear with an uneasy, forced, rumbling laugh, and eyes that crept about like rats in a hole. Had he had armorial bearings they would have been a glass and a bottle of vodka rampant.

The proceedings opened. After a couple of minutes Bob and I hissed in our Commissioner's ear, 'It's B.' Speaking note B was then read out.

The Soviets were greatly impressed. One of them approached me in the first coffee break. 'That was brilliant,' he said. 'Your Commissioner answered the most detailed points straight away. He is a genius.' With Bob grinning at my side, I said gravely that he was a man of remarkable qualities.

The meeting – as we knew it would – came to naught. So did a further meeting in Brussels some time later. The Soviets were more interested in Community bashing than trade. Progress would have to await the great thaw at the end of the 1980s.

In 1991 COMECON was disbanded. The European Union now has its own (Commission) Ambassador in Moscow.

DEALINGS MULTILATERAL

There was also much multilateral business, some of it concerning the poorer countries.

In the 1950s they had come knocking on the door in Geneva. They wanted to have the benefits of the world trading system, but could not afford the full subscription – in terms of compliance with all the GATT rules and opening up their markets to all comers. So it was agreed that they should have the benefits of membership without the obligations; these they would one day be able to assume when they had become better off. This seemed to us all a reasonable solution if the GATT were to be a one-world system and not simply a club for the rich.

So the membership of the GATT rapidly expanded. In the beginning there were twenty-three countries; after little more than a decade this number had trebled, and the Palais des Nations in Geneva began to resemble the United Nations. So did the debates; the quiet matter-of-fact discussions of the early days about how obstacles to trade could be removed began to yield to fiery ideological speeches on the urgent need for the meek to inherit the earth. It became apparent from the occasional expression of barely controlled rage on the face of Wyndham White, as the custodian of the GATT, that in his view the meek had started to get above themselves.

In 1965 a new institution was set up, UNCTAD – the United Nations Conference on Trade and Development. This produced much in the way of rhetoric, little in the way of practical help. So cries came for madder music and stronger wine. The developed countries were called reactionary. They should give more and more; it was their duty. During my time in Brussels a conference of UNCTAD was called in Manila. With a small team I attended. Someone found out that I had served in the old Indian Army. 'There, you see,' he cried. 'He is still at heart a colonialist!'

I felt an almost irresistible temptation to cry in a stentorian voice that if the developing countries were to follow the example of Hong Kong and Singapore, stop begging for aid, stop spending the proceeds of what they had received on useless prestige projects like steel mills and inefficient airlines, and stop lining the pockets of a corrupt few back home, if they were to institute honest government and change to a free enterprise economy, then they would be much better served. But this would have been regarded as laughably reactionary. Topsy Turvy Land ruled.

Other economic meetings proliferated, too dreary to record. But there was one regular meeting in the Community designed, as they used to say in the cavalry, to bring some tone to what would otherwise have been a vulgar brawl. This was the monthly meeting on political cooperation – the jargon word for attempting to formulate a common Community foreign policy – and was attended by the Political Directors of the Foreign Offices of the Member States. It was certainly sensible for the Community to aim at the greatest degree of common foreign policy it could achieve, since its impact on the world stage would thus be greater and our interests further advanced. But there was about the whole thing a certain spurious glitter. Glitter because foreign affairs – mysterious emissaries arriving at the dead of night in marbled palaces and deciding on peace or war – had an enchantment far beyond a haggle over the level of the tariff on dried goatskins. Thus Doctor Johnson's maxim of patriotism being the last refuge of the scoundrel was transmuted into political cooperation being the last refuge of those who had neither time nor understanding for economics. Spurious because the road to a common foreign policy would be long and rocky. There has to be (with the odd exception) a common trade policy because the Community is a customs union with one common tariff. But for Member States to yield up the right to cut a figure on the world stage, so much beloved by Heads of Government, will be the last straw. There was much talk but little progress. Lengthy declarations were issued from time to time. I remember with particular pleasure one to the effect that the 'Foreign Ministers of the Twelve expressed their sympathy with the plight of camels in Somalia.'

My own boiling point came fairly early in my time in the

Commission. I was wondering whether it was really sensible, given our massive other preoccupations, to spend two days a month in a gathering which regarded economics as something from outer space, when I had to listen for three quarters of an hour to a discussion on who should attend the funeral of an Archbishop in Madrid. I stole away never to return and arranged for my place to be taken by someone from the Secretariat General of the Commission.

But the greatest show on earth – short of that great meeting in the sky, which one day we shall all attend – was the annual Summit of the Industrialised Countries. I have written of the meeting in London in 1977 and the one in Bonn in 1978. At the latter I sat at the back for the discussion on the Tokyo Round. Normally my role was only tangential. The Summits were prepared by the personal representatives of the Heads of Government – the Sherpas, the ones who scaled the heights. In the case of the Commission, the Sherpa was the Chef de Cabinet of the President, for most of my time Crispin Tickell, who was cooperative and efficient. I would brief him on trade matters and accompany the team in case advice was needed on the spot. Normally all one had to do was to drift about for a day and a half in dignified and comfortable circumstances and talk to colleagues from other capitals.

There was one exception. In 1981, when Gaston Thorn, then President of the Commission, was about to set off for Ottawa, where that year the Summit was being held, I got to Brussels airport to find that his Chef de Cabinet and Sherpa, Fernand Spaak, had died in tragic circumstances the day before. There being little alternative at short notice, I was catapulted into the position of Sherpa. So together with the other Sherpas, who gave a kindly welcome to a temporary new boy, I was able to sit at the back of the proceedings and observe the great at play.

Pierre Trudeau was in the chair, a curious cross between a Left Bank intellectual and a lizard, with the occasional rapid smile subsituting for a flickering tongue.

Mrs Thatcher, in that uniquely cooing voice, addressed the President of the United States as 'Ron'. He did not seem to mind, but I could think of many Americans both past and present who would have. President Reagan appeared for this, his first Summit, with the dazed affability of a cowboy, wondrously transported to International Babble Land and dazing his companions in turn with homey anecdotes from life on the range. Helmut Schmidt had been to all the previous Summits and his manner showed it. He knew it all and conveyed this at great length. The Japanese Prime Minister gave every appearance of mistaken identity; I suspected that he was in fact from Neptune, or some other distant planet, his visit the result of some misrouted galactic telephone call. President Mitterand was present for his first Summit. He gave a tolerable imitation of one of the stone carvings in the Invalides suddenly equipped with human voice. But he seemed to me very much on the ball. He had discovered, he said, with some dismay that a whole tribe of 'Sherpas' had grown up, handsomely paid no doubt and with commensurate pensions. What these gentlemen had done in the course of their lifelong occupation was to produce a draft communiqué the length of a minor telephone directory, through which, he gathered, Heads of Government were expected to toil through most of the second day in the manner of middle level bureaucrats. He suggested a very much shorter text. Lizard, in the chair, flickered his tongue with some effect and the discussion moved on.

Over lunch the other Sherpas explained to me that, as I had been able to see that morning, eight of the most distinguished figures of the industrialised world, meeting for inside of two days, when a *tour de table* on a single subject might take a couple of hours, could not decide much. Nor by the nature of things was any such gathering equipped to take major new decisions. These nowadays, at any rate in the economic field, were of such horrid complexity that lengthy discussion between experts and departmental Ministers would first be necessary.

241

In the brief span of a Summit there was simply not enough time. What they could do was to endorse some major decisions, which had been adequately prepared. And this could have real weight – as when the Bonn Summit put its authority behind the deal emerging in the Tokyo Round. But why then this interminable communiqué? It was explained that it would be thought intolerable by the chattering classes if some of the themes dear to their hearts seemed to be ignored. What, they would say, the great of the world have met and completely ignored the problem of the tsetse fly in Ethiopia or the approach of the ice age/global warming (or whatever the nostrum of the moment was)? So a good deal of boiler plate was presentationally necessary.

All right, I said, but, as a wartime poster in Britain used to ask, 'Is your journey really necessary?'

The answer was quick and clear. First of all, Heads of Government like these meetings. They are photographed in the company of their peers – that is good for their image. Every so often they are the host – and then they are like a cat with two tails. But also they like sizing each other up. X can take Y aside before lunch and say, 'That speech you made last week. What was really biting you?' Then he would get an answer he wouldn't get from his Ambassador. Summits are high-level maintenance of the international tram lines. They are worth it. Later that afternoon President Reagan made the same point: 'I guess its a good thing to have an idea of the guy at the other end of the telephone.'

MOVING ON

The year 1982 marked my fifth with the Commission; it seemed to me no bad time to take stock.

The change of administration in Washington had brought a new level of friction in our relations with the Americans. The Reagan

Administration had come in with a conviction – which occurs from time to time there when there is a change – that their predecessors had been soft on foreigners. The Republicans – led by the way-out right-wing Californians – announced that they were not going to put up with any more nonsense from foreigners; they would sock it to them.

They began to. Massive anti-dumping suits were brought against European steel exports to the United States. We pointed out in vain that there was nothing in the international trading rules against dumping (a good deal of European steel was certainly subsidised); only when it could be shown to have caused 'material injury' could counter-measures be justified. And European steel exports, though important to us, formed only a tiny proportion of US domestic production.

Our representations were brushed aside. Unless we cut back our exports drastically – in an action laughably called 'voluntary restraint' – we would be clobbered. We began negotiations. It proved to be tough sledding.

The threats were not limited to steel. We were lectured that all subsidies were bad. For one visit to Washington I had armed myself with a copy of the Subsidies Code painfully negotiated in the Tokyo Round. At least I thought I had – in a hurried departure I had brought the wrong agreement. But rising above such trivia I produced it one evening in discussion with an American Cabinet member. I pulled it out of my pocket in the manner of a US attorney in a B film. 'There!' I cried, 'That is what the US agreed to.'

The Cabinet member was horrified. Pointing to the cover, which was red, he shouted, 'That's what I thought. It's a Commie document!' I was told later that he was joking. I do not believe it.

Then, after a misunderstanding at the Versailles Summit in June 1981, the US Government banned exports of American equipment which could be used in the construction of a pipeline conveying Soviet natural gas to Western Europe. This provoked a major uproar.

Simultaneously a war of words began over the preparations for the GATT Ministerial Meeting now fixed for November 1982. The Americans wanted a declaration outlawing agricultural subsidies. We pointed out that this for us was politically impossible; we knew that for the Americans, abolishing aid to dairy farmers and sugar producers was equally impossible. But we were talking to ideologues. Exchanges were frequent; communication was nil.

All this meant that the amount of attention I had to devote in Brussels to American affairs rose sharply. In the first half of 1982 I had to go there on four occasions; some two thirds of my remaining time – including a good slice of the afternoon on the telephone to Washington – was spent on American trade problems

Then two other things happened. In the summer of 1982 – quite unconnected with these events – the Commission decided to move, after only two years, our man in Washington. And that summer saw a steady deterioration in my relations with the Commissioner nominally responsible for external affairs.

Stevy Davignon thought up an ingenious solution. I would go as Community Ambassador to Washington and deal with the Americans on the spot. If I wanted to return to Brussels to DG1 after a couple of years this would be perfectly acceptable. He told me later that someone had doubted – given the major storm approaching in our relations with the US – whether I would think it wise to accept, and he had replied that he knew me pretty well: he did not think I would refuse to rise to a challenge.

Of course this meant leaving a job that I liked enormously; it was the best I had ever had. And in DG1 I had the friendship and the help of some marvellously talented people. We were a happy and effective ship, and I was proud to be its captain. I would be fifty-eight that year; in the Commission retirement was at sixty-five. But the physical strain of the job was such that I did not think that after five years I could last more than another couple. A third of the year on long distance travel, but carefully timed so as not to miss any really important meeting in Brussels, meant boarding a plane one evening, getting a few hours' fitful sleep on the overnight journey, going straight into meetings all day when I got there, either sitting up late in discussion or negotiating all night, then another overnight journey back with meetings to attend as soon as I got off the plane in Brussels. For someone nearing sixty, this was not a recipe for longevity, particularly with the increase in dealings with the United States. My two predecessors had retired early on grounds of ill health; one had since died. I did not want to retire early; I would have been bored. Nor did I want to move to another Directorate General: trade policy and external relations had been my life.

I had been prepared to support another candidate for Washington, but this offer struck me as heaven sent. In the world of trade policy there were two superpowers; I would be moving from one capital to the other, but the burden would not be as crushing. I consulted Moya. When we married I was on loan to the Foreign Office in Geneva, and had promised at her request never to become a diplomat. But as a good soldier's wife she agreed straight away to 'pay, pack and follow'.

Thereupon I accepted with alacrity. Stevy told me that if I ever needed help in Washington I could count on him. Ortoli asked me to call, poured me a generous brandy, and said the same. They were both as good as their word.

Moya and I moved to Washington in September 1982. We were to spend seven years there and to enjoy it hugely. But that is another chapter of another tale.

SIX

Impressions, Reflections, Conclusions

IMPRESSIONS

I joined the Civil Service in the immediate aftermath of the Second World War. Most of the entrants had served in the war, from Europe to the Western Desert and Burma. One had become Brigade Major on the Italian front at the age of twenty-three. Another had become Second Mate on the Atlantic convoys and had developed at an early age a personality which would not have been daunted by Nebuchadnezzar. A third, who was to become the permanent head of the Department of Education, had been Intelligence Officer in my Brigade in Burma and had been so forceful in voicing in the Mess *New Statesman*-type opinions that the Brigadier had placed him under close arrest.

It follows that the new entrants were not only of some ability, because they would not otherwise have been passed a stiff competitive examination, they were very far from the popular legend of a desiccated calculating machine unconnected to the outside world. And with this variety of background they developed widely different talents. One able and dynamic woman I worked for, who would have become one of the leading lights of Whitehall, became in her forties the head of an Oxford college. I suspect another colleague would have been happier running a band of mercenaries. One was offered a City job not

246

because of a fashionable old school tie but because a leading City banker, temporarily in Government service, saw that his bank could make a wad of money with this young man. (Despite hard pressure to accept he declined, to his later regret, because, like many of us, he had been brought up poor and was loath to abandon the security of government service.) Another, though I have no evidence that his private life was other than irreproachable, had an eye for the ladies, an instinctive knowledge of form (anyone who thinks I am referring to racehorses is an idiot), and in the more relaxed circumstances of a Mediterranean country would have run a very successful brothel.

Of course, in time, 20,000 hours of cattle-truck commuting and thirty-five years of cash-strapped suburbia dimmed the bright flame to a flickering glow. But the upper reaches of the Civil Service were more varied in outlook and interests than popular legend admits. Serving with them was fun.

My second impression relates to the power of the Civil Service. This was certainly considerable. But a distinction needs to be made between the execution and the determination of policy. The Civil Service regards the devising and introduction of radical new policies as an affair for politicians. They do so because civil servants are well aware that they have not been elected. New policies can only properly be introduced by people who have a mandate from the electorate. Civil servants will happily advise on how new ideas can best be implemented. But unless otherwise instructed they will devote their energies to the not inconsiderable task of keeping the ship humming safely along with those minor changes of course every now and again made necessary by the political wind and the tides.

I can recall only two occasions over the last fifty years when civil servants sought to bring about radical change.

The first was when Treasury officials, led by brilliant and forceful ex-*Financial Times* journalist 'Otto' Clarke (Sir Richard Clarke), proposed in 1952 that sterling should be made convertible at a floating rate. In the immediate post-war epoch of fixed exchange rates and careful rationing of non-sterling expenditure, this was a revolutionary proposal. But it was also a neat solution to the perennial balance of payments crises which had dogged the British economy since the war. Sterling would fall but would stabilise at a lower rate. The major difficulty lay in the political consequences. Devaluation would mean a rise in prices; diversion of resources to exports would mean a rise in unemployment. Treasury officials, with the support of the Bank of England, convinced the Chancellor of the Exchequer that whatever the disadvantages Britain's economic position was so dire that there was no alternative. Accordingly he recommended the plan (named ROBOT) to the Cabinet.

There the plan foundered. The Chancellor was R. A. Butler, new in the job and largely ignorant of economics. He was supported by the only industrialist in the Cabinet, Oliver Lyttleton. But the argument that won the day was that however severe Britain's economic problems might be, attempting to solve them by a financial conjuring trick could lead to inflation and unemployment on a convulsive enough scale to threaten the Government's survival.

The second occasion was when a Treasury Permanent Secretary, Sir Frank Lee, persuaded Prime Minister Harold Macmillan in 1961 to apply for membership of the European Economic Community. Frank Lee was not by origin a Treasury man with that Department's ingrained contempt for European entanglements; he had a wider view. He had started in the Colonial Office and had served in Rhodesia; he spent most of the war in Washington and had served as permanent head of the Ministry of Food and then the Board of Trade. In a memorandum circulated to the Cabinet in July 1961 he argued forcefully for British entry. And he was blunt about the longer term: 'We cannot join the Common Market on the cheap. Joining means taking some far-reaching decisions. First we must accept that there will have to be political content in our action – we must show that we are prepared to join with the Six in their institutional arrangements and in any development to closer political integration.'

Macmillan took his advice, but he was only half convinced. He dallied so long over objections from the Commonwealth and British agriculture that the negotiations ran out of steam and De Gaulle, seeing an ebbing of British popular support, was able to torpedo them in January 1963.

In both these cases Civil Service advice was many years ahead of its time. Seventeen years after Otto Clarke's ROBOT plan, exchange control was abolished and sterling freed. Twelve years after Frank Lee's memorandum, Britain joined the European Community. Neither of these two visionaries lived to see the day.

But of course while a plan might ultimately be right does not mean that it is saleable years in advance. This must be a political judgement and cannot be left to unelected officials.

It can reasonably be argued that on both occasions the politicians were timorous. In 1952 the real problem was that Britain was living in a dream world. Virtually bankrupted by the war, it was hardly in a position simultaneously to afford both a generous welfare state and armed forces on an imperial scale. Again, both in 1961 and for the last forty years, the crucial point in joining an integrating Europe was not the sort of commercial or financial arrangements to be made but whether we were 'prepared to join in . . . closer political integration.' In neither case did politicians judge it advisable to put these issues to the people.

But that is the democratic system. Civil servants administer existing policies and can justifiably be faulted if they fail in this task. They can advise major changes but whether these are accepted and how they are sold to the public is the task of elected politicians and the new breed of political adviser. These do not always rise to their responsibilites.

249

But as Churchill once remarked, 'Democracy is the worst form of government except all those other forms which have been tried.'

REFLECTIONS

Even if the Civil Service has talent and even if it can hardly be expected on its own to change the course of British history, a number of critical questions remain. I would choose four.

First, has Britain got its Civil Service right? Has the service absorbed too much of the nation's talent? Can Whitehall rub along on a Volkswagen or does it need a Rolls Royce?

Second, what sort of a job has the Civil Service done? Bureaucracy has few friends. But most would agree that from the 1870s, when entry on merit began, Whitehall has been free from corruption and general standards of administration have been thought to compare well with those of other countries. A detailed assessment of how it has fared in dealing with activities as disparate as the maintenance of lunatic asylums, the treatment of vagabonds and the preservation of wild birds would take many volumes. But let us limit this brief review to the biggest question facing Britain over the last fifty years, its relationship with an integrating Europe. A British newspaper headline is once supposed to have read, 'FOG IN THE CHANNEL – CONTINENT ISOLATED'. Has Whitehall been able to see through the fog?

Third, has there been too much Government secrecy? Pretty well every outside report about the workings of government laments the hole-in-the-corner way in which government seems to do business. Let light shine into the darkest crevices, cry the commentators. Let us see how decisions are made. Let there be transparency.

Fourth is the continuing dogfight among Ministers today. Minister A is rubbished in the press by shadowy sources (seemingly including civil servants, who used to be politically impartial). This is promptly followed by anonymous attacks on Minister B, who by a mysterious chance is known to be opposed to Minister A. Recently the Prime Minister's office announced that he and the Chancellor had agreed a joint approach to the euro, only to have this rubbished by the Chancellor's office. Far from joined-up government, we have a Government whose joints at any moment seem on the point of flying apart. Is this a momentary aberration? Can we expect one day to return to placid normality?

Does Whitehall need a Rolls Royce?

A Civil Service exists to serve the state. Up to the Second World War Britain was the head of a great empire, ranking at the Potsdam Conference in 1945 with the two other victorious world powers, the United States of America and the Soviet Union.

While it lasted, the Empire imposed its values. Our forefathers thought that the British Empire needed to be governed in style. In the late Victorian years of headlong economic expansion and a widening empire, Gladstone had to decide how the governors should be recruited. Devoted to sound finance and probity in public expenditure, he rejected the jobbery of the Regency years and brought in competitive examinations. So year after year some of the brightest and best from Oxford and Cambridge passed a stiff examination and entered the service of the Crown. It was not lacking in trappings of grandeur. In the Indian Civil Service or the Colonial Service a young man of twenty-five could find himself governing several million people and by forty-five be the Governor of a province as huge as Bengal, with greater responsibilities than many a European Prime Minister and all the splendour of a maharajah. When Edward VIII, as Prince of Wales, stayed with the Governor of Bombay, he remarked that he had never known before how royalty lived. Others passed the Foreign Office examination and rose to head an imposing Embassy and deal with

251

heads of state. When Lord Halifax arrived in Washington as Ambassador in 1941 he did so in one of Britain's newest battleships and the President of the United States sailed out to greet him. Those with less of a taste for foreign adventure could join the ranks of the Higher Civil Service and help to decide behind the tall windows of Whitehall the policies of one of the leading powers of the world.

The result was what John Gunther, an American journalist, called a Civil Service 'which is the incorruptible spinal column of England. My office boy, if he were reasonably presentable and adaptable, could conceivably fill the office of Chancellor of the Exchequer or Minister of War; the permanent staff would carry on.'[1] He went on to describe the permanent heads of the great Departments as 'among the characters who really rule England' but who avoid the limelight and flourish in the shadows.

There was one side effect that was little regarded in the years of glory. Industry and commerce ranked little in popular appeal for the brightest of the young. Why should they be interested? Britain was a great imperial power. The defence of its interests across the world was a suitable task for its élite. Of course the saloon bar would always be full of commercial travellers, what the elect of the Indian Civil Service referred to as 'boxwallahs'. But, as the British Ambassador in St Petersburg once wrote to a British businessman, 'Pray remember that I am not here to be bothered with questions about trade.' Quite apart from social prestige, the manufacture of dogfood or cotton knickers did not pose the intellectual challenge which would interest a First in Greats. Nor did those who manufactured such commodities make any effort to attract undergraduates. So a large number of the brightest from Oxbridge preferred the distinction of passing a difficult competitive examination, agreeably civilised companions and the chance of a distinguished career, to the hurly burly of the saloon bar.

With this distribution of national talent came an unspoken compact between the politicians and the clerks. There reigned a certain mutual respect. Politicians knew that the civil service was incorruptible, loyal, and had some of the best brains in the land. If the minister were a booby, which not infrequently he was, then his civil servants, in the manner immortalised on television by Sir Humphrey Appleby, would guide him smoothly into channels which required minimum change and trouble. If he were not, civil servants would produce a version of his ideas which had the best chance of being saleable to his colleagues and Parliament. When the Liberals introduced their ground-breaking social reforms in 1908 and Labour the welfare state from 1945, there was no complaint about lack of cooperation from Whitehall.

For their part the Civil Service knew that their advice would be listened to with respect. They fully accepted that ministers had been elected and had the last word. But they knew that subject to this they could argue for changes designed to make a new policy more accept-able or workable, and not be sacked for doing so.

But the days of Britain as a great power were not to last. At Potsdam in 1945 an American referred to the 'two and a half great powers'. And already far earlier one of its proconsuls had seen the shape of things to come. 'When India has gone and the great colonies have gone,' asked Lord Curzon in 1908, 'do you suppose that we can stop there? . . . England, from having been the arbiter, would sink at best into the inglorious playground of the world. Our antiquities, our natural beauties, our relics of a once mighty sovereignty, our castles and cathedrals, our mansion houses and parks, would attract a crowd of wandering pilgrims. People would come and see us just as they climb the Acropolis at Athens or ascend the waters of the Nile . . . England would become a sort of glorified Belgium.'[2]

At the beginning of a new century Curzon's prophecy has come true. Britain is Belgium, though the British do not know it yet, and in terms of income per head they are not as well off. The national theme park foreseen by Curzon is blazoned in advertisements across the world's press. Twenty-five million visitors a year swarm over the sceptred isle and its remnants of the past. 'Without their crowns and coronets,' the novelist John Updike wondered once in the *New Yorker*, 'how could the English be distinguished from the Icelanders?'[3]

Inexorably this decline in power has had its implications for Whitehall. The Indian Civil Service and the Colonial Office have long since gone. The Foreign Service no longer represents a world power. Sir Con O'Neill, who led our team in the negotiations to enter the European Communities in 1970–72, reflected to me once that when he had joined the Foreign Office in 1936, it was then quite something to have done so. As a First Secretary in Cairo, if the High Commissioner were on leave and the Counsellor off duck shooting, you could run Egypt. If he had been a young man forty years later, he would not have chosen to enter the Foreign Office.

The decline in world power has also had its effect on the governance of Britain. Lord Curzon would have wondered why the administration of a theme park needed a galaxy of Oxbridge double firsts. And world status is not the only thing which has changed. The age of deference has melted away and with it the compact between politicians and clerks. Politicians are no longer prepared to regard chief civil servants as the real, albeit shadowy, rulers of the land. A rash of political advisers has appeared in Whitehall. They seem to have taken over the Prime Minister's office and largely run the Treasury. A Minister from the 1930s would have found it difficult to understand why they were necessary. The Minister's job was to know about politics; he saw his constituency at the weekends; he saw his colleagues regularly; his Parliamentary Private Secretary, a bright young MP, starting his career on the Government ladder, would brief him on feeling in the House. But the ambitious young political advisers of today have no doubt why they are there. They want a slice of the action. They not only want to make sure that the old fossils of Whitehall do not dilute programmes dear to their Labour (or Conservative) hearts. They want to have the fun of dealing with Ministers on major issues of policy without the tiresome necessity of passing a stiff competitive examination and serving a long apprenticeship. For their part, Ministers now seem to find it easier, when they put forward ideas, to have the uncritical support of young enthusiasts than face a sober appraisal of their work-ability by an experienced official. Slowly Britain is moving towards the American Presidential system with its hordes of political appointees. An American friend once told me that this was bound to happen: 'Every so many years Britain follows the American example, choosing with unerring skill the wrong thing to follow.'

The biggest change in Whitehall happened in the Thatcher revolu-tion. She was a radical reformer. She wanted no part of 'a nicely calcu-lated less or more'. She was on good terms with a few civil servants, mostly those who became her acolytes. But for the most part she despised them. Her heroes were those who earned huge salaries in the City; those who worked for the state were by definition second-raters. To them she made clear that she wanted instant compliance with her wishes, otherwise heads would roll. She ruined the careers of two senior civil servants of undoubted ability, who had dared to argue with her. Alan Clark recounts in his diaries that 'officials were all completely terrified of the Lady.' In the case of one of them, 'She marked his card on the spot and he is going to take early retirement . . . This was early in the 1979 Parliament before the old nostra had been undermined and these changes confirmed by the electorate.'[4] In time her extremism, on Europe and on the poll tax, did for her, as they usually do for dictators, and she ended not on the gibbet but in tears, driving away from No. 10. But what lasted was the effect on Whitehall. The Civil Service found itself openly and publicly despised by its political masters and told that the role of the most senior was that of courtier. Ever adaptable to the wishes of Ministers, the Seniors became courtiers. The quality of their advice suffered. So did the quality of the Service.

Political advisers are not the only ones who have broken into the once cosy Whitehall world. The media have played a major part. They have changed their function from that of reporting and commenting to become a major entertainment industry, dumbing down, chasing gossip and sensation in a ruthless maximisation of sales. With this they have become brasher and more intrusive. Douglas Hurd has said that after a typical ministerial statement in the House of Commons, he could expect to conduct five to six interviews, possibly four for television and two for radio. If he did not, then critics and commentators would fill the gap – the justification of policy had become as important as its execution.[5] Two management consequences have followed. The first is a growing workload for Ministers. Geoffrey Howe has talked of taking home, when Foreign Secretary, three boxes a night for six nights a week.[6] Presentation has thus tended to squeeze out analysis and reflection. The second is that even if time for reflection were found it has become difficult to discuss long-term policy for fear of the political embarrassment when details of the options are leaked.

The political consequence has been an enormous increase in the power of the press. In 1919 Lord Northcliffe, the great press baron of his day, wanted what the Prime Minister thought too much say in government. Lloyd George told him to go to hell. In 1931 Lord Beaverbrook wanted the same. Baldwin coined the memorable public phrase that what the press wanted 'was the prerogative of the harlot throughout the ages: power without responsibility'. Now the Government is fearful of the press. Mr Blair has attributed the size of his election victory in 1997 to the support of the *Sun*. He knows that victory in 2004 will depend in large measure on the support of the Murdoch press.

Five signs show how the balance has changed between politicians and the press.

~ Before the Second World War a newspaper editor was paid a third of the salary of the Prime Minister; before the last election editors were paid three times as much as the Prime Minister. They know it. At the 1997 Labour Party conference the editor of the *Mirror*, who was giving lunch to Mr Blair, found hilarious a discussion of a freeze on the pay of Cabinet Ministers. He threw across a £20 note and bellowed, 'Hey, Tony, buy the kids some toys!'[7]

~ Alistair Campbell, the Prime Minister's Head of Communications (and former press secretary), has been given access to the Prime Minister and powers to coordinate Whitehall's dealings with the media which are unprecedented. Some have considered his position to be effectively that of Deputy Prime Minister. The impression was not gainsaid by a television documentary made by Alistair Campbell and screened in the autumn of 2000 showing him in magisterial command of a retinue in which Mr Blair had a minor walk-on part.

~ After three years in office and only a year before the next general election, Mr Blair capitulated to the press barons. He spent the Easter Sunday of 2000 penning to the editor of the *Sun*, Rupert Murdoch's main British newspaper, a cringing hand-written plea for more sympathetic coverage. The paper published it in full, and with relish, under the headline 'RATTLED'.

~ The date of the General Election in June 2001 was announced not by the Prime Minister to Parliament but by the Political Editor of the *Sun*, Trevor Kavanagh.

~ Later in 2001 the Whips (the MPs concerned to maintain at all times a Parliamentary majority for the party in office and to advise the Prime Minister on any trends in party opinion which might threaten this) were moved out of their traditional home in No. 12 Downing Street and their place taken by Alistair Campbell and his advisers. Partly, of course, this reflects the low regard which the Blair administration has for a Parliament which a huge Labour majority in the House of Commons has rendered powerless. But it also amounts to a striking symbol of the triumph of the spin doctors.

Those who recall how things were fifty or even thirty years ago would mostly regard the politicisation and tabloidisation of Whitehall as a slow and melancholy descent to Hades and hope against hope that one day the march might be reversed.

On several counts they would be wrong. There is no putting back the clock. The days have gone for ever when the bowler-hatted barons of Whitehall could discreetly run the country's affairs. Deference has gone the way of plumed hats and maharajahs. The media will get brasher; political advisers more influential; special interest groups more insistent.

Should this matter? Americans make no bones about the fact that their national administration is staffed by second- or third-raters and the key posts given to political appointees. Yet the United States has won two world wars, gone on to win the Cold War without a single missile being fired, and is as yet unchallenged as the richest and most powerful country in the world. In the United States intellectual talent goes into business or the law. As President Coolidge once said, 'The chief business of the American people is business.'[8] In a national emergency, someone from their ranks can always be found to save the state. A deployment of the best and the brightest to the service of the state has not been found necessary for its preservation.

Indeed, the deployment in Britain for several generations of its best and brightest to the higher ranks of Government service was an aberration. The Empire could have been efficiently administered without a yearly input of double firsts. Britain's survival as a great trading nation depended on its remaining competitive. And this meant harnessing more of its talents to manufacturing industry, to engineering and to trading. But the elegantly educated young were conditioned to turn up their noses at these callings as not suitable for gentlemen. That is why Britain, from being before 1914 one of the richest countries in the world, has slipped steadily down the scale.

Fortunately the trend of talented young away from the public service has already set in. They can hardly be encouraged by the present day trend to 'open up the top jobs', in other words to award Permanent Secretary posts not to the ablest of those who have spent their careers preparing for them but to trendy amateurs or cronies of politicians. From the Civil Service Selection Board there are unofficial reports that, while there is a steady flow of applicants, their quality has dropped. The major companies now regularly trawl the universities to seek recruits. Mega bonuses in the City attract a wider circle to investment banking. The head of an Oxford College recently surprised a politician from an earlier generation with the news that the top choice for his brightest young men and women was now the media. Whether this will arrest Britain's decline in world influence or simply portray it more vividly is not clear. But at least the national talent is being more widely spread.

It is high time it was. Because as a much reduced Britain enters the twenty-first century, Whitehall does not need a Rolls Royce.

Did Whitehall see through the fog in the Channel?
The answer must be that officials very largely did not. The first of the decisive moments in the British post-war relationship with Europe happened in 1950. Then the French Foreign Minister, Robert Schuman, proposed the setting up of a Coal and Steel Community to pool coal and steel production between France and Germany, and other European countries willing to join. But the intention went much wider. The ultimate aim, as the declaration made clear, was the creation of a European Federation.

Official advice in London was firmly against. Sir William Strang, the Foreign Office Permanent Under Secretary wrote, 'The decision which the French are now summoning us to take is, in fact, the decision whether or not we are to bind ourselves irrevocably to the European community.' This was 'something I cannot bring myself to recommend.'[9] But it was not just a failure of perception on the part of the Foreign Office. The official head of the Treasury, Sir Edward Bridges, submitted: 'It has been our settled policy hitherto that in view of our world position and interests, we should not commit ourselves irrevocably to Europe unless we could measure the extent and effects of the commitment.'[10]

When British Ministers considered the French proposal they hardly needed these encouraging words. Their reactions were a mixture of indignation and alarm: indignation that one of the defeated rabble of Continental countries had dared to propose a new order ('There was general agreement that the French Government had behaved extremely badly in springing this proposal on the world without any attempt at consultation with Her Majesty's Government and the US Government'); alarm at 'a regrettable tendency to move away from the concept of the Atlantic Community and in the direction of a European Federation.'

So Britain refused to take part in the establishment of the Coal and Steel Community. In 1955 the Foreign Ministers of its six founding members met in Messina to discuss the next steps. A committee was set up – the Spaak Committee – to work out the details of a customs union. The British sent an observer, a civil servant, an Under Secretary from the Board of Trade, Russell Bretherton. After the first few months he walked out. A European customs union, the European Community, was founded without British participation. Britain remained aloof from Europe.

The reasoning behind this in Whitehall had two strands.

The first was a profound conviction that Britain was a great power. As Oliver Franks, an academic turned major mandarin and then Ambassador in Washington, wrote in 1954, 'It is part of the formation of our minds that Britain should continue as a great power.'[11] Thus Britain could not possibly weaken its position as head of the Commonwealth and a special favoured ally of the United States by merging itself with a group of second-rank Continentals which it had either beaten or liberated.

The second was an equally strong conviction that the plan for a Continental customs union would not work. Bretherton is alleged to have said when leaving the Spaak Committee that the treaty they were discussing had no chance of being negotiated, even if agreed it had no chance of being ratified and if ratified had no chance of being applied. He has been criticised for this. Alternatively, some have doubted whether he ever in fact said anything quite so epigrammatic. In fact, Bretherton was merely voicing a sentiment shared by all senior officials in Whitehall.

Sir Roger Makins, one of the most powerful figures in the Foreign Office and its most strident anti-European, by this time Ambassador in Washington, explained to the State Department in November 1955 that the proposed customs union had 'an air of unreality since the real French position seemed very questionable . . . he doubted very much whether, when the chips were down, the French would be prepared to make the internal adjustments which would be necessary for progress towards a common market.'[12] Gladwyn Jebb, another Foreign Office panjandrum, Ambassador in Paris, predicted that progress from Messina 'will be purely verbal.'[13]

These doubts were not limited to the Foreign Office; they were strongly held in the Treasury and the Board of Trade. Nor at the time did they seem wholly implausible. France had been a highly protected economy for three hundred years since Colbert. Was it conceivable that it would agree to throw its markets open to the formidable competition of German industry? (Indeed Robert Marjolin, a notable French technocrat and the first Secretary General of the OEEC, records in his memoirs that opposition to a customs union was almost universal in Paris.[14]) Even if a treaty on these lines were negotiated, surely the French Chamber of Deputies would not ratify it, just as it had refused to approve the European Defence Community? And even if the treaty were to become law, the citizens of France would refuse to accept it.

But the doubts did not prevail. The French realised that, after having vetoed the European Defence Community, they could not impose a second veto and retain the leadership of a uniting Europe. The Treaty of Rome, setting up a customs union of the Six, was signed in March 1957 and came into effect on 1 January 1958. Against British doubts, it was to prove a resounding success. Once again Britain had missed the boat.

Britain thrashed about. The fiasco of Suez had shown the illusion of the Commonwealth connection. An attempt to dilute the customs union of the Six by a Europe-wide free trade area failed. Britain formed a free trade area with the Swiss, the Austrians, the Portuguese and the Scandinavians, but this was widely regarded as a sideshow.

The senior Foreign Office official dealing with economic affairs, later its Permanent Secretary, Sir Paul Gore-Booth wrote of this time:

> With hindsight, I feel that neither we nor our posts in Europe had quite caught the wind of change that was blowing through the Community countries at that time. What should have been clear was that whereas up to, say 1955, it had been assumed that a radical economic reorganisation of Western Europe would not be possible without Britain, the only major OEEC country not overwhelmed by defeat or occupation, the Messina meeting had changed all that.[15]

But even with hindsight he was wrong. The wind of change that was blowing through the chancelleries of Europe came from the horrors of defeat and occupation. The Continental countries which had known them were passionately determined to banish their return for ever by forming a federation. The British had not had this experience and did not understand. For them the war was a time of victory and glory. Jean Monnet understood. He came to London in 1950 to try and convince the British of the need to join the Coal and Steel Community. Later in his memoirs he wrote, 'England had known neither defeat nor occupation. She had no need to exorcise the past.'

Even without understanding this, however, Britain did become increasingly uneasy at being left out of a growing European success. Then something in Whitehall changed. The most formidable senior civil servant of the post-war years, Frank Lee, speaking not a word of any foreign language, saw that the world had changed and that Britain needed to change with it. He browbeat the Treasury and browbeat Macmillan. But you can browbeat someone without filling him with ironclad Cromwellian conviction. And Macmillan always had about him the air of an elegant poseur. A witty French Commission official, Jean François Deniau, remarked that the negotiation was not about Britain joining the Community but the Community joining the Commonwealth.[16] When General De Gaulle brought the negotiations to an end in January 1963, several of the shrewdest Continental observers thought he was right.

Then Frank Lee retired and Whitehall returned happily to its Eurosceptic ways, the Foreign Office with relief because it was only slowly emerging from the period when any trade question was considered below the salt. The barons of the Treasury and the Board of Trade were relieved that they could return undistracted to the Anglo-American-Commonwealth world of finance and trade. One senior official fulminated that on trade matters the Europeans were refusing to be dealt with directly; they had the impertinence to insist on being approached through some new anonymous body called the Commission.

Even when Edward Heath led the Conservatives to a surprise victory in the general election of 1970 and began to negotiate our entry into the European Communities, Whitehall did not change much. The Permanent Secretary of the Foreign Office, Sir Denis Greenhill, opined that trying to enter Europe was 'flogging a dead horse'.[17] Sir John Hunt, who dealt with European affairs from the Cabinet Office from 1972 and became Cabinet Secretary in 1973, thought that to be aggressively keen on Europe was 'proof of a slight eccentricity'. He considered that those on the negotiating team were 'mavericks . . . not naturally people who were going to go to the top of the mainstream Civil Service . . . some of them had been shoved into this job because it was one that nobody else was keen to do and they happened to believe in it.'[18]

But when the negotiation had been successfully concluded two changes took place. The first was that the Foreign Office swung behind the European venture. Michael Palliser, the new Permanent Representative in Brussels to the European Communities, partly brought up in France, twice in our Embassy in Paris, and married to a daughter of Paul Henri Spaak, was impeccably European. In 1975 he was to become Foreign Office Permanent Secretary. The Foreign Office began to see that to be European was no longer a sign of dangerous eccentricity.

Indeed David Owen (Foreign Secretary 1977–79) thought darkly that the Foreign Office harboured a nest of federalists. It did not. The Foreign Office line had changed and close and friendly relations with our partners in the European Communities were now important. But this was far from recognising that membership of the EEC would inexorably involve two further steps, a single currency and then a political union. As long ago as the 1930s a League of Nations working party on customs unions had concluded that 'when there is free movement of goods, persons and capital in any area, diverse economic policies concerned with maintaining economic activity cannot be pursued. To ensure uniformity of policy some political mechanism is required. The greater the interference of the state, the greater must be

the political integration within a customs union.'[19] As Walter
Hallstein, the first President of the European Commission said in
1958, 'Customs union, economic union, political union.' Yet John
Major's Foreign Office Private Secretary (later British Permanent
Representative in Brussels) Sir Stephen Wall is credited by some with
helping him to refer, in an *Economist* article in 1994, to economic and
monetary union as having 'all the quaintness of a rain dance and about
the same potency'. Since then, monetary union has gained some
support among Foreign Office officials but political union still seems
to be regarded as Utopian. A senior Foreign Office official declared in
a discussion open to the public in 1999 that federation was simply a
concept of the immediate post-war years.

The second change was a growing shift in power over European
issues in Whitehall from the Foreign Office to the Treasury. The
accession negotiations had been under Foreign Office control. But
once in the European club, Britain's day-to-day business became that
of European economic integration. Trade policy, industrial policy,
regional policy, transport and the environment were all matters of
which the Foreign Office knew little. Policy on these issues was coordinated in Whitehall under Cabinet Office chairmanship. But of all
the Whitehall departments the Treasury has always been the most
powerful since it has control over expenditure. After the retirement of
Sir Frank Lee in 1961, the Treasury happily reverted to its role as the
most anti-European department because it did not want its power
challenged. Douglas Allen, the Permanent Secretary from 1968 to
1974, is recorded by Hugo Young as 'roused to unusually vigorous
displays of disdain' when the economic arguments for entry into
Europe were put before him.[20] (Indeed, documents released at the
beginning of 2002 show that in 1971 Treasury officials sent Edward
Heath a warning of the power the Treasury would lose over the basic
instruments of national economic management if Continental plans

for a single currency by 1980 were to be realised and we were by then a member of the EEC. The paper was not shown to Ministers nor circulated interdepartmentally. It was meant as a private warning which might cool Heath's enthusiasm for Europe. It did not succeed.) The Treasury approach seems no warmer under Gordon Brown. The Foreign Office may lament the lack of influence in Europe which remaining outside the euro brings. But in Whitehall the Treasury rules.

Nor is it likely to be challenged by the other Home Departments. Their Permanent Secretaries mostly speak no foreign language, know nothing of Europe and its history. They would see no value in tilting for an unknown cause at the windmills of the Treasury. They would not relish in the five years or so before retirement their power and influence being trimmed back by a motley throng of foreigners in Brussels. And habits of deference still linger too. A decision to enter Europe would seem to them so far-reaching as to be essentially political. They would happily advise on road building or the construction of prisons. But handing over the government of the country to foreigners is so revolutionary as to be an affair exclusively for politicians.

There has been one other unfortunate consequence of this Whitehall distrust of European integration. Its attitude towards staffing the Commission has been one of haughty disdain. The then official head of the Treasury, Sir William Armstrong, visited Brussels in 1973 shortly after our accession. He was taken round the Commission and met some of their most senior staff. Asked later what he thought of them, he said with a barely concealed sneer that he had the impression of talking to the lowest basic grade in Whitehall.[21]

So the word went round Whitehall that the Commission was the equivalent of some Latin American comic opera army. Hardly surprisingly there followed a general lack of enthusiasm for joining it. In the twenty-eight years of our membership only one Permanent Secretary has gone from Whitehall to the Commission. Heads were shaken on his departure, but it was explained that he was an eccentric Europhile who had volunteered. The general practice has been to put forward for the most senior jobs someone markedly lower in rank. This may seem an obsession with bureaucratic hierarchy. But if it were a question of staffing a European Army, and we were to put forward for a general's job a colonel or a brigadier, under the unspoken, arrogant assumption that he would amply equal a comic opera European general, we would not end up with a great deal of influence.

Some minor changes have been made. For some years a 'European stream' scheme has been in operation whereby new recruits to the Civil Service have been encouraged to apply for bottom-rung jobs in the European Commission. It has had little if any effect on the general decline in British influence, given the length of time they must take to rise to top jobs and the gradual drifting of Britain away from Europe. One example shows its extent.

There are six official level jobs which are crucial in the Commission: Secretary General, Head of the Legal Service, Chef de Cabinet (head of the personal staff) of the President, and the three Directors General where the Commission has real powers under the treaties, external trade, competition and agriculture. None of these jobs is held by a British national. Two are held by Frenchmen, the others by an Irishman, a German, a Dane and a Spaniard. The three top jobs serving the Council of Ministers (the equivalent of the British Cabinet Office) and including the Council's special representative for foreign and security policy, are held by a Spaniard, a Frenchman and a German. That shows the extent to which an arrogant insularity has cost Britain power and influence in Europe.

So the answer to the question whether Whitehall has been able to see through the fog in the Channel is, for the most part, No. The Department best qualified to peer ahead was the Foreign Office but its vision was late and partial. Bizarrely, the one official who did see clearly the European future was a Home Civil Servant who had started life in the Colonial Office and progressed through the Ministry of Food and the Board of Trade to the top of the Treasury. But he was not around long enough.

Of course, even if Whitehall had perceived how Europe would develop and had been able to present clearly to Ministers the choice between impotent isolation and the role Britain could have played as a leading member of a new European superpower, it is most unlikely that Ministers would have accepted their advice. With few exceptions, the British political class over the last fifty years has known as much about Europe as of outer Mongolia and has been as terrified of risking votes by advocating closer links with it as Baldwin was of defending rearmament in the 1930s. Even now, if Mr Blair does decide to risk a referendum on the euro before the election of 2004 (and if Mr Gordon Brown allows him to), he will not dare to tell the British people that the next irrevocable step is the formation of some European political union.

As a very distinguished Belgian diplomat, Philippe de Schoutheete (a former Belgian Permanent Representative in Brussels) wrote in the *Financial Times* of 29 August 2001, 'contrary to the initial hopes of Belgium and the Netherlands, successive British governments have never been able to exert an influence on European affairs comparable with that of France or Germany. Leadership presupposes shared aspirations. In the case of Britain there were none or too few.'

In the late 1930s there was much talk of '*la trahison des clercs*' (betrayal by the intellectuals). In Britain in the coming years people will talk of how in the second half of the twentieth century their politicians were frightened to tell them the truth about what was happening in Europe and thus betrayed them. But this in no way absolves the mandarins of the day from their duty to give realistic advice about the choices open to us.

Do we need more transparency?

R. A. Butler (Chancellor of the Exchequer in the early 1950s), the son of a distinguished member of the Indian Civil Service, who could himself have become a top civil servant, once said that government flourished best in the dark. This nowadays would arouse journalists and academics to fury. Bureaucratic arrogance!, they would cry. But two examples show that in voicing this view Butler had sense on his side.

Firstly, the forum in which the ultimate decisions about our affairs are taken. This used to be the Cabinet; now it is a small group clustered round the Prime Minister. Should their deliberations be held in public?

The result of any public discussion would be no agreement. The settling of any hard-fought issue involves what an eminent trade unionist once called a 'dirty compromise'. Positions held with passion for years have to be partially abandoned. Defending the deal after-wards is difficult enough, but reference can be made to the advantages which have been secured. Conceding a vital point in front of the tele-vision cameras to the groans and catcalls of his supporters would make even the most seasoned politician blanch. This is why the rare public sessions of the American Cabinet result in ponderous agreement on the virtues of motherhood and apple pie.

The second example relates to the advice given to Ministers. In the 1950s, when contact between Government and industry was much closer than now because of the wartime and post-war controls, a Board of Trade Minister once needed to discuss some delicate issues with the managing committee of a trade association; later he had lunch with them. He had been carefully briefed by the Head of Division in the Department respon-sible for this particular industry and he handled his task with skill and discretion. He was obviously familiar with the issues raised, had a sure grasp of the personalities involved and was able to agree, after some tough discussion, compromises which were just about acceptable.

The civil servant who had done the briefing and who had accompanied his Minister returned to the Department well content. But his content was short-lived. The Secretary of the Association came on the telephone. In tones so chilly that one could almost hear the grinding of the ice floes, he reported that the Minister had left behind a document 'of a confidential nature which I am returning to you forthwith. I regret to say that the document appears to bear your signature.'

It was the brief for the Minister. It set out clearly and accurately the problems to be discussed, possible solutions and it gave an equally accurate sketch of the personalities involved. One senior industrialist was described as 'a blockhead', another as 'vain as a peacock', and a third as 'devious almost beyond belief'. Of course, the brief should not have been left behind. And it did for a while cause some friction. But it greatly helped the Minister; had the brief been prepared with an eye to publication, it would have been far more discreet and far less useful. After all, an old established solicitor in a country town does not advertise on a placard in his window the advice he is giving his client.

All this should not remove the need for a full debate both before and after Government decisions. But it does show that without an element of confidentiality, government business is much more difficult to transact. That is why parties in Opposition often proclaim the virtues of transparency, yet are strangly hesitant to pursue the matter once they take office.

To the public, the picture nowadays presented by the Government is one of endless backbiting. Memoir follows biography and biography memoir at relentless intervals. Shadowy sources continually brief the media and try to do each other down. These now include not just politicians but civil servants. The author of a recent revelatory book on conflicts in the government (Andrew Rawnsley, *Servants of the People: The Inside Story of New Labour*) was criticised for not revealing sources. Anyone who had served in Whitehall could have told the critics that for him to quote the civil servants who had spoken to him would not only have meant ugly consequences for them, but that no one in an official position would ever have spoken to him again.

The exasperated citizen watching this spectacle must wonder whether there was really a golden age when, despite a stately divergence once in a while on policy, national Government sailed on majestically like one of the great ocean liners of old.

The short answer is that, with rare intervals, rivalry, treachery and backbiting are as natural to politics as grouse to moors. Those who join the political game are not shrinking violets. They are in competition for fame and glory and are well aware that there is no friendship at the top. Let us not go back to Robert Walpole but simply to the last century. In the early years of the First World War the brilliant and mercurial Lloyd George served as a supposedly loyal colleague under Asquith, rubbished him in private ('I will now give my celebrated imitation of Mr Asquith leaving a restaurant', acting forthwith the weaving and swaying of the post-prandial, inebriated Prime Minister), and then cut his political throat in 1916. In 1922, as head of a coalition of Liberal and Conservative MPs, Lloyd George was in turn despatched by the seemingly indolent and placid Baldwin, who rallied the Conservative Party against him in a meeting at the Carlton Club. He acknowledged that Lloyd George was a 'dynamic force' but 'a dynamic force is a very terrible thing; it may crush you, but it is not necessarily right.'[22]

In the Labour Government of 1945–51 Harold Wilson began to emerge as one of its rising stars. But he was distrusted as more than usually slippery by the old Labour leadership under Attlee (in which judgement they were not entirely wrong). Ernest Bevin, annoyed once because he thought Wilson, through his trade deals in Moscow, was interfering in his own (Foreign Office) area, lambasted him so severely in Cabinet that Wilson returned to the Board of Trade (where I was his Private Secretary) in a state of shellshock. And I still remember the rage on Wilson's face when we learnt that Hugh Gaitskell, then junior to Wilson, was going – on Herbert Morrison's advice – to succeed Stafford Cripps in 1950 as Chancellor of the Exchequer. Of course Wilson outlived or outfought his rivals – only to find himself, as Prime Minister, in a state of war with George Brown and abandoned by Callaghan on trade union reform. So the gavotte went on; the dissension in the Major Cabinet was as legendary as it was recent.

So Cabinet infighting is nothing new. What is new is the attitude of the public and the press. Up to comparatively recently there was a certain public reticence about the private affairs of the great. It was long known in a limited circle that Harold Macmillan's wife was the mistress of another Conservative MP, Bob Boothby. Equally it was known that Hugh Gaitskell had a long affair with Anne Fleming. But, as with the innumerable affairs of President Kennedy, nothing appeared in the press.

Nor was this reticence confined to sexual matters. In 1912–13 Lloyd George was able to survive his involvement in the Marconi scandal (where insider dealing in shares was alleged) as well as the charge of misleading the House of Commons on the subject. It seems most unlikely that he would have escaped today. In the late 1930s a particularly close collaboration developed between two long-time associates, Beaverbrook, proprietor of the *Daily Express* and Sir Samuel Hoare, Home Secretary in 1937 and previously the holder of several distinguished Ministerial posts including that of Foreign Secretary. In November 1938 Hoare's wife wrote Beaverbrook a begging letter: 'If [Sam] is not to retire at this election he must be relieved of financial anxiety . . . if he goes, I believe it will be a great loss to this country.' Beaverbrook promptly sent him £2,000 (equivalent to nearly £70,000 in today's money). The same amount was sent in September 1939, and again in November 1939.[23] At the same time Churchill, also heavily in debt, was lent £18,000 (some

£600,000 in present day money) by Sir Henry Strakosch, a South African financier of Czech origin who was known fiercely to oppose German demands for the return of the Sudetenland.[24]

Whether Hoare had urged Chamberlain, as he later hinted, to take Beaverbrook into his Cabinet and whether Churchill felt under any obligation to Sir Henry Stakosch cannot now be established and in any case is hardly relevant. We are discussing differences between today and yesterday. Today deals of this kind would in all probability have leaked out and would have caused an immense uproar. Lloyd George and Hoare would have had to resign; Churchill would have found the episode damaging to say the least.

Whether this would have been worth while is another matter. It could have deprived us of two great wartime Prime Ministers. But the change in attitudes did not happen because of any idealistic campaign for probity in public life. It happened for several reasons.

First is a coincidence between two factors already mentioned – the end of the age of deference and the increasing power of a steadily more intrusive media. Even in the 1960s things had progressed since Kitchener left his tent at Omdurman, and finding a small group of British journalists gathered, cried, 'Out of my way, you drunken swabs!' But even in the 1960s a journalist interviewing a Minister returning from a mission abroad, would be tugging his forelock, 'And now, Sir, I hope you will be having a good few days' rest,' he would end reverentially. The no-holds-barred interrogation of the *Today* programme and the merciless satire of the Parliamentary sketch writers are part of a different world.

Second is the fact that the Great nowadays are more than anxious to oblige the press. Already in opposition New Labour was shaping a press control machine superior to anything which had gone before. To be sure politicians have talked to the press since time immemorial and their carrots and sticks – exclusive interviews balanced by refusal of information – are equally well known. But Peter Mandelson and Alistair

Campbell developed this into the finest of black arts. A journalist writing 'off message' (i.e. something which did not reflect the government line) would be given a week or several weeks in quarantine (meaning that no Government source would speak to him). His editor would be telephoned. He might be sacked. Goebbels would have approved. Even Peter Mandelson subsequently admitted the ill effects of overspinning.

A third reason is the absence under Blair of Cabinet Government. Richard Crossman, a clever fool, wrote of the Wilson Administration in the 1960s that it had become Presidential. He was thirty years out. Up to 1997, Cabinet meetings lasted nearly all morning. Decisions were sometimes reached by narrow majorities. But everyone had their say. I remember a Cabinet meeting in the summer of 1976 when Callaghan was Prime Minister and Tony Crosland Foreign Secretary. Callaghan set out a certain line of action. Sitting opposite him was Crosland. He said, 'No, Jim, that won't run.' He said it quietly, and there was no intake of breath and stormy protest. Callaghan changed course.

Again in the late 1970s, when Britain desperately needed an IMF loan and the Cabinet was split over whether to accept the cutbacks in Government expenditure demanded, Callaghan held meeting after meeting of the Cabinet. Every alternative was thrashed out. In the end the Cabinet reached an agreed solution.

Now exchanges of this kind, perhaps a good deal more tempestuous, take place between Blair and Gordon Brown, but they do so in private, not before the assembled Cabinet. Of course, even if a Cabinet does reach an agreed solution on a difficult question this is no guarantee that there will be no leaks. But the incentive for Ministers to let their own view be known is much greater if they have no chance to be heard and are simply informed of key decisions in a cursory half-hour meeting in Downing Street.

This latter phenomenon has been helped by what I suspect has been a steady decline in the quality of those attracted by a parliamentary career in what is no longer a great power. Anyone voicing this sentiment must be prepared for the comment that one of the signs of growing old is that policemen seem younger. But while it is difficult to measure, there does seem to be a qualitative difference between the immediate post-war generation of politicians and the ones now emerging.

CONCLUSIONS

~ In the latter part of the nineteenth century, Britain overinvested in its public service. And in tackling the most important problem before it over the last fifty years, our relationship with an integrating Europe, the public service mostly got it wrong. Even if they had got it right, they would not have succeeded in persuading politicians. For Whitehall, even in retrospect, this cannot be seen as other than a minor consolation.

~ The attractions of the public service have diminished. In today's world, talent needs to be shifted from the public to the private sector. Fortunately this is already happening. Civil servants now seem to be despised by the leaders of the Conservative Party and distrusted by Labour. Key jobs are being filled by party cronies. Spin doctors rule. The press becomes steadily more intrusive. Britain's role on the world stage now being a minor one, the country no longer attracts the best and the brightest to its service.

~ The best and the brightest now go in increasing numbers not just to traditional occupations offering high rewards, such as banking and the law, but to the media and the new internet technologies. This is not to be deplored but to be welcomed, for this shift will enliven and enrich the country.

~ This needs a minor caveat. When Britain does eventually join the European federation now in the making, Whitehall will find its role change from the administration of a minor power to what will essentially be the local government of a state within a major one. Then thought will need to be given to how we can best protect our local interests by sending, as the French already do, a small number of able officials to the Federation's centre. But that will be for another generation.

NOTES

1.   John Gunther, *Inside Europe*, 1938, p. 241.
2.   Lord Curzon, *The True Imperialism*, 1908, pp. 157-8.
3.   John Updike, 'Shirley Temple Reigns', *New Yorker*, 22 April 1996.
4.   Alan Clark, *Diaries*, 1994, p. 22.
5.   M. Stuart, *Douglas Hurd: The Public Servant*, 1990, p. 329.
6.   Geoffrey Howe, *Conflict of Loyalty*, 1995, p. 568.
7.   Nick Cohen, 'Hacking their way to a fortune', *New Statesman*, 22 May 2000.
8.   Speech by Calvin Coolidge in New York on 17 January 1925.
9.   Hugo Young, *This Blessed Plot*, 1998. p. 63.
10. ibid., p. 64.
11. John Coles, *Making Foreign Policy*, 2000, p. 37.
12. Trevor Salmon and Sir William Nicoll, *Building European Union*, 1997, p. 62. Memo of a conversation with Sir Roger Makins, Department of State, Washington, November 1955.
13. Hugo Young, op. cit., p. 82.
14. Robert Marjolin, *Architect of European Union: Memoirs 1911-86*, 1989.
15. Sir Paul Gore-Booth, *With Great Truth and Respect*, 1974, p. 248.
16. Conversation with the author, Brussels, June 1978.
17. Hugo Young, op. cit., p. 225.
18. ibid., p. 224.
19. *Customs Unions. A League of Nations contribution to the study of customs unions*, United Nations, 1947, p. 74.
20. Hugo Young, op. cit., p. 225.
21. Private information.
22. Peter Clarke, *Hope and Glory: Britain 1900-1990*, 1996, p. 150.
23. Anne Chisholm and Michael Davis, *Beaverbrook: A Life*, 1992, p. 352.
24. John Charmley, *Churchill: The End of Glory*, 1993, p. 356.

INDEX

278